RECESS PIECES

RECESS PIECES

Story and Art by

Bob Fingerman

Dark Horse Books

PUBLISHER Mike Richardson

EDITOR Dave Land

ASSISTANT EDITOR Katie Moody

DESIGNER Amy Arendts

Dedicated to my wife, Michele, for her unyielding love and encouragement; George A. Romero, for his maverick spirit and the gift of his living dead tetralogy; and to my junior high school chum, Charlie "Tripper" Bonet, for having had the balls to see the unrated original *Dawn of the Dead* first run and then regale me as we warmed the bench in gym class with detailed orations of its goriest moments because at the time I lacked the moxie to witness them firsthand.

RECESS PIECES

Dark Horse Books
A division of Dark Horse Comics, Inc.
10956 SE Main Street
Milwaukie, OR 97222

darkhorse.com

To find a comics shop in your area, call the Comic Shop Locator Service: (888) 266-4226

First edition: August 2006
ISBN-10: 1-59307-450-6
ISBN-13: 978-1-59307-450-0

10 9 8 7 6 5 4 3 2 1
Printed in China

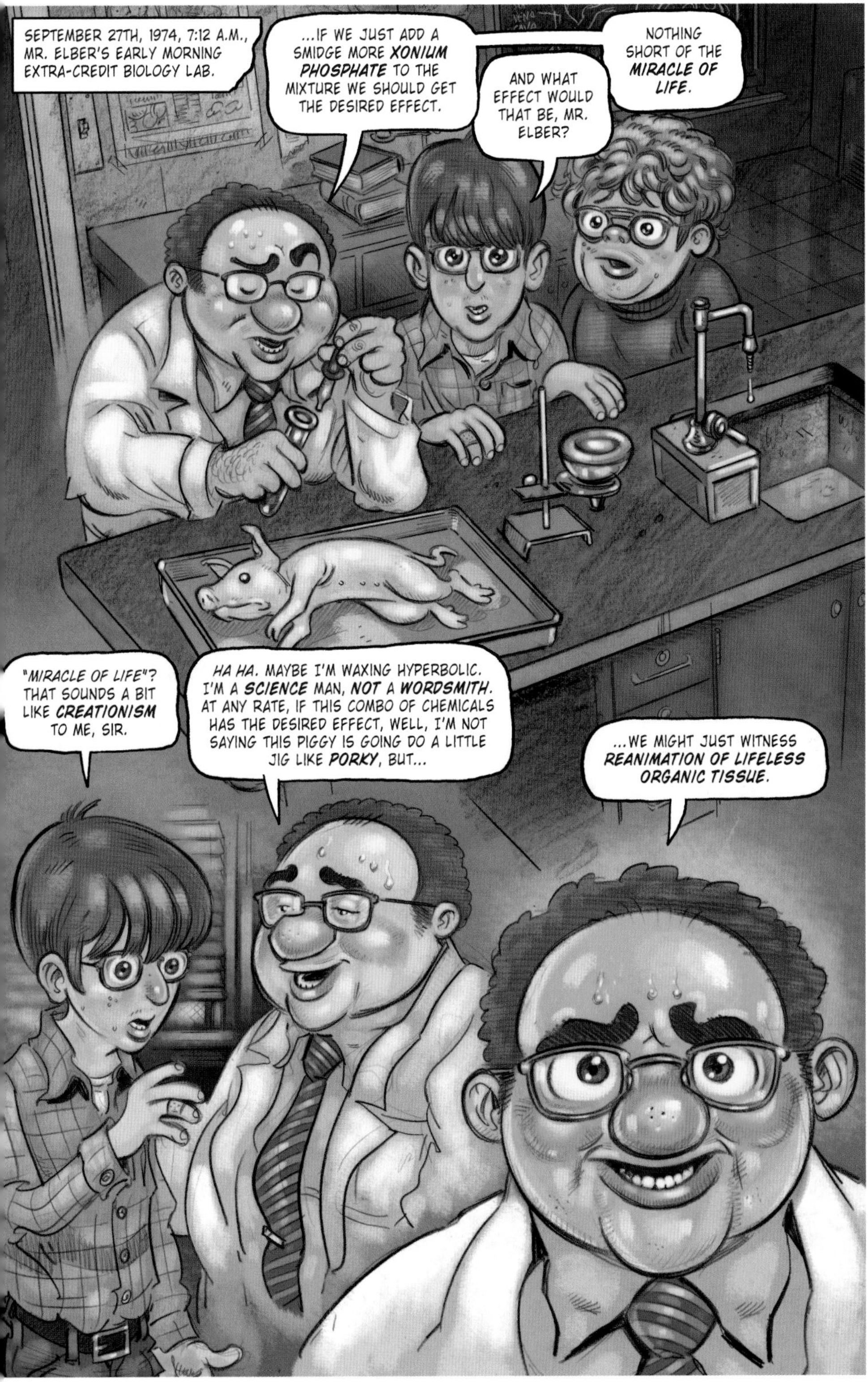
SEPTEMBER 27TH, 1974, 7:12 A.M., MR. ELBER'S EARLY MORNING EXTRA-CREDIT BIOLOGY LAB.
...IF WE JUST ADD A SMIDGE MORE XONIUM PHOSPHATE TO THE MIXTURE WE SHOULD GET THE DESIRED EFFECT.
AND WHAT EFFECT WOULD THAT BE, MR. ELBER?
NOTHING SHORT OF THE MIRACLE OF LIFE.
"MIRACLE OF LIFE"? THAT SOUNDS A BIT LIKE CREATIONISM TO ME, SIR.
HA HA. MAYBE I'M WAXING HYPERBOLIC. I'M A SCIENCE MAN, NOT A WORDSMITH. AT ANY RATE, IF THIS COMBO OF CHEMICALS HAS THE DESIRED EFFECT, WELL, I'M NOT SAYING THIS PIGGY IS GOING DO A LITTLE JIG LIKE PORKY, BUT...
...WE MIGHT JUST WITNESS REANIMATION OF LIFELESS ORGANIC TISSUE.

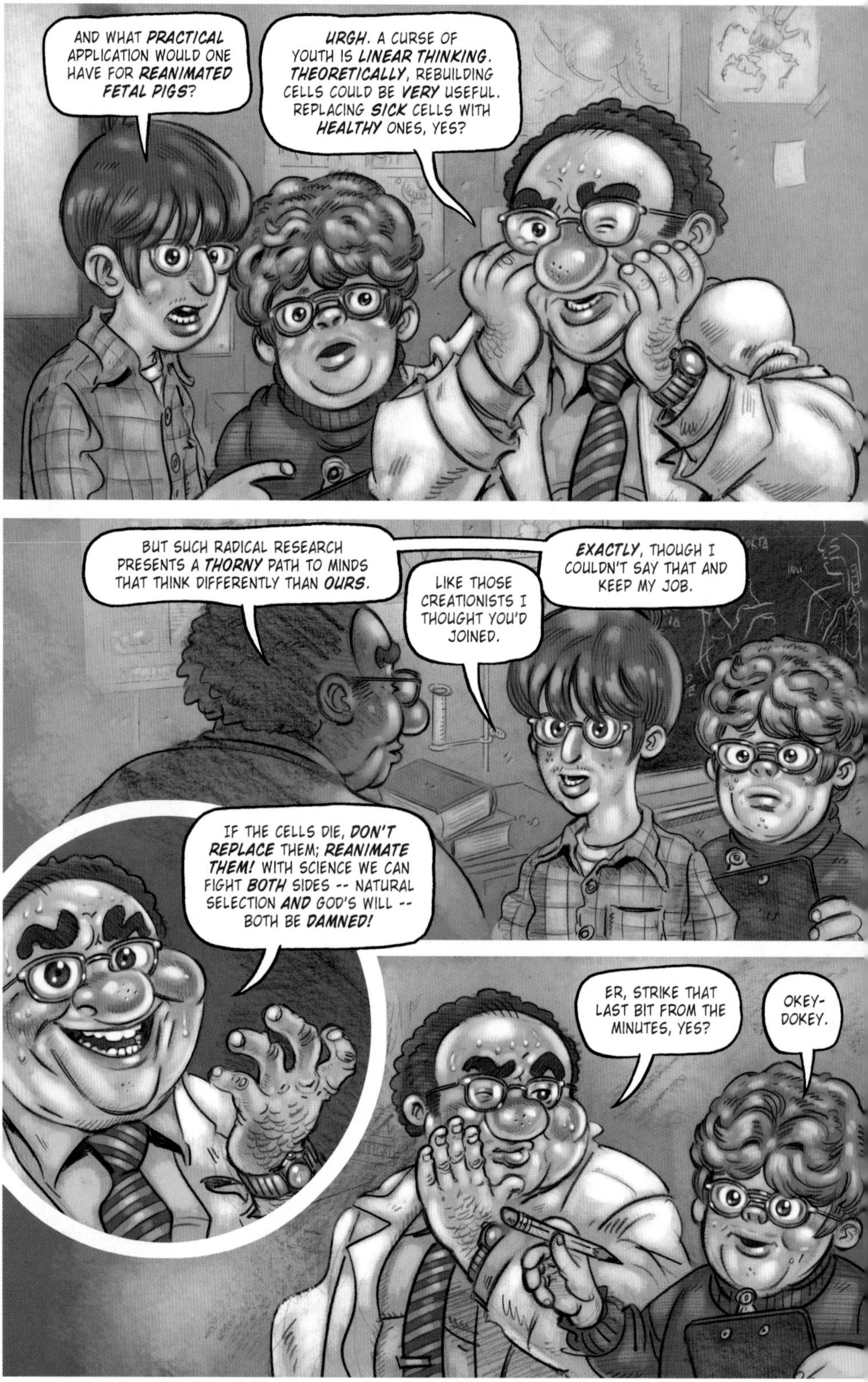
AND WHAT PRACTICAL APPLICATION WOULD ONE HAVE FOR REANIMATED FETAL PIGS?
URGH. A CURSE OF YOUTH IS LINEAR THINKING. THEORETICALLY, REBUILDING CELLS COULD BE VERY USEFUL. REPLACING SICK CELLS WITH HEALTHY ONES, YES?
BUT SUCH RADICAL RESEARCH PRESENTS A THORNY PATH TO MINDS THAT THINK DIFFERENTLY THAN OURS.
LIKE THOSE CREATIONISTS I THOUGHT YOU'D JOINED.
EXACTLY, THOUGH I COULDN'T SAY THAT AND KEEP MY JOB.
IF THE CELLS DIE, DON'T REPLACE THEM; REANIMATE THEM! WITH SCIENCE WE CAN FIGHT BOTH SIDES -- NATURAL SELECTION AND GOD'S WILL -- BOTH BE DAMNED!
ER, STRIKE THAT LAST BIT FROM THE MINUTES, YES?
OKEY-DOKEY.

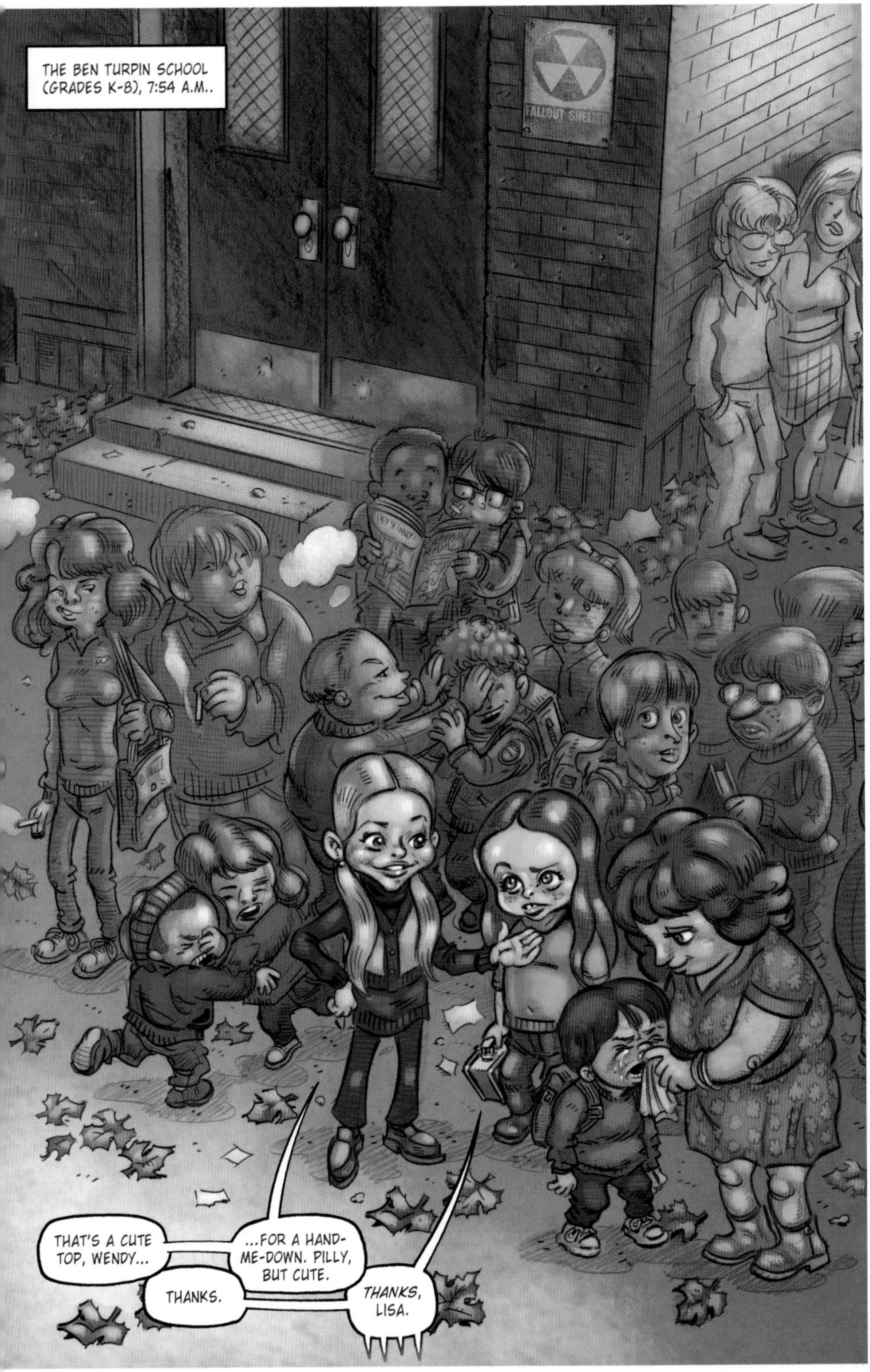
THE BEN TURPIN SCHOOL (GRADES K-8), 7:54 A.M..
FALLOUT SHELTER
THAT'S A CUTE TOP, WENDY...
...FOR A HAND-ME-DOWN. PILLY, BUT CUTE.
THANKS.
THANKS, LISA.

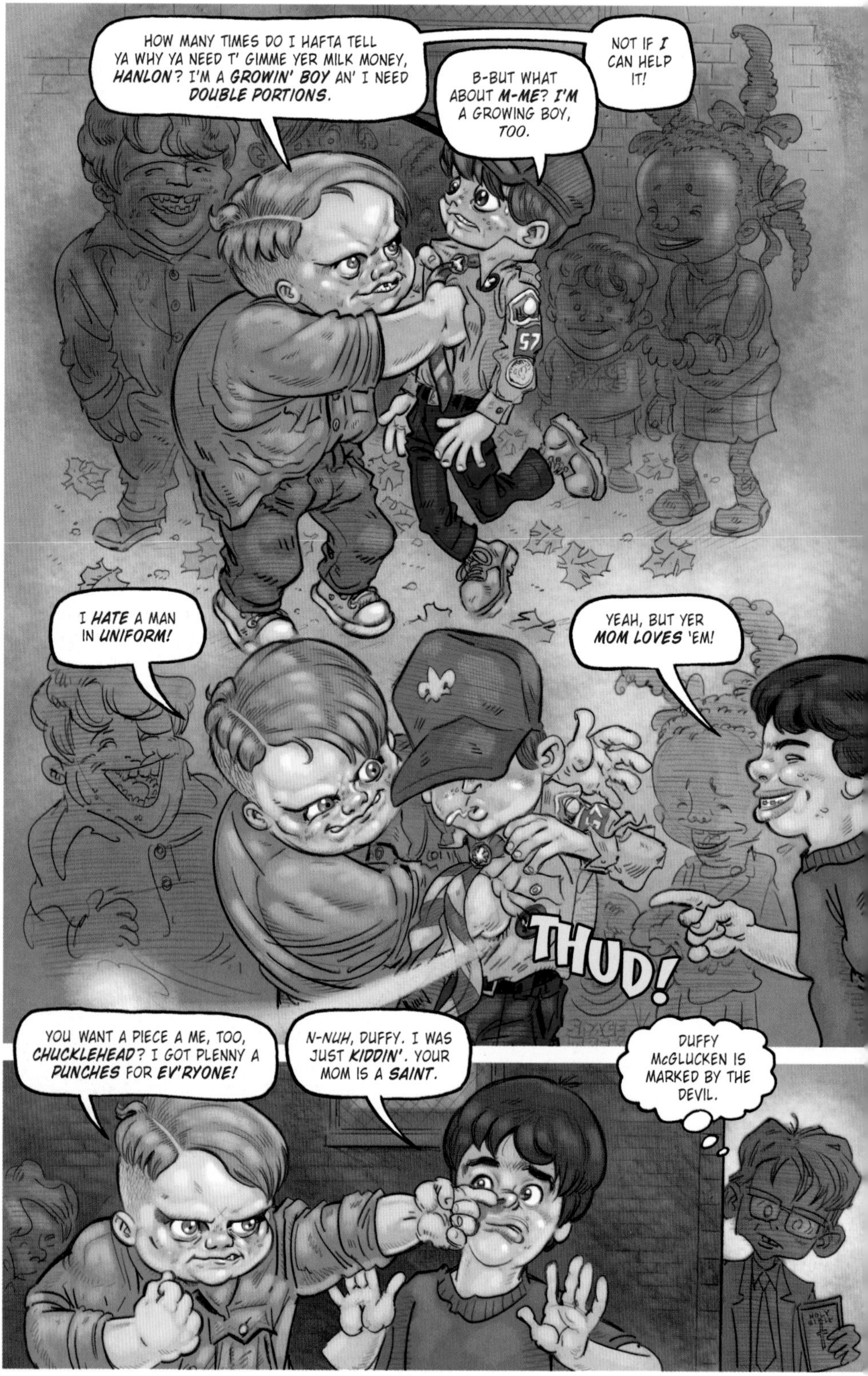

HOW MANY TIMES DO I HAFTA TELL YA WHY YA NEED T' GIMME YER MILK MONEY, HANLON? I'M A GROWIN' BOY AN' I NEED DOUBLE PORTIONS.
B-BUT WHAT ABOUT M-ME? I'M A GROWING BOY, TOO.
NOT IF I CAN HELP IT!
I HATE A MAN IN UNIFORM!
YEAH, BUT YER MOM LOVES 'EM!
THUD!
YOU WANT A PIECE A ME, TOO, CHUCKLEHEAD? I GOT PLENNY A PUNCHES FOR EV'RYONE!
N-NUH, DUFFY. I WAS JUST KIDDIN'. YOUR MOM IS A SAINT.
DUFFY McGLUCKEN IS MARKED BY THE DEVIL.

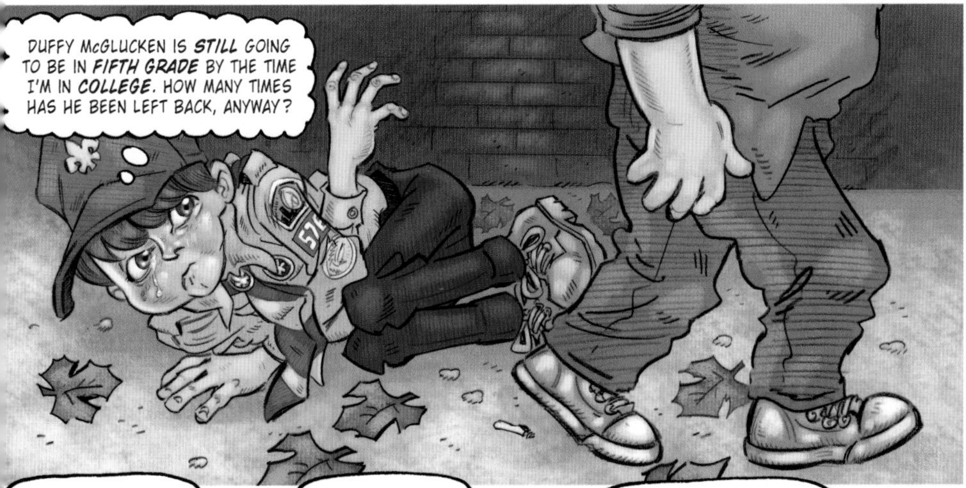
DUFFY McGLUCKEN IS STILL GOING TO BE IN FIFTH GRADE BY THE TIME I'M IN COLLEGE. HOW MANY TIMES HAS HE BEEN LEFT BACK, ANYWAY?

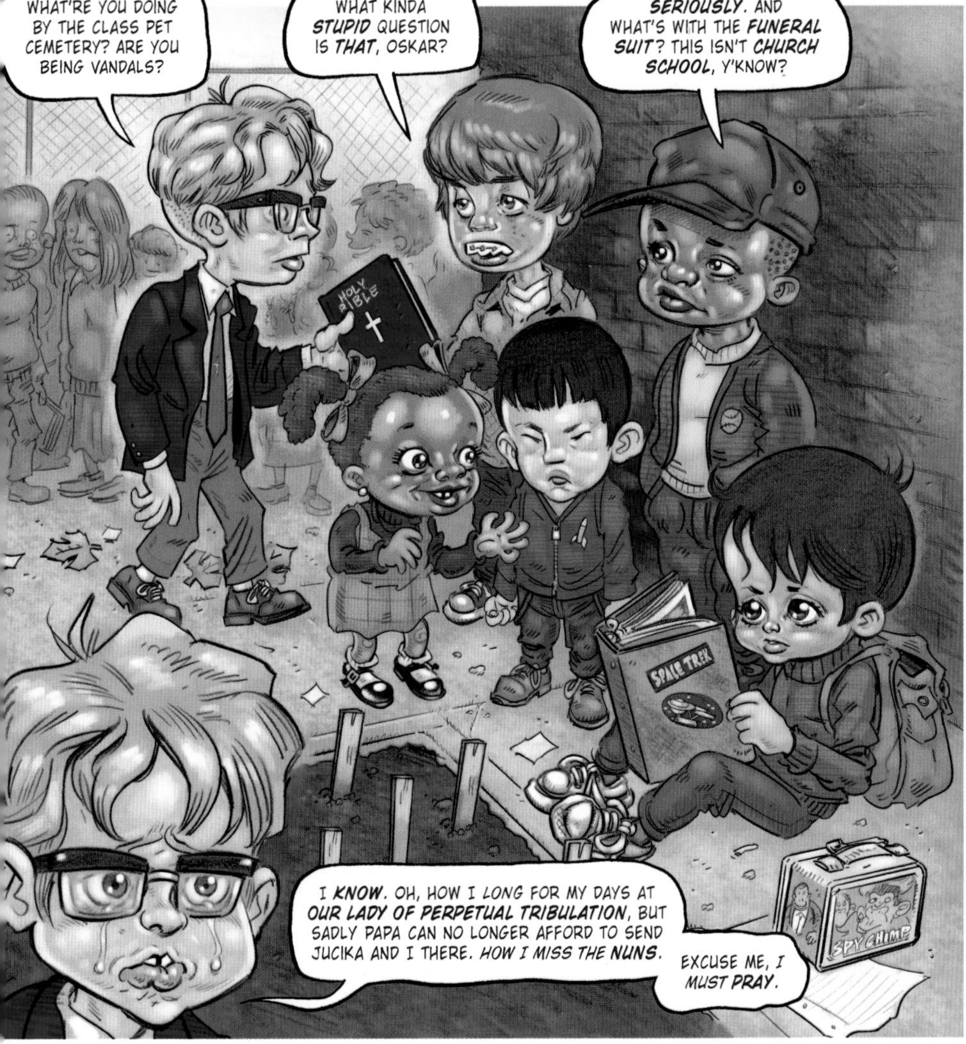
WHAT'RE YOU DOING BY THE CLASS PET CEMETERY? ARE YOU BEING VANDALS?
WHAT KINDA STUPID QUESTION IS THAT, OSKAR?
SERIOUSLY. AND WHAT'S WITH THE FUNERAL SUIT? THIS ISN'T CHURCH SCHOOL, Y'KNOW?
HOLY BIBLE
SPACE TREK
I KNOW. OH, HOW I LONG FOR MY DAYS AT OUR LADY OF PERPETUAL TRIBULATION, BUT SADLY PAPA CAN NO LONGER AFFORD TO SEND JUCIKA AND I THERE. HOW I MISS THE NUNS.
EXCUSE ME, I MUST PRAY.
SPY CHIMP

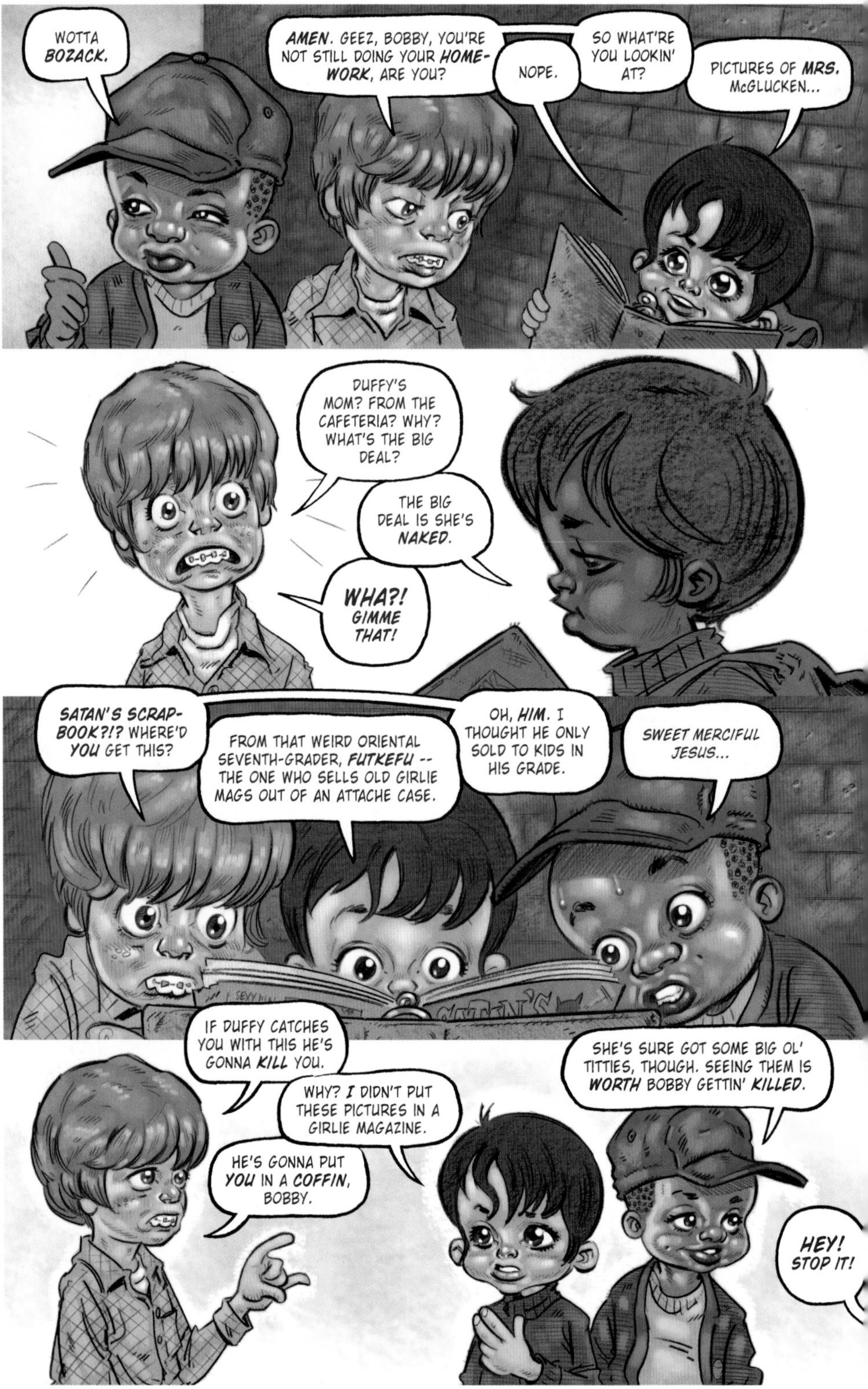
WOTTA BOZACK.
AMEN. GEEZ, BOBBY, YOU'RE NOT STILL DOING YOUR HOMEWORK, ARE YOU?
NOPE.
SO WHAT'RE YOU LOOKIN' AT?
PICTURES OF MRS. McGLUCKEN...
DUFFY'S MOM? FROM THE CAFETERIA? WHY? WHAT'S THE BIG DEAL?
THE BIG DEAL IS SHE'S NAKED.
WHA?! GIMME THAT!
SATAN'S SCRAPBOOK?!? WHERE'D YOU GET THIS?
FROM THAT WEIRD ORIENTAL SEVENTH-GRADER, FUTKEFU -- THE ONE WHO SELLS OLD GIRLIE MAGS OUT OF AN ATTACHE CASE.
OH, HIM. I THOUGHT HE ONLY SOLD TO KIDS IN HIS GRADE.
SWEET MERCIFUL JESUS...
IF DUFFY CATCHES YOU WITH THIS HE'S GONNA KILL YOU.
WHY? I DIDN'T PUT THESE PICTURES IN A GIRLIE MAGAZINE.
HE'S GONNA PUT YOU IN A COFFIN, BOBBY.
SHE'S SURE GOT SOME BIG OL' TITTIES, THOUGH. SEEING THEM IS WORTH BOBBY GETTIN' KILLED.
HEY! STOP IT!

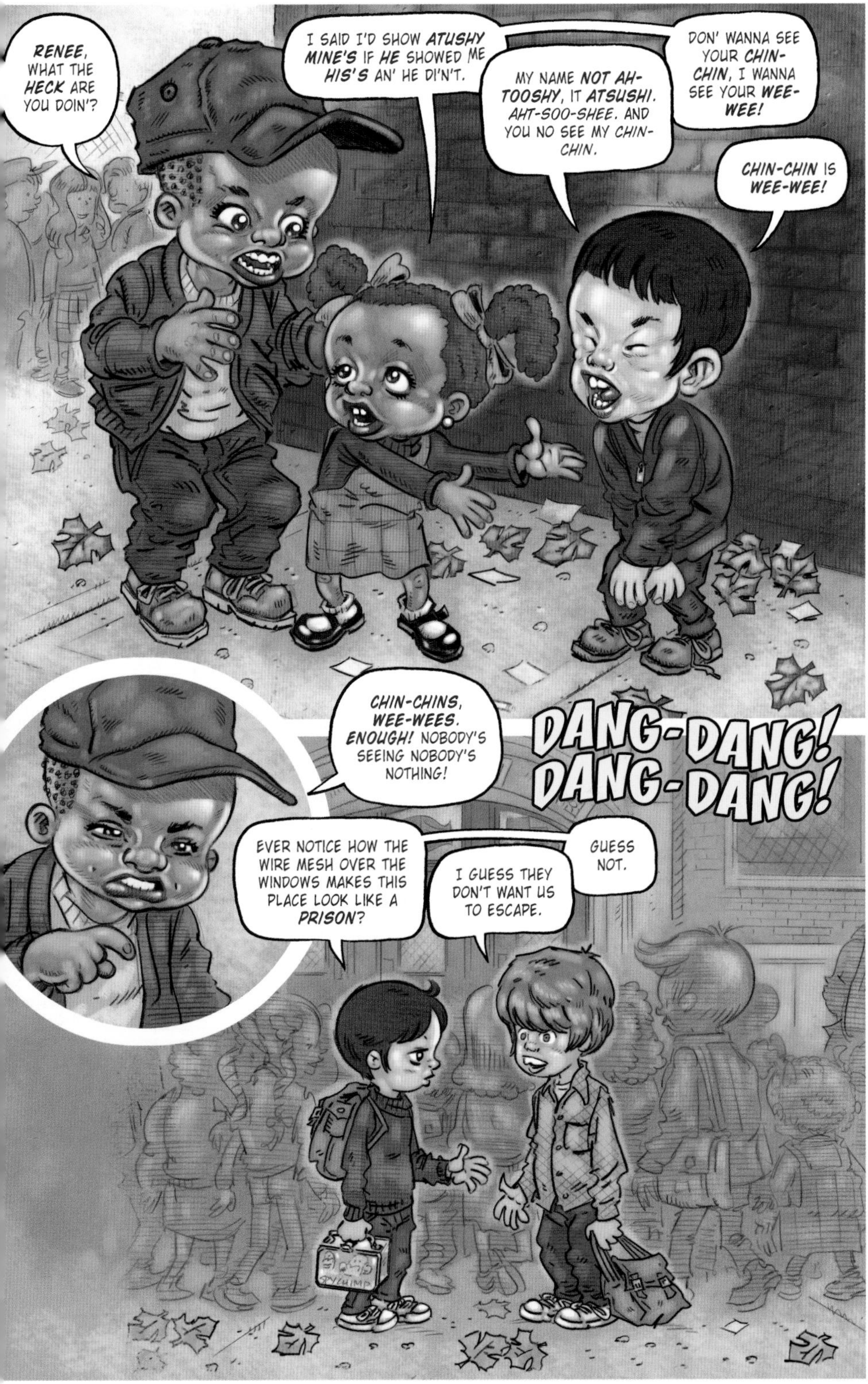
RENEE, WHAT THE HECK ARE YOU DOIN'?
I SAID I'D SHOW ATUSHY MINE'S IF HE SHOWED ME HIS'S AN' HE DI'N'T.
MY NAME NOT AH-TOOSHY, IT ATSUSHI. AHT-SOO-SHEE. AND YOU NO SEE MY CHIN-CHIN.
DON' WANNA SEE YOUR CHIN-CHIN, I WANNA SEE YOUR WEE-WEE!
CHIN-CHIN IS WEE-WEE!
CHIN-CHINS, WEE-WEES. ENOUGH! NOBODY'S SEEING NOBODY'S NOTHING!
DANG-DANG! DANG-DANG!
EVER NOTICE HOW THE WIRE MESH OVER THE WINDOWS MAKES THIS PLACE LOOK LIKE A PRISON?
I GUESS THEY DON'T WANT US TO ESCAPE.
GUESS NOT.

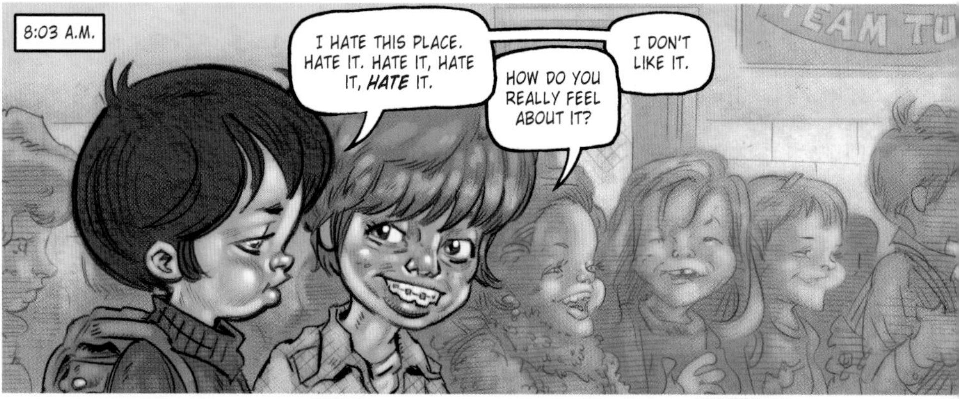
8:03 A.M.
I HATE THIS PLACE. HATE IT. HATE IT, HATE IT, HATE IT.
I DON'T LIKE IT.
HOW DO YOU REALLY FEEL ABOUT IT?
TEAM TU

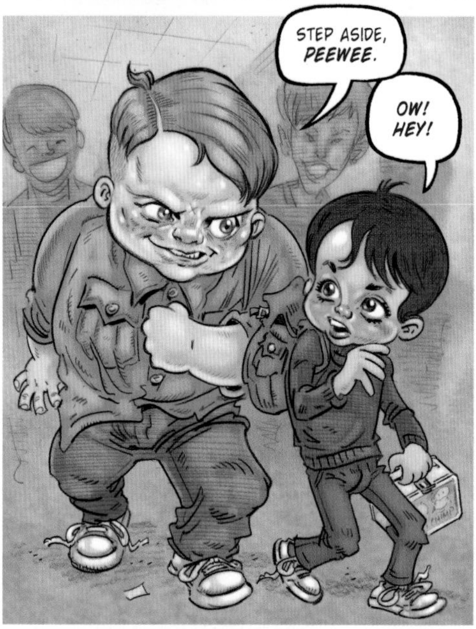
STEP ASIDE, PEEWEE.
OW! HEY!

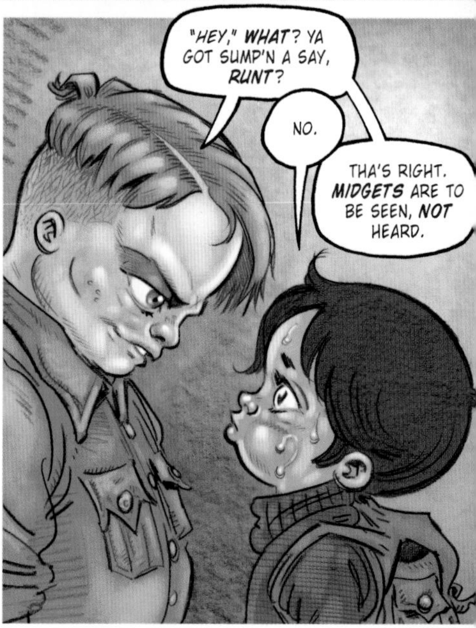
"HEY," WHAT? YA GOT SUMP'N A SAY, RUNT?
NO.
THA'S RIGHT. MIDGETS ARE TO BE SEEN, NOT HEARD.

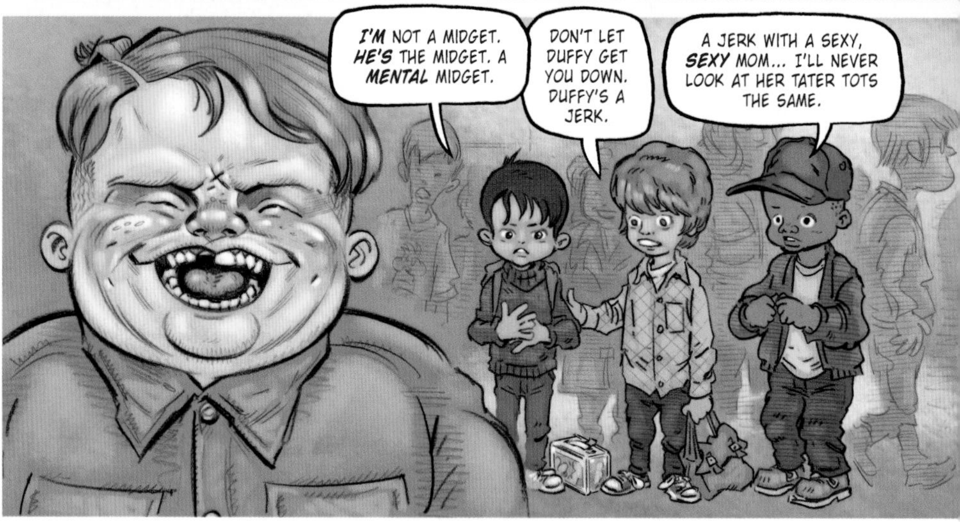
I'M NOT A MIDGET. HE'S THE MIDGET. A MENTAL MIDGET.
DON'T LET DUFFY GET YOU DOWN. DUFFY'S A JERK.
A JERK WITH A SEXY, SEXY MOM... I'LL NEVER LOOK AT HER TATER TOTS THE SAME.

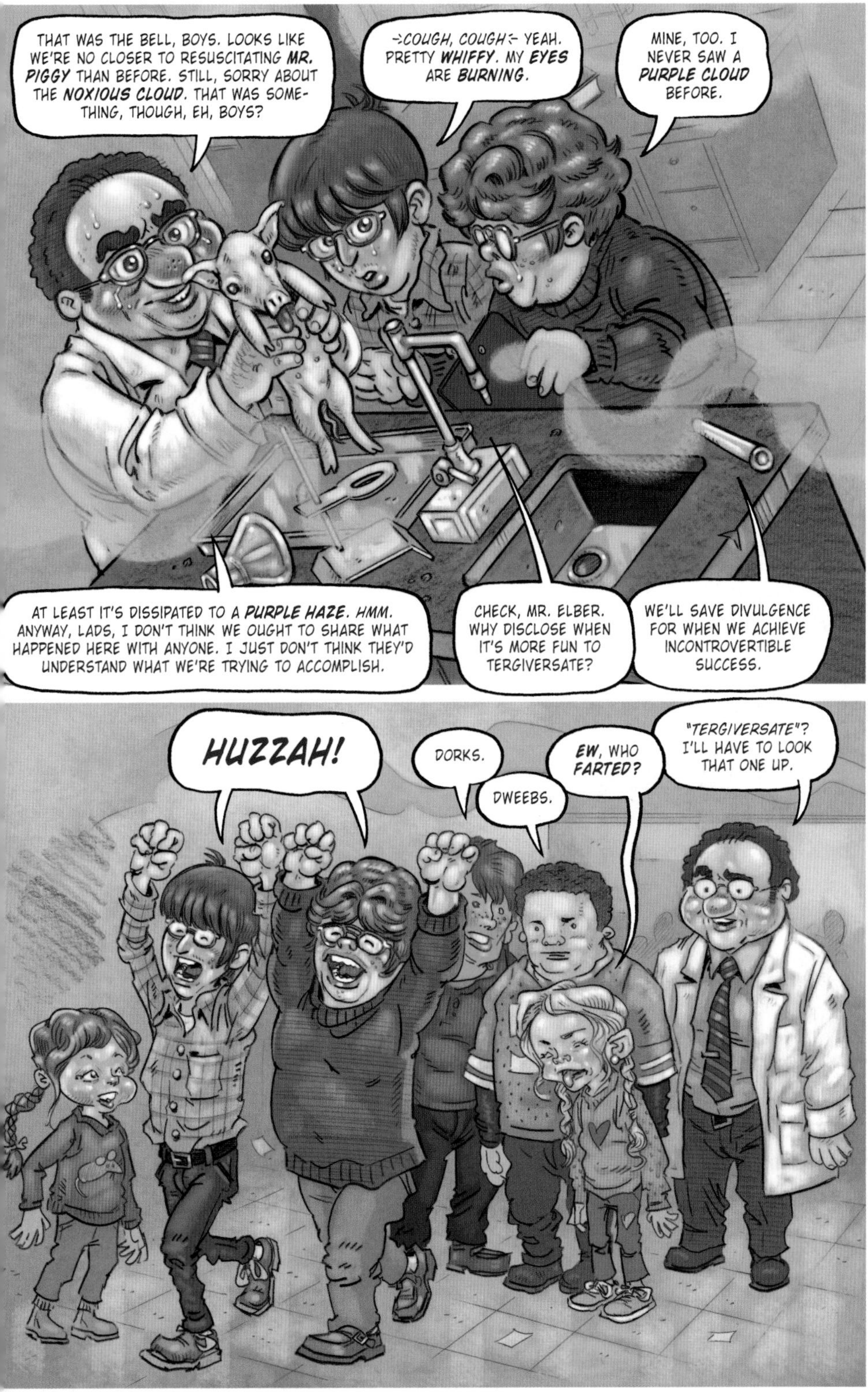
THAT WAS THE BELL, BOYS. LOOKS LIKE WE'RE NO CLOSER TO RESUSCITATING **MR. PIGGY** THAN BEFORE. STILL, SORRY ABOUT THE **NOXIOUS CLOUD**. THAT WAS SOMETHING, THOUGH, EH, BOYS?
-:*COUGH, COUGH*:- YEAH. PRETTY **WHIFFY**. MY **EYES** ARE **BURNING**.
MINE, TOO. I NEVER SAW A **PURPLE CLOUD** BEFORE.
AT LEAST IT'S DISSIPATED TO A **PURPLE HAZE**. *HMM.* ANYWAY, LADS, I DON'T THINK WE OUGHT TO SHARE WHAT HAPPENED HERE WITH ANYONE. I JUST DON'T THINK THEY'D UNDERSTAND WHAT WE'RE TRYING TO ACCOMPLISH.
CHECK, MR. ELBER. WHY DISCLOSE WHEN IT'S MORE FUN TO TERGIVERSATE?
WE'LL SAVE DIVULGENCE FOR WHEN WE ACHIEVE INCONTROVERTIBLE SUCCESS.
HUZZAH!
DORKS.
DWEEBS.
EW, WHO **FARTED?**
"*TERGIVERSATE*"? I'LL HAVE TO LOOK THAT ONE UP.

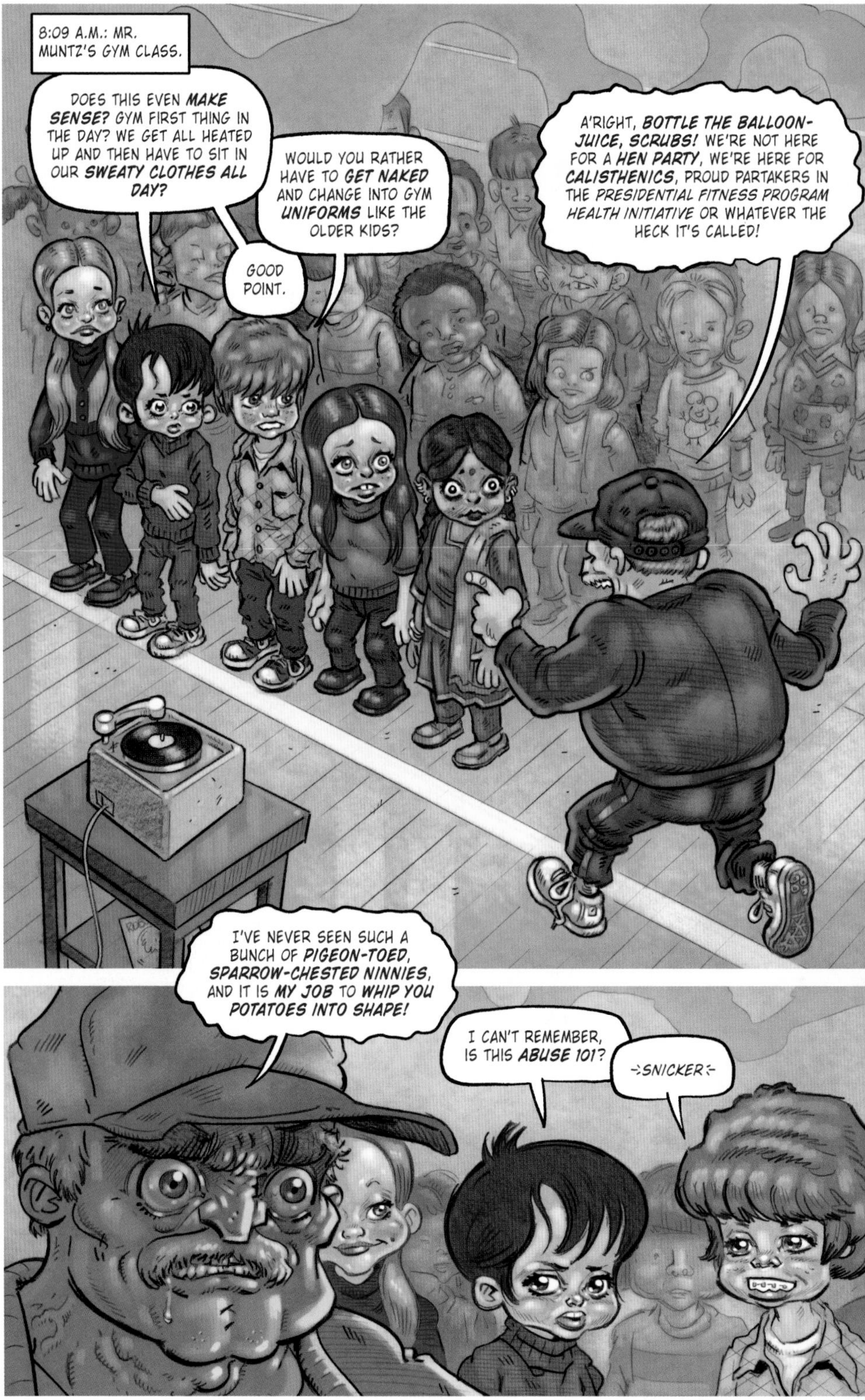
8:09 A.M.: MR. MUNTZ'S GYM CLASS.
DOES THIS EVEN MAKE SENSE? GYM FIRST THING IN THE DAY? WE GET ALL HEATED UP AND THEN HAVE TO SIT IN OUR SWEATY CLOTHES ALL DAY?
WOULD YOU RATHER HAVE TO GET NAKED AND CHANGE INTO GYM UNIFORMS LIKE THE OLDER KIDS?
GOOD POINT.
A'RIGHT, BOTTLE THE BALLOON-JUICE, SCRUBS! WE'RE NOT HERE FOR A HEN PARTY, WE'RE HERE FOR CALISTHENICS, PROUD PARTAKERS IN THE PRESIDENTIAL FITNESS PROGRAM HEALTH INITIATIVE OR WHATEVER THE HECK IT'S CALLED!
I'VE NEVER SEEN SUCH A BUNCH OF PIGEON-TOED, SPARROW-CHESTED NINNIES, AND IT IS MY JOB TO WHIP YOU POTATOES INTO SHAPE!
I CAN'T REMEMBER, IS THIS ABUSE 101?
SNICKER

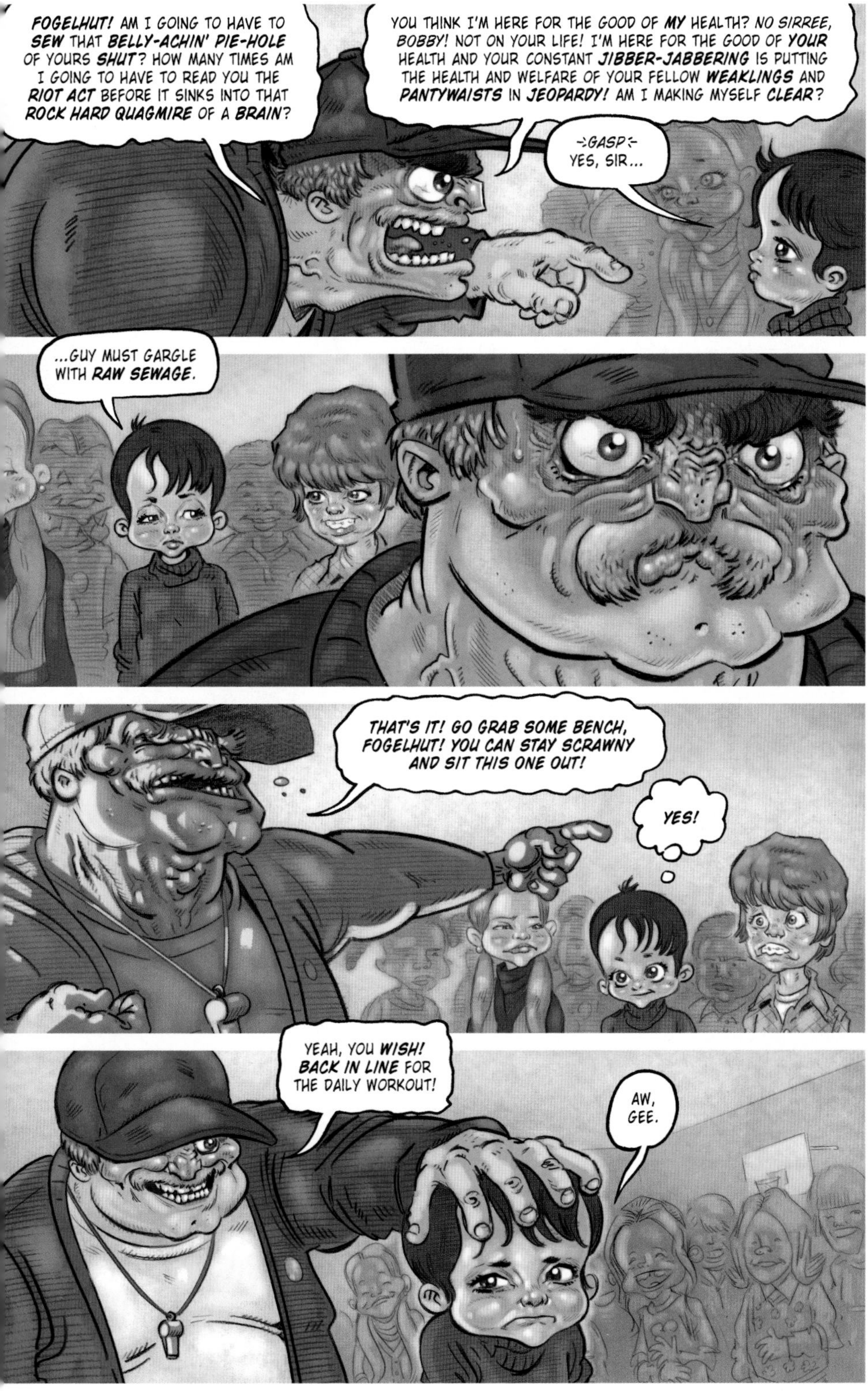
FOGELHUT! AM I GOING TO HAVE TO SEW THAT BELLY-ACHIN' PIE-HOLE OF YOURS SHUT? HOW MANY TIMES AM I GOING TO HAVE TO READ YOU THE RIOT ACT BEFORE IT SINKS INTO THAT ROCK HARD QUAGMIRE OF A BRAIN?
YOU THINK I'M HERE FOR THE GOOD OF MY HEALTH? NO SIRREE, BOBBY! NOT ON YOUR LIFE! I'M HERE FOR THE GOOD OF YOUR HEALTH AND YOUR CONSTANT JIBBER-JABBERING IS PUTTING THE HEALTH AND WELFARE OF YOUR FELLOW WEAKLINGS AND PANTYWAISTS IN JEOPARDY! AM I MAKING MYSELF CLEAR?
GASP YES, SIR...
...GUY MUST GARGLE WITH RAW SEWAGE.
THAT'S IT! GO GRAB SOME BENCH, FOGELHUT! YOU CAN STAY SCRAWNY AND SIT THIS ONE OUT!
YES!
YEAH, YOU WISH! BACK IN LINE FOR THE DAILY WORKOUT!
AW, GEE.

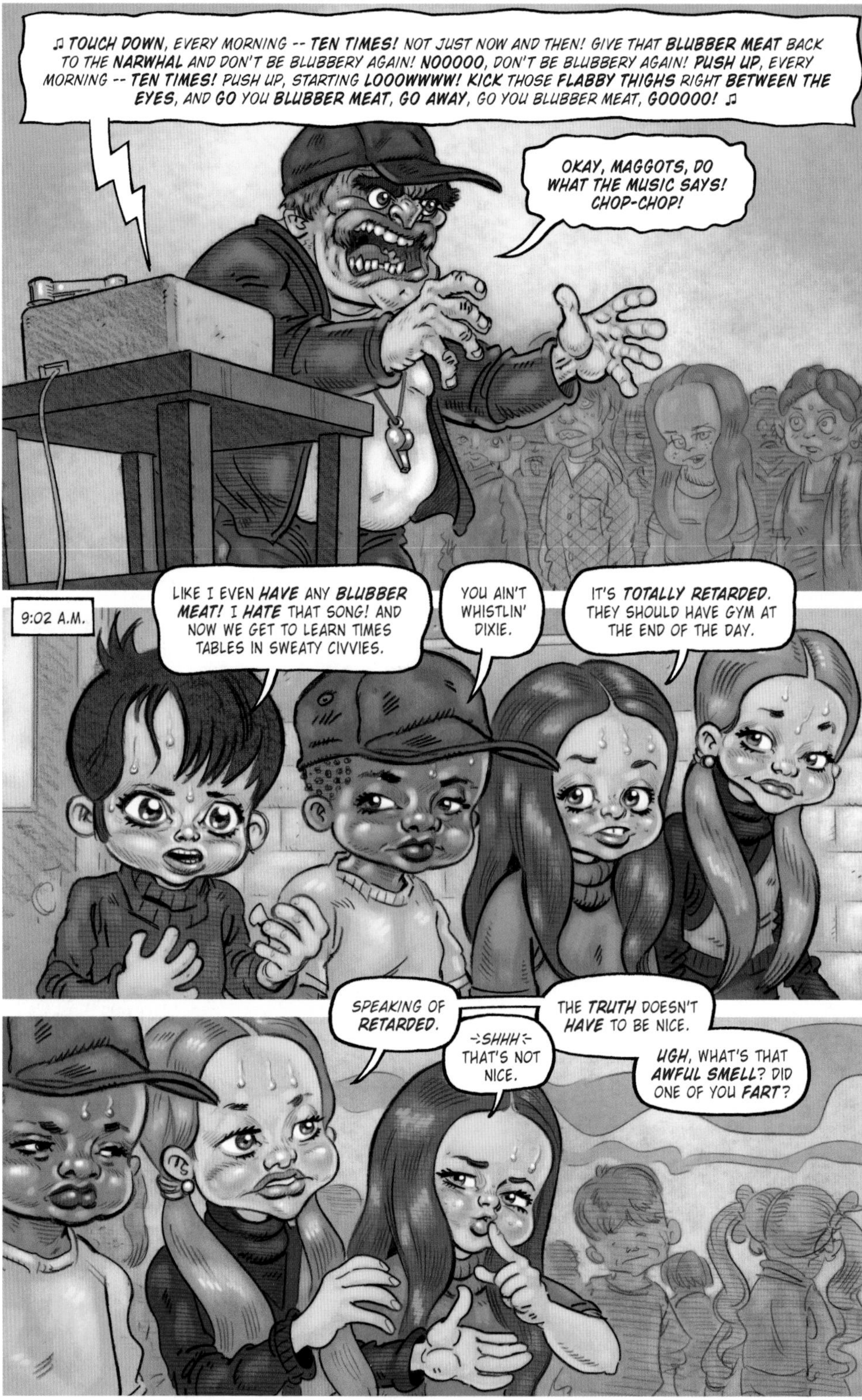
♫ TOUCH DOWN, EVERY MORNING -- TEN TIMES! NOT JUST NOW AND THEN! GIVE THAT BLUBBER MEAT BACK TO THE NARWHAL AND DON'T BE BLUBBERY AGAIN! NOOOOO, DON'T BE BLUBBERY AGAIN! PUSH UP, EVERY MORNING -- TEN TIMES! PUSH UP, STARTING LOOOWWWW! KICK THOSE FLABBY THIGHS RIGHT BETWEEN THE EYES, AND GO YOU BLUBBER MEAT, GO AWAY, GO YOU BLUBBER MEAT, GOOOOO! ♫
OKAY, MAGGOTS, DO WHAT THE MUSIC SAYS! CHOP-CHOP!
9:02 A.M.
LIKE I EVEN HAVE ANY BLUBBER MEAT! I HATE THAT SONG! AND NOW WE GET TO LEARN TIMES TABLES IN SWEATY CIVVIES.
YOU AIN'T WHISTLIN' DIXIE.
IT'S TOTALLY RETARDED. THEY SHOULD HAVE GYM AT THE END OF THE DAY.
SPEAKING OF RETARDED.
SHHH THAT'S NOT NICE.
THE TRUTH DOESN'T HAVE TO BE NICE.
UGH, WHAT'S THAT AWFUL SMELL? DID ONE OF YOU FART?

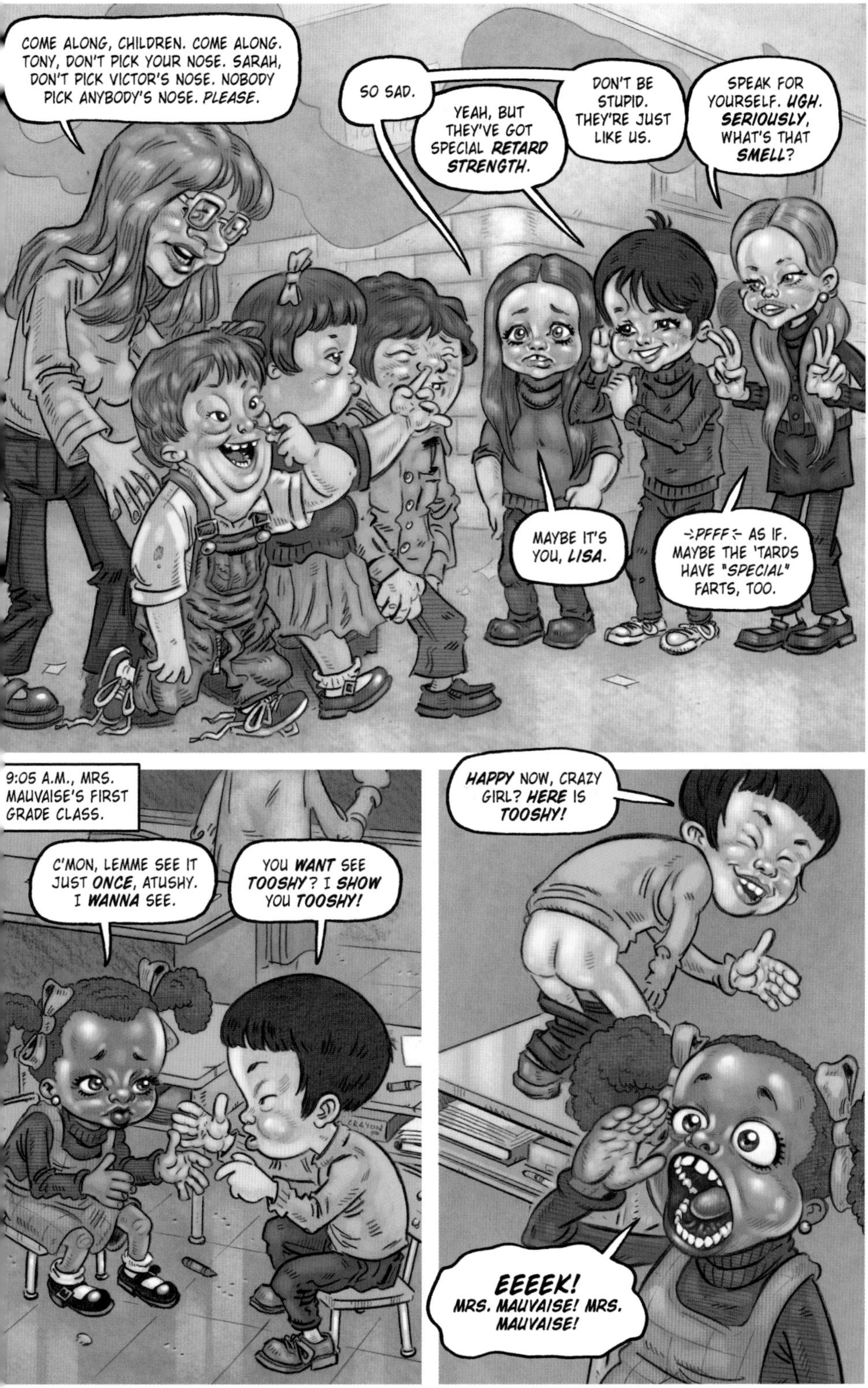
COME ALONG, CHILDREN. COME ALONG. TONY, DON'T PICK YOUR NOSE. SARAH, DON'T PICK VICTOR'S NOSE. NOBODY PICK ANYBODY'S NOSE. *PLEASE.*
SO SAD.
YEAH, BUT THEY'VE GOT SPECIAL ***RETARD STRENGTH.***
DON'T BE STUPID. THEY'RE JUST LIKE US.
SPEAK FOR YOURSELF. ***UGH. SERIOUSLY,*** WHAT'S THAT ***SMELL?***
MAYBE IT'S YOU, ***LISA.***
PFFF AS IF. MAYBE THE 'TARDS HAVE "*SPECIAL*" FARTS, TOO.
9:05 A.M., MRS. MAUVAISE'S FIRST GRADE CLASS.
C'MON, LEMME SEE IT JUST ***ONCE,*** ATUSHY. I ***WANNA*** SEE.
YOU ***WANT*** SEE ***TOOSHY?*** I ***SHOW*** YOU ***TOOSHY!***
HAPPY NOW, CRAZY GIRL? ***HERE*** IS ***TOOSHY!***
EEEEK! MRS. MAUVAISE! MRS. MAUVAISE!

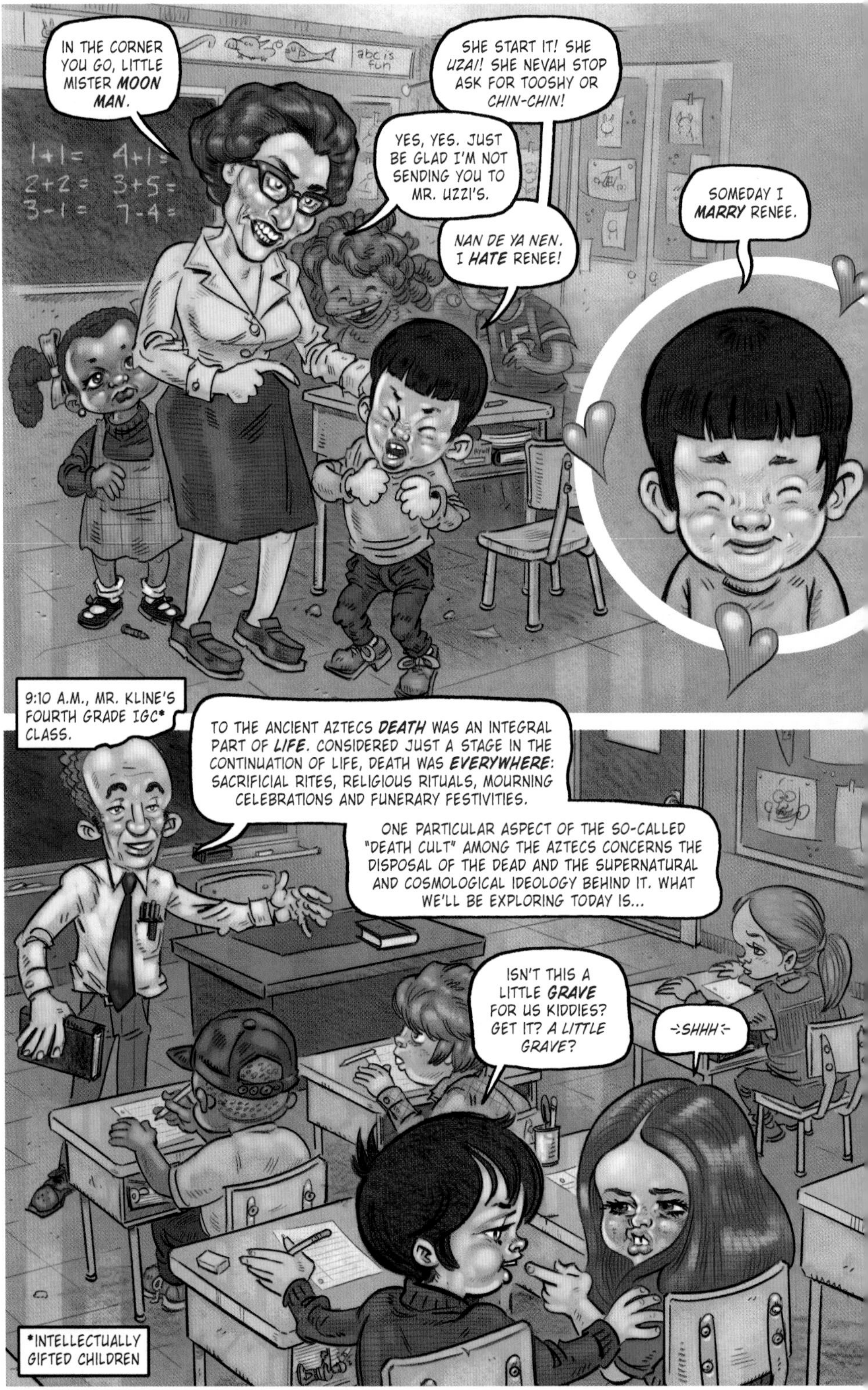
IN THE CORNER YOU GO, LITTLE MISTER MOON MAN.
SHE START IT! SHE UZAI! SHE NEVAH STOP ASK FOR TOOSHY OR CHIN-CHIN!
YES, YES. JUST BE GLAD I'M NOT SENDING YOU TO MR. UZZI'S.
NAN DE YA NEN. I HATE RENEE!
SOMEDAY I MARRY RENEE.
9:10 A.M., MR. KLINE'S FOURTH GRADE IGC* CLASS.
TO THE ANCIENT AZTECS DEATH WAS AN INTEGRAL PART OF LIFE. CONSIDERED JUST A STAGE IN THE CONTINUATION OF LIFE, DEATH WAS EVERYWHERE: SACRIFICIAL RITES, RELIGIOUS RITUALS, MOURNING CELEBRATIONS AND FUNERARY FESTIVITIES.
ONE PARTICULAR ASPECT OF THE SO-CALLED "DEATH CULT" AMONG THE AZTECS CONCERNS THE DISPOSAL OF THE DEAD AND THE SUPERNATURAL AND COSMOLOGICAL IDEOLOGY BEHIND IT. WHAT WE'LL BE EXPLORING TODAY IS...
ISN'T THIS A LITTLE GRAVE FOR US KIDDIES? GET IT? A LITTLE GRAVE?
SHHH
*INTELLECTUALLY GIFTED CHILDREN

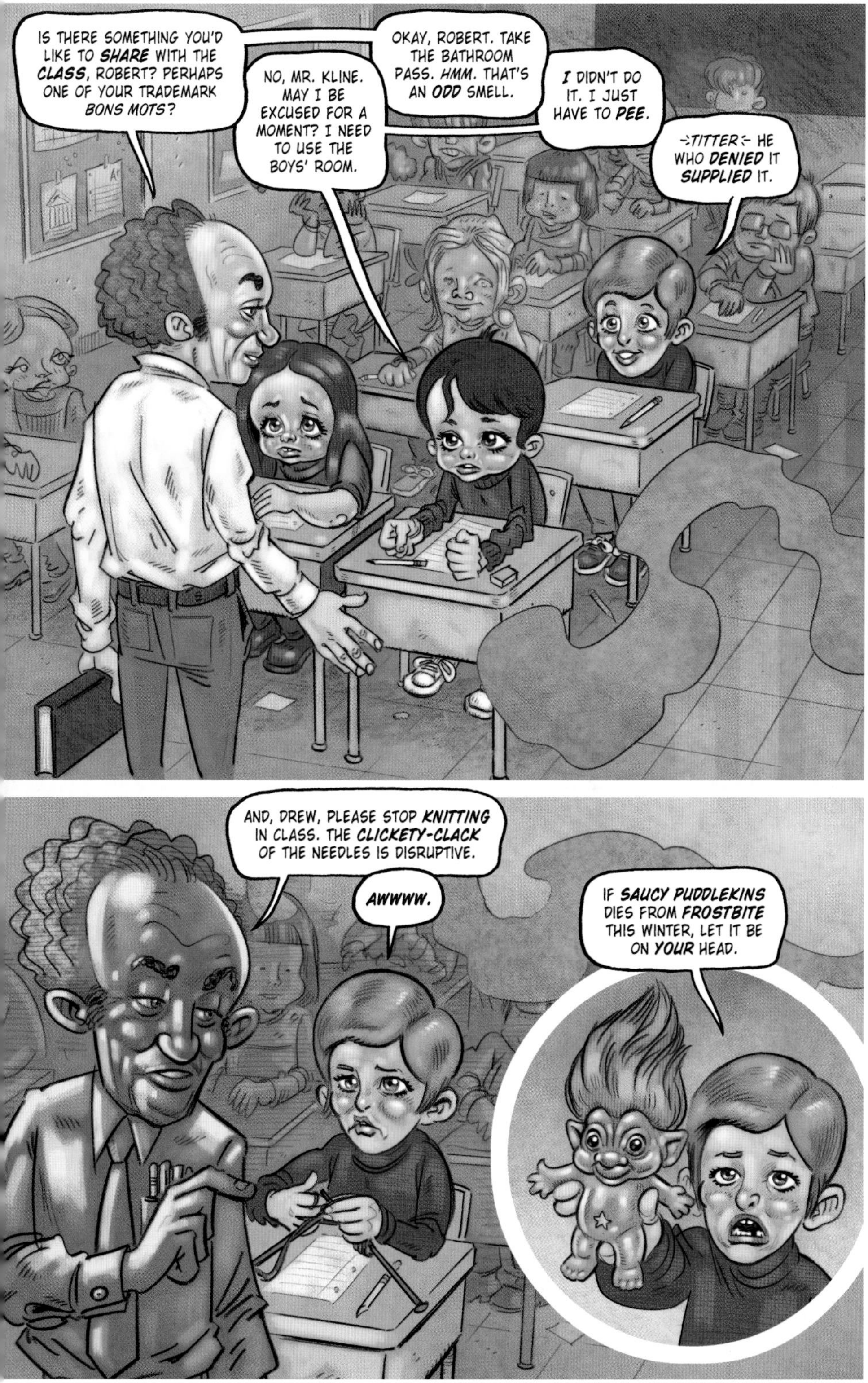
IS THERE SOMETHING YOU'D LIKE TO SHARE WITH THE CLASS, ROBERT? PERHAPS ONE OF YOUR TRADEMARK BONS MOTS?
NO, MR. KLINE. MAY I BE EXCUSED FOR A MOMENT? I NEED TO USE THE BOYS' ROOM.
OKAY, ROBERT. TAKE THE BATHROOM PASS. HMM. THAT'S AN ODD SMELL.
I DIDN'T DO IT. I JUST HAVE TO PEE.
TITTER HE WHO DENIED IT SUPPLIED IT.
AND, DREW, PLEASE STOP KNITTING IN CLASS. THE CLICKETY-CLACK OF THE NEEDLES IS DISRUPTIVE.
AWWWW.
IF SAUCY PUDDLEKINS DIES FROM FROSTBITE THIS WINTER, LET IT BE ON YOUR HEAD.

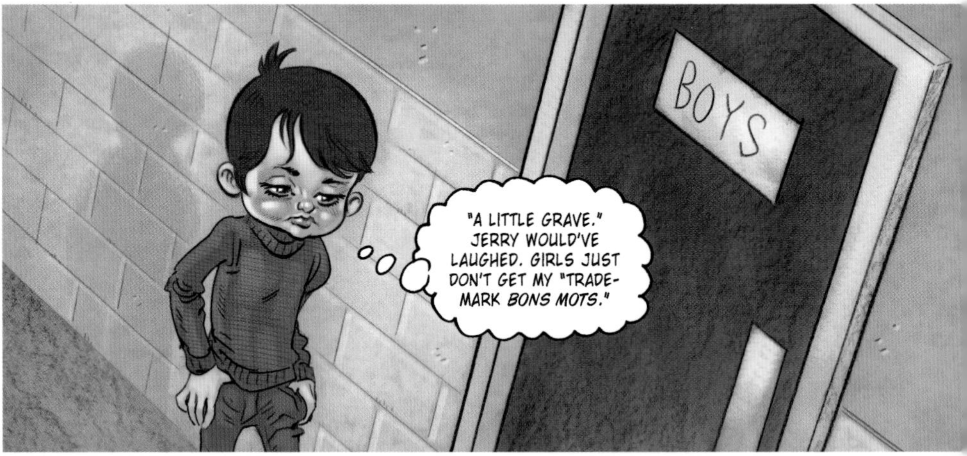
BOYS
"A LITTLE GRAVE." JERRY WOULD'VE LAUGHED. GIRLS JUST DON'T GET MY "TRADE-MARK *BONS MOTS*."

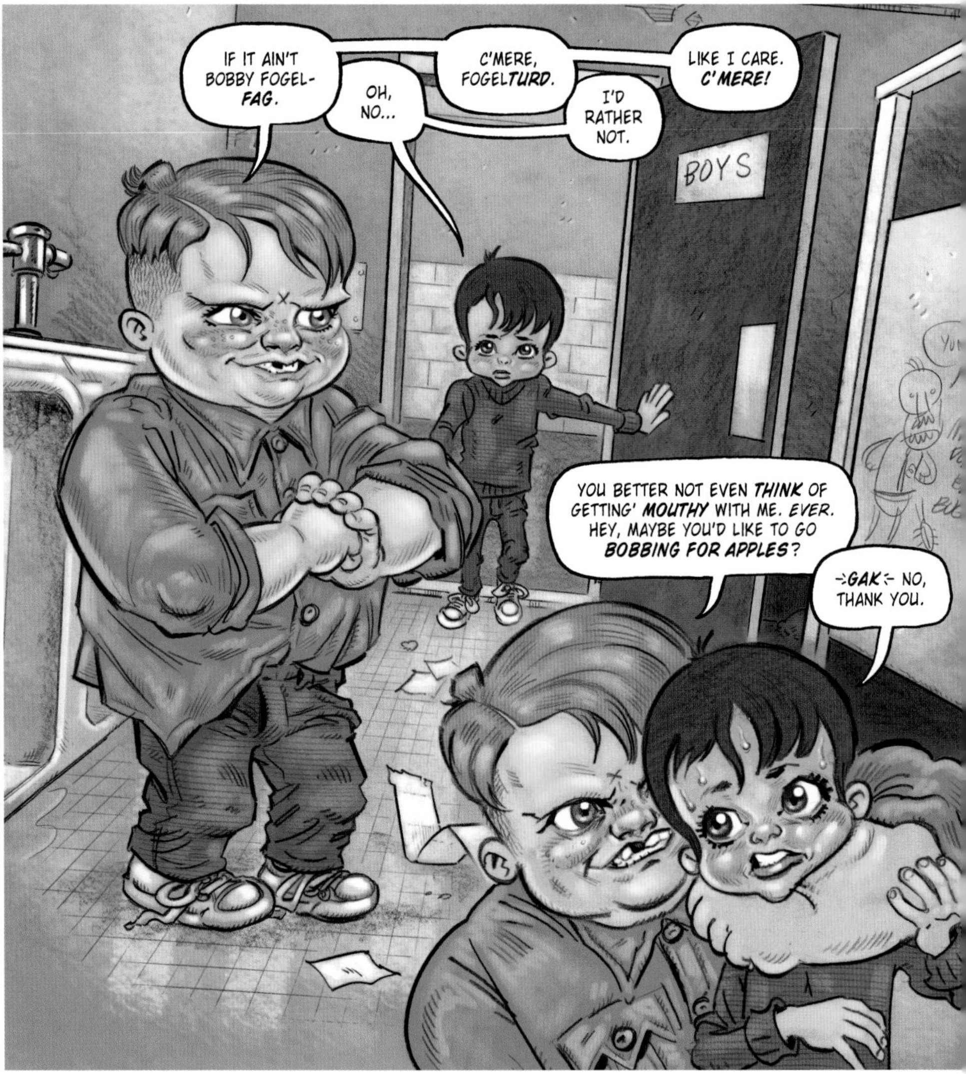
IF IT AIN'T BOBBY FOGEL-**FAG**.
OH, NO...
C'MERE, FOGEL**TURD**.
I'D RATHER NOT.
LIKE I CARE. ***C'MERE!***
BOYS
YOU BETTER NOT EVEN ***THINK*** OF GETTING' ***MOUTHY*** WITH ME. *EVER*. HEY, MAYBE YOU'D LIKE TO GO ***BOBBING FOR APPLES***?
-***GAK***- NO, THANK YOU.

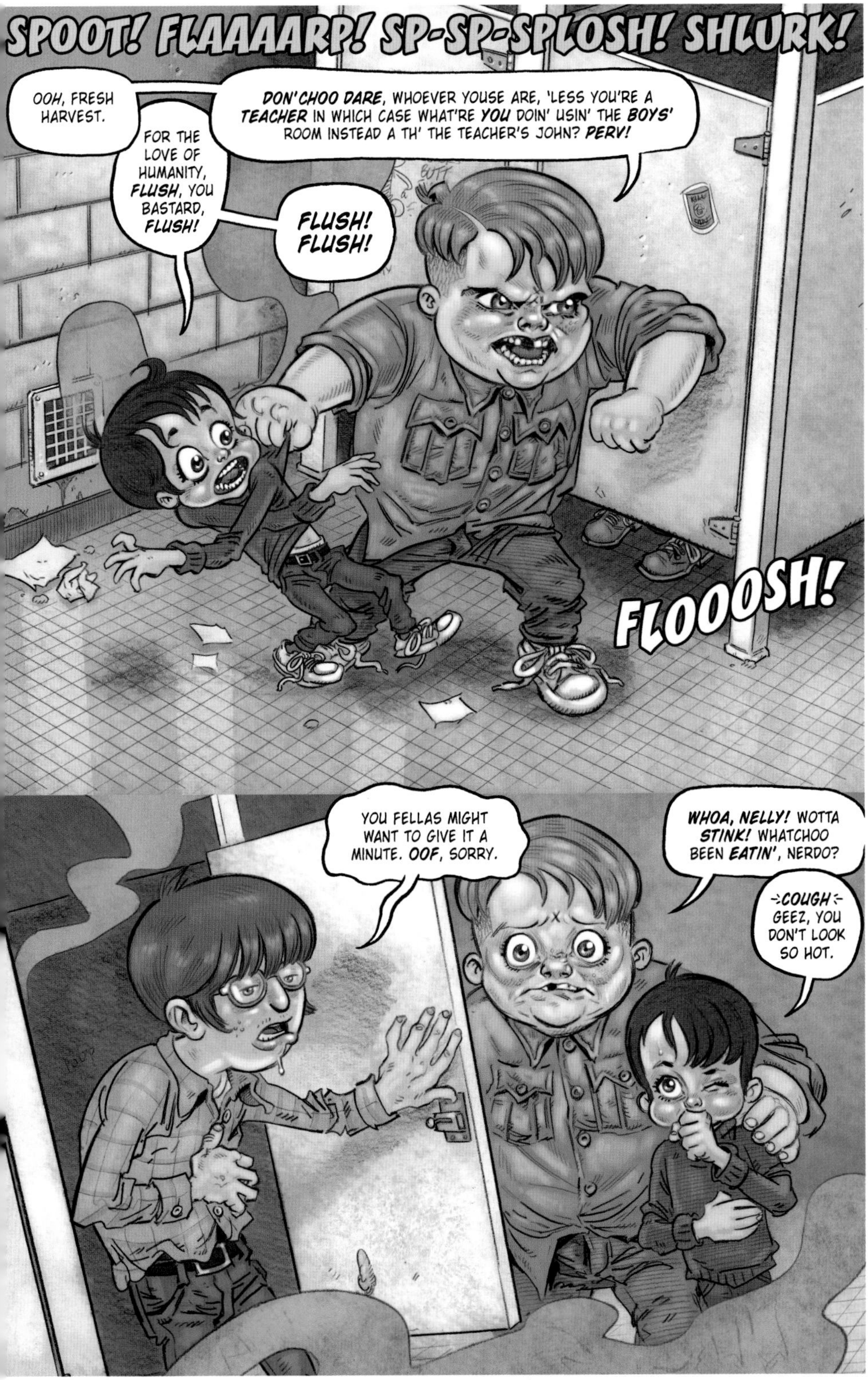
SPOOT! FLAAAARP! SP-SP-SPLOSH! SHLURK!
OOH, FRESH HARVEST.
FOR THE LOVE OF HUMANITY, FLUSH, YOU BASTARD, FLUSH!
FLUSH! FLUSH!
DON'CHOO DARE, WHOEVER YOUSE ARE, 'LESS YOU'RE A TEACHER IN WHICH CASE WHAT'RE YOU DOIN' USIN' THE BOYS' ROOM INSTEAD A TH' THE TEACHER'S JOHN? PERV!
FLOOOSH!
YOU FELLAS MIGHT WANT TO GIVE IT A MINUTE. OOF, SORRY.
WHOA, NELLY! WOTTA STINK! WHATCHOO BEEN EATIN', NERDO?
COUGH GEEZ, YOU DON'T LOOK SO HOT.

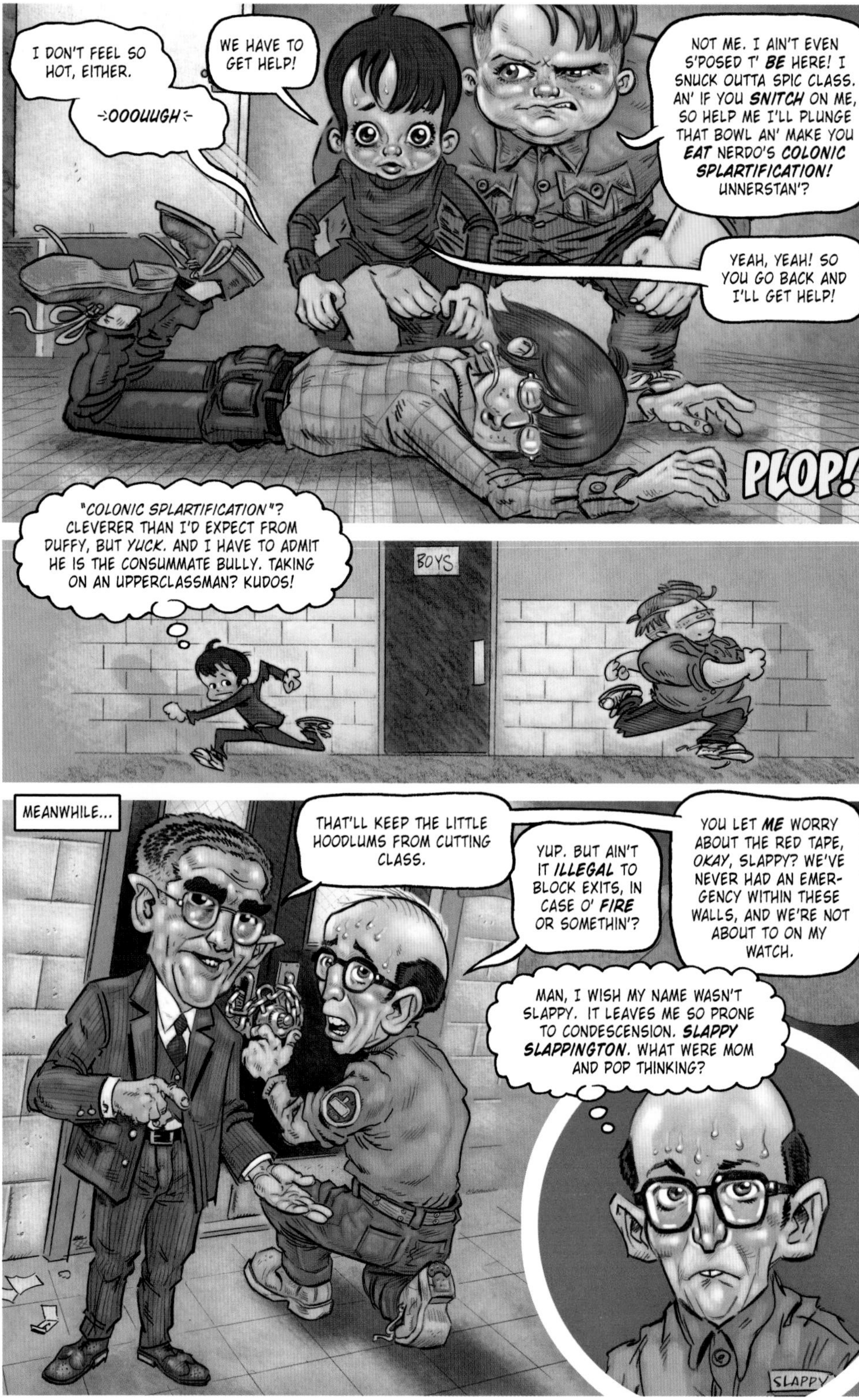
I DON'T FEEL SO HOT, EITHER.
-OOOUUGH-
WE HAVE TO GET HELP!
NOT ME. I AIN'T EVEN S'POSED T' BE HERE! I SNUCK OUTTA SPIC CLASS. AN' IF YOU SNITCH ON ME, SO HELP ME I'LL PLUNGE THAT BOWL AN' MAKE YOU EAT NERDO'S COLONIC SPLARTIFICATION! UNNERSTAN'?
YEAH, YEAH! SO YOU GO BACK AND I'LL GET HELP!
PLOP!
"COLONIC SPLARTIFICATION"? CLEVERER THAN I'D EXPECT FROM DUFFY, BUT YUCK. AND I HAVE TO ADMIT HE IS THE CONSUMMATE BULLY. TAKING ON AN UPPERCLASSMAN? KUDOS!
BOYS
MEANWHILE...
THAT'LL KEEP THE LITTLE HOODLUMS FROM CUTTING CLASS.
YUP. BUT AIN'T IT ILLEGAL TO BLOCK EXITS, IN CASE O' FIRE OR SOMETHIN'?
YOU LET ME WORRY ABOUT THE RED TAPE, OKAY, SLAPPY? WE'VE NEVER HAD AN EMERGENCY WITHIN THESE WALLS, AND WE'RE NOT ABOUT TO ON MY WATCH.
MAN, I WISH MY NAME WASN'T SLAPPY. IT LEAVES ME SO PRONE TO CONDESCENSION. SLAPPY SLAPPINGTON. WHAT WERE MOM AND POP THINKING?
SLAPPY

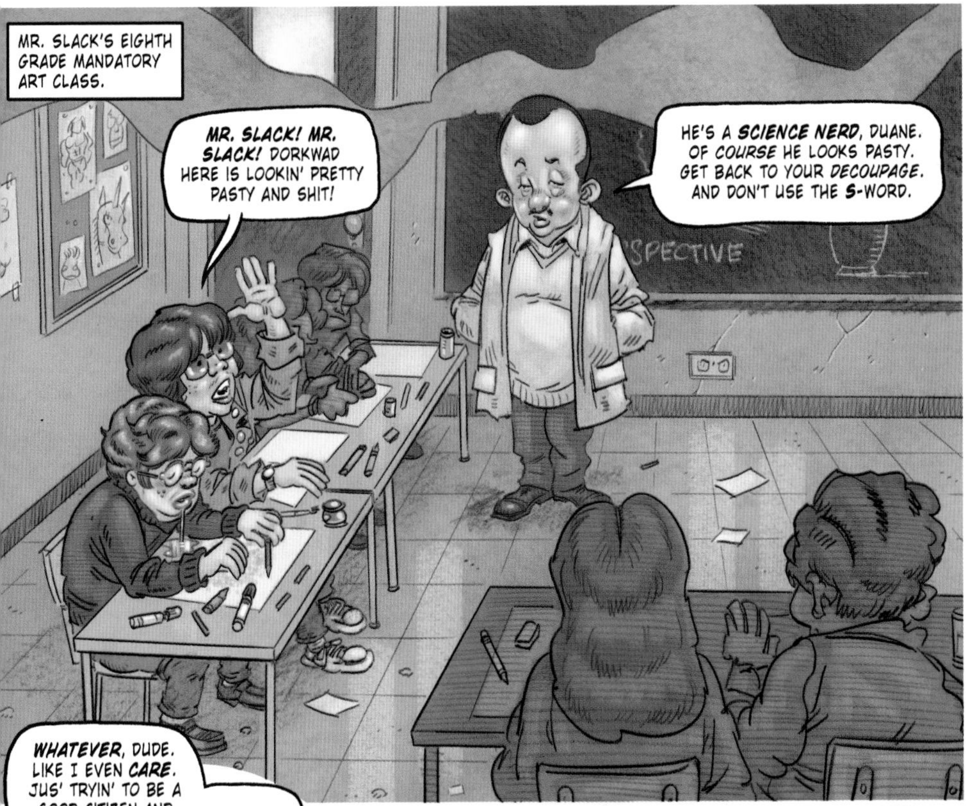
MR. SLACK'S EIGHTH GRADE MANDATORY ART CLASS.
MR. SLACK! MR. SLACK! DORKWAD HERE IS LOOKIN' PRETTY PASTY AND SHIT!
HE'S A SCIENCE NERD, DUANE. OF COURSE HE LOOKS PASTY. GET BACK TO YOUR DECOUPAGE. AND DON'T USE THE S-WORD.
SPECTIVE

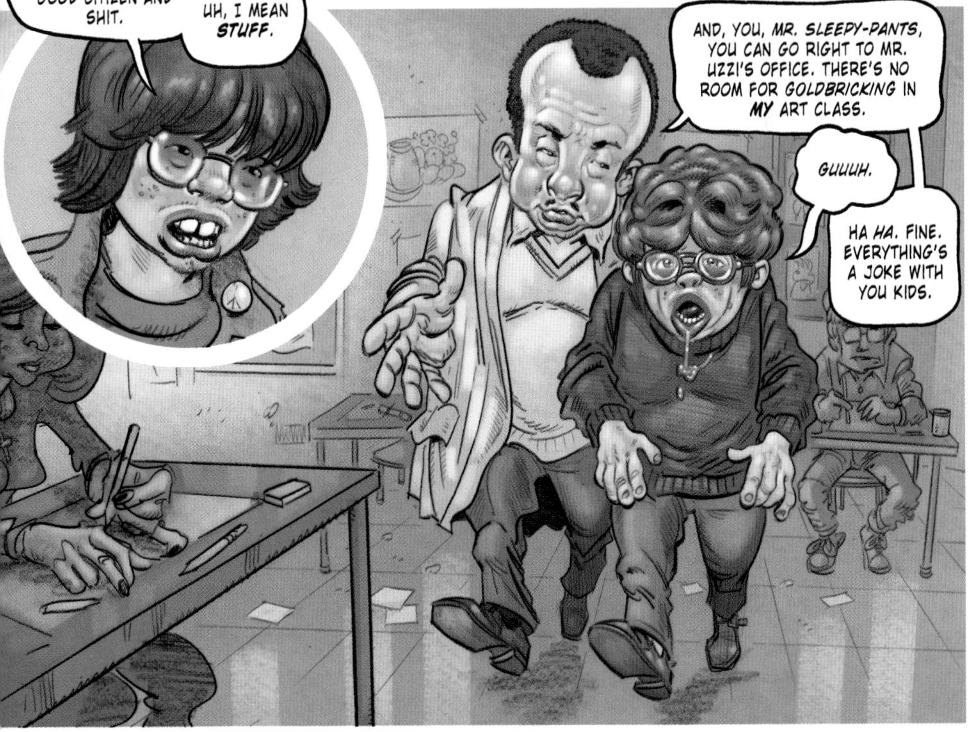
WHATEVER, DUDE. LIKE I EVEN CARE. JUS' TRYIN' TO BE A GOOD CITIZEN AND SHIT.
UH, I MEAN STUFF.
AND, YOU, MR. SLEEPY-PANTS, YOU CAN GO RIGHT TO MR. UZZI'S OFFICE. THERE'S NO ROOM FOR GOLDBRICKING IN MY ART CLASS.
GUUUH.
HA HA. FINE. EVERYTHING'S A JOKE WITH YOU KIDS.

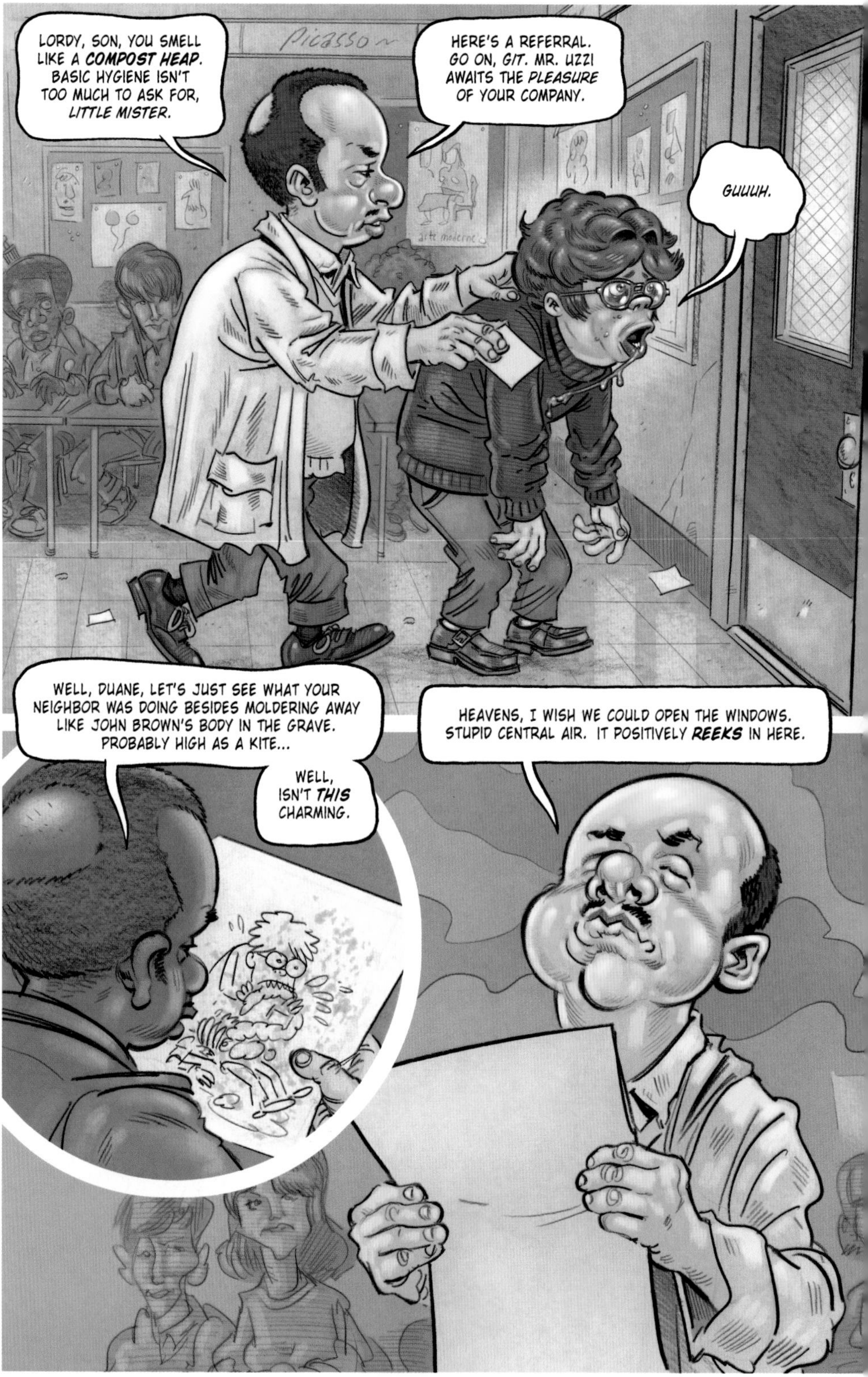
LORDY, SON, YOU SMELL LIKE A ***COMPOST HEAP***. BASIC HYGIENE ISN'T TOO MUCH TO ASK FOR, *LITTLE MISTER*.
HERE'S A REFERRAL. GO ON, *GIT*. MR. UZZI AWAITS THE *PLEASURE* OF YOUR COMPANY.
GUUUH.
WELL, DUANE, LET'S JUST SEE WHAT YOUR NEIGHBOR WAS DOING BESIDES MOLDERING AWAY LIKE JOHN BROWN'S BODY IN THE GRAVE. PROBABLY HIGH AS A KITE...
WELL, ISN'T ***THIS*** CHARMING.
HEAVENS, I WISH WE COULD OPEN THE WINDOWS. STUPID CENTRAL AIR. IT POSITIVELY ***REEKS*** IN HERE.

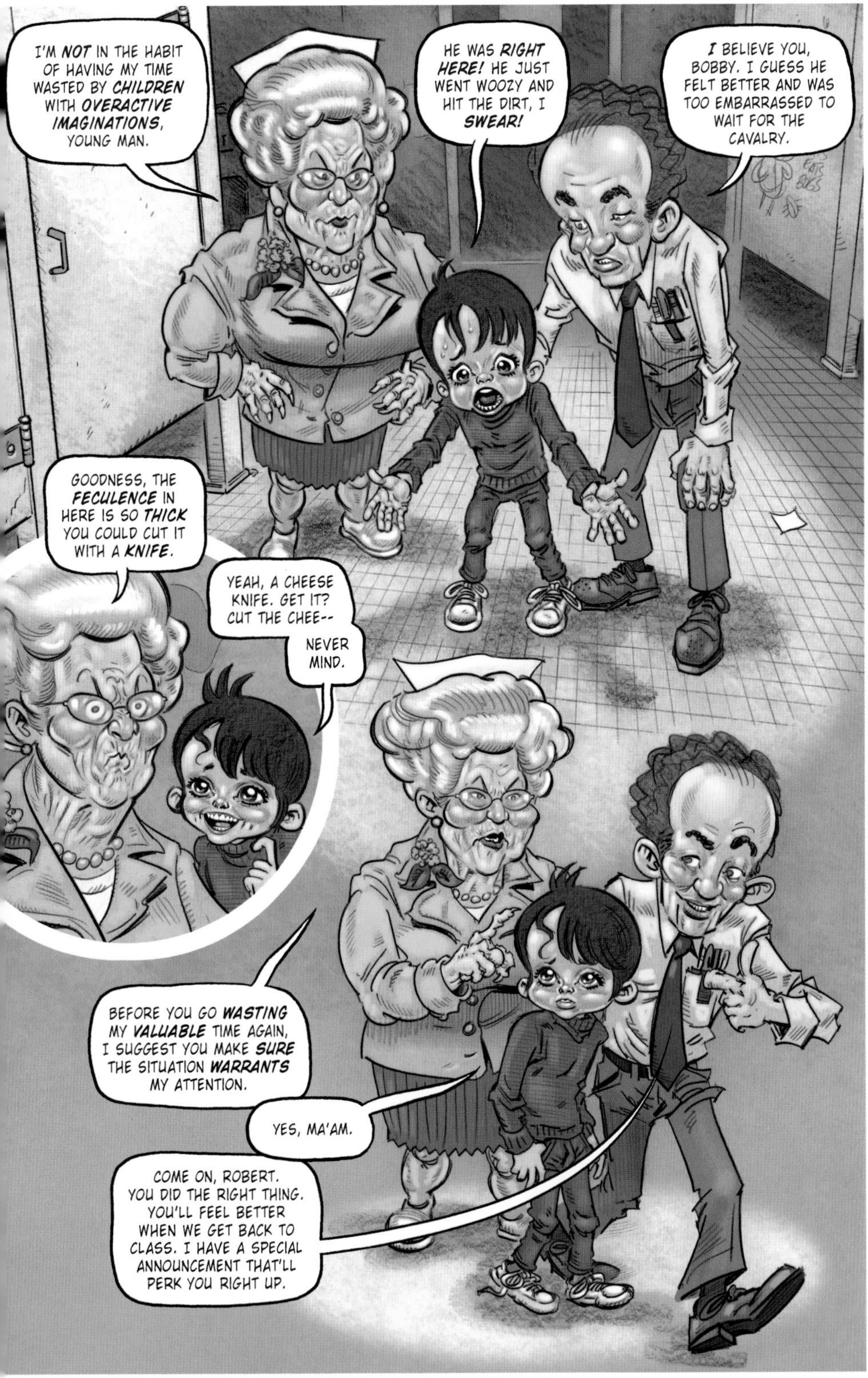

I'M NOT IN THE HABIT OF HAVING MY TIME WASTED BY CHILDREN WITH OVERACTIVE IMAGINATIONS, YOUNG MAN.
HE WAS RIGHT HERE! HE JUST WENT WOOZY AND HIT THE DIRT, I SWEAR!
I BELIEVE YOU, BOBBY. I GUESS HE FELT BETTER AND WAS TOO EMBARRASSED TO WAIT FOR THE CAVALRY.
GOODNESS, THE FECULENCE IN HERE IS SO THICK YOU COULD CUT IT WITH A KNIFE.
YEAH, A CHEESE KNIFE. GET IT? CUT THE CHEE--
NEVER MIND.
BEFORE YOU GO WASTING MY VALUABLE TIME AGAIN, I SUGGEST YOU MAKE SURE THE SITUATION WARRANTS MY ATTENTION.
YES, MA'AM.
COME ON, ROBERT. YOU DID THE RIGHT THING. YOU'LL FEEL BETTER WHEN WE GET BACK TO CLASS. I HAVE A SPECIAL ANNOUNCEMENT THAT'LL PERK YOU RIGHT UP.

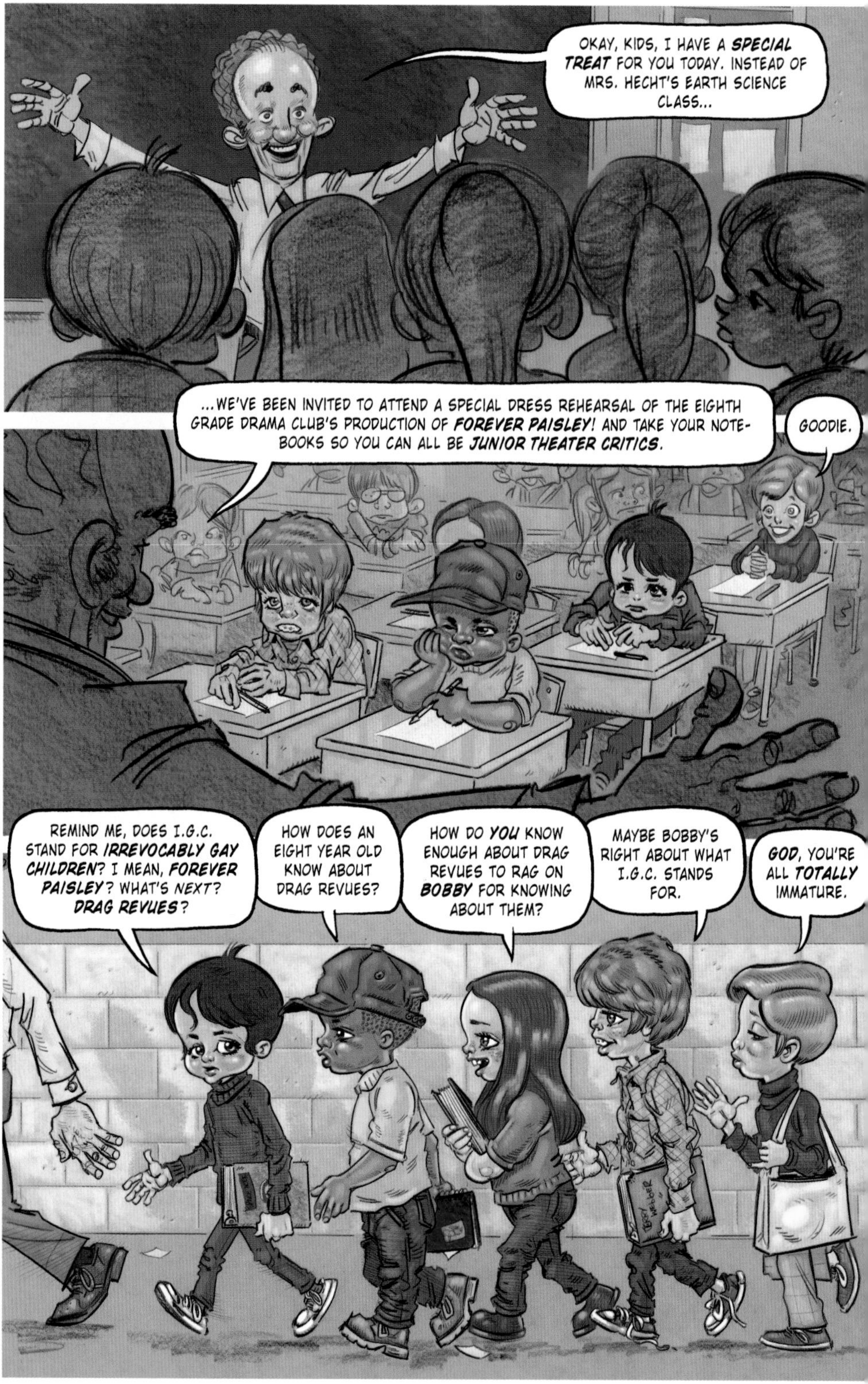
OKAY, KIDS, I HAVE A SPECIAL TREAT FOR YOU TODAY. INSTEAD OF MRS. HECHT'S EARTH SCIENCE CLASS...
...WE'VE BEEN INVITED TO ATTEND A SPECIAL DRESS REHEARSAL OF THE EIGHTH GRADE DRAMA CLUB'S PRODUCTION OF FOREVER PAISLEY! AND TAKE YOUR NOTE-BOOKS SO YOU CAN ALL BE JUNIOR THEATER CRITICS.
GOODIE.
REMIND ME, DOES I.G.C. STAND FOR IRREVOCABLY GAY CHILDREN? I MEAN, FOREVER PAISLEY? WHAT'S NEXT? DRAG REVUES?
HOW DOES AN EIGHT YEAR OLD KNOW ABOUT DRAG REVUES?
HOW DO YOU KNOW ENOUGH ABOUT DRAG REVUES TO RAG ON BOBBY FOR KNOWING ABOUT THEM?
MAYBE BOBBY'S RIGHT ABOUT WHAT I.G.C. STANDS FOR.
GOD, YOU'RE ALL TOTALLY IMMATURE.

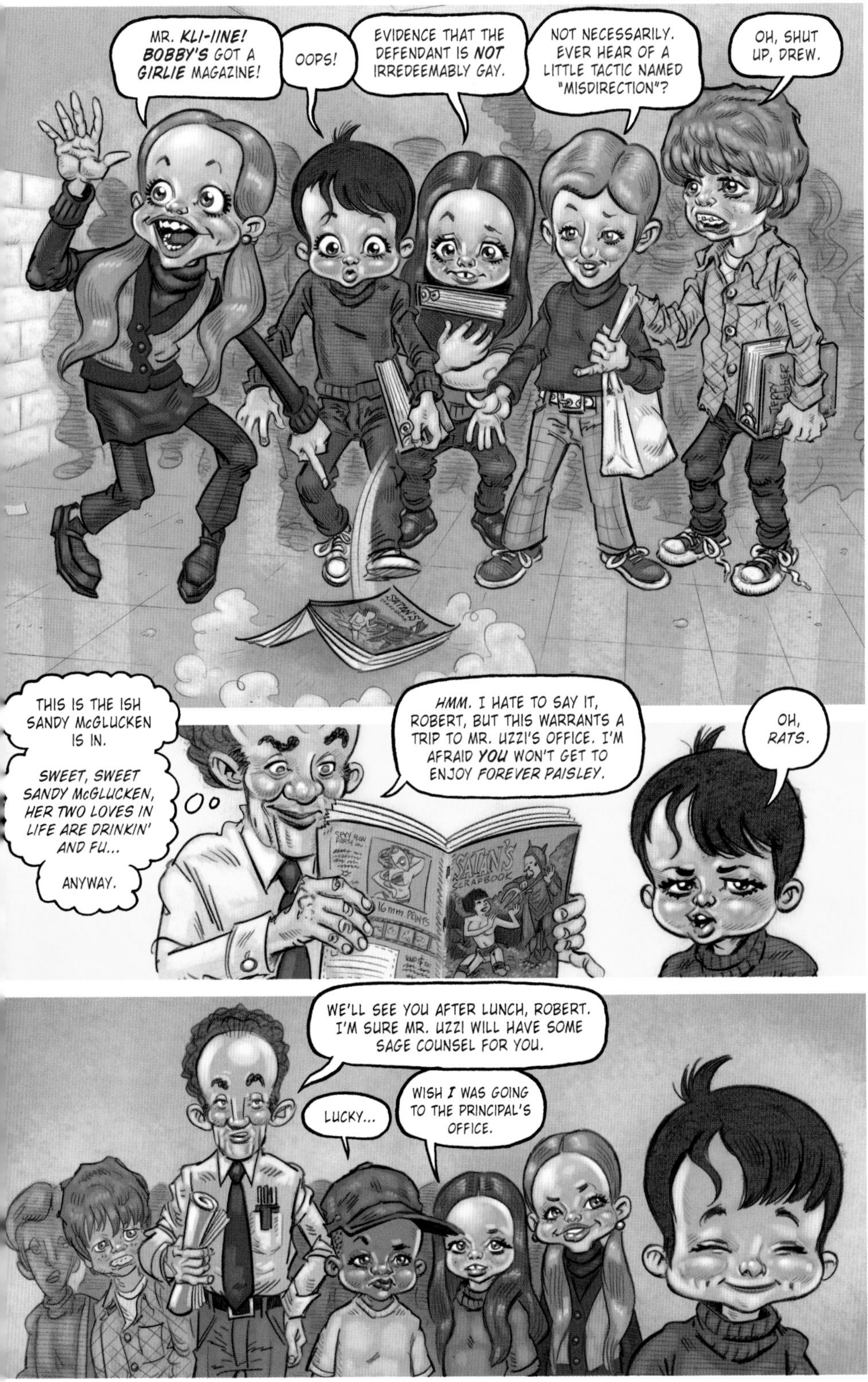
MR. KLI-IINE! BOBBY'S GOT A GIRLIE MAGAZINE!
OOPS!
EVIDENCE THAT THE DEFENDANT IS NOT IRREDEEMABLY GAY.
NOT NECESSARILY. EVER HEAR OF A LITTLE TACTIC NAMED "MISDIRECTION"?
OH, SHUT UP, DREW.
THIS IS THE ISH SANDY McGLUCKEN IS IN.
SWEET, SWEET SANDY McGLUCKEN, HER TWO LOVES IN LIFE ARE DRINKIN' AND FU...
ANYWAY.
SATAN'S SCRAPBOOK
HMM. I HATE TO SAY IT, ROBERT, BUT THIS WARRANTS A TRIP TO MR. UZZI'S OFFICE. I'M AFRAID YOU WON'T GET TO ENJOY FOREVER PAISLEY.
OH, RATS.
WE'LL SEE YOU AFTER LUNCH, ROBERT. I'M SURE MR. UZZI WILL HAVE SOME SAGE COUNSEL FOR YOU.
LUCKY...
WISH I WAS GOING TO THE PRINCIPAL'S OFFICE.

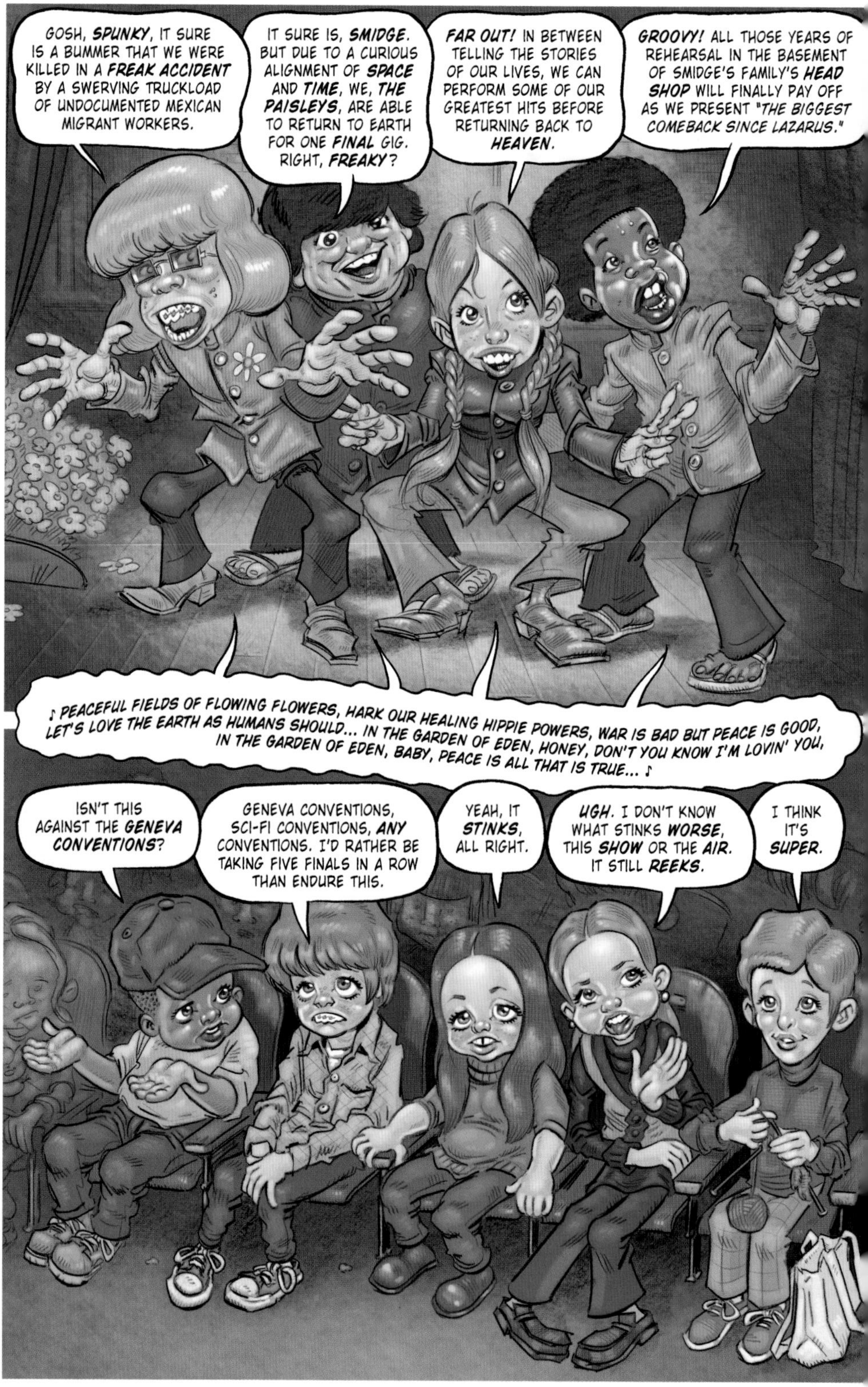
GOSH, SPUNKY, IT SURE IS A BUMMER THAT WE WERE KILLED IN A FREAK ACCIDENT BY A SWERVING TRUCKLOAD OF UNDOCUMENTED MEXICAN MIGRANT WORKERS.
IT SURE IS, SMIDGE. BUT DUE TO A CURIOUS ALIGNMENT OF SPACE AND TIME, WE, THE PAISLEYS, ARE ABLE TO RETURN TO EARTH FOR ONE FINAL GIG. RIGHT, FREAKY?
FAR OUT! IN BETWEEN TELLING THE STORIES OF OUR LIVES, WE CAN PERFORM SOME OF OUR GREATEST HITS BEFORE RETURNING BACK TO HEAVEN.
GROOVY! ALL THOSE YEARS OF REHEARSAL IN THE BASEMENT OF SMIDGE'S FAMILY'S HEAD SHOP WILL FINALLY PAY OFF AS WE PRESENT "THE BIGGEST COMEBACK SINCE LAZARUS."
♪ PEACEFUL FIELDS OF FLOWING FLOWERS, HARK OUR HEALING HIPPIE POWERS, WAR IS BAD BUT PEACE IS GOOD, LET'S LOVE THE EARTH AS HUMANS SHOULD... IN THE GARDEN OF EDEN, HONEY, DON'T YOU KNOW I'M LOVIN' YOU, IN THE GARDEN OF EDEN, BABY, PEACE IS ALL THAT IS TRUE... ♪
ISN'T THIS AGAINST THE GENEVA CONVENTIONS?
GENEVA CONVENTIONS, SCI-FI CONVENTIONS, ANY CONVENTIONS. I'D RATHER BE TAKING FIVE FINALS IN A ROW THAN ENDURE THIS.
YEAH, IT STINKS, ALL RIGHT.
UGH. I DON'T KNOW WHAT STINKS WORSE, THIS SHOW OR THE AIR. IT STILL REEKS.
I THINK IT'S SUPER.

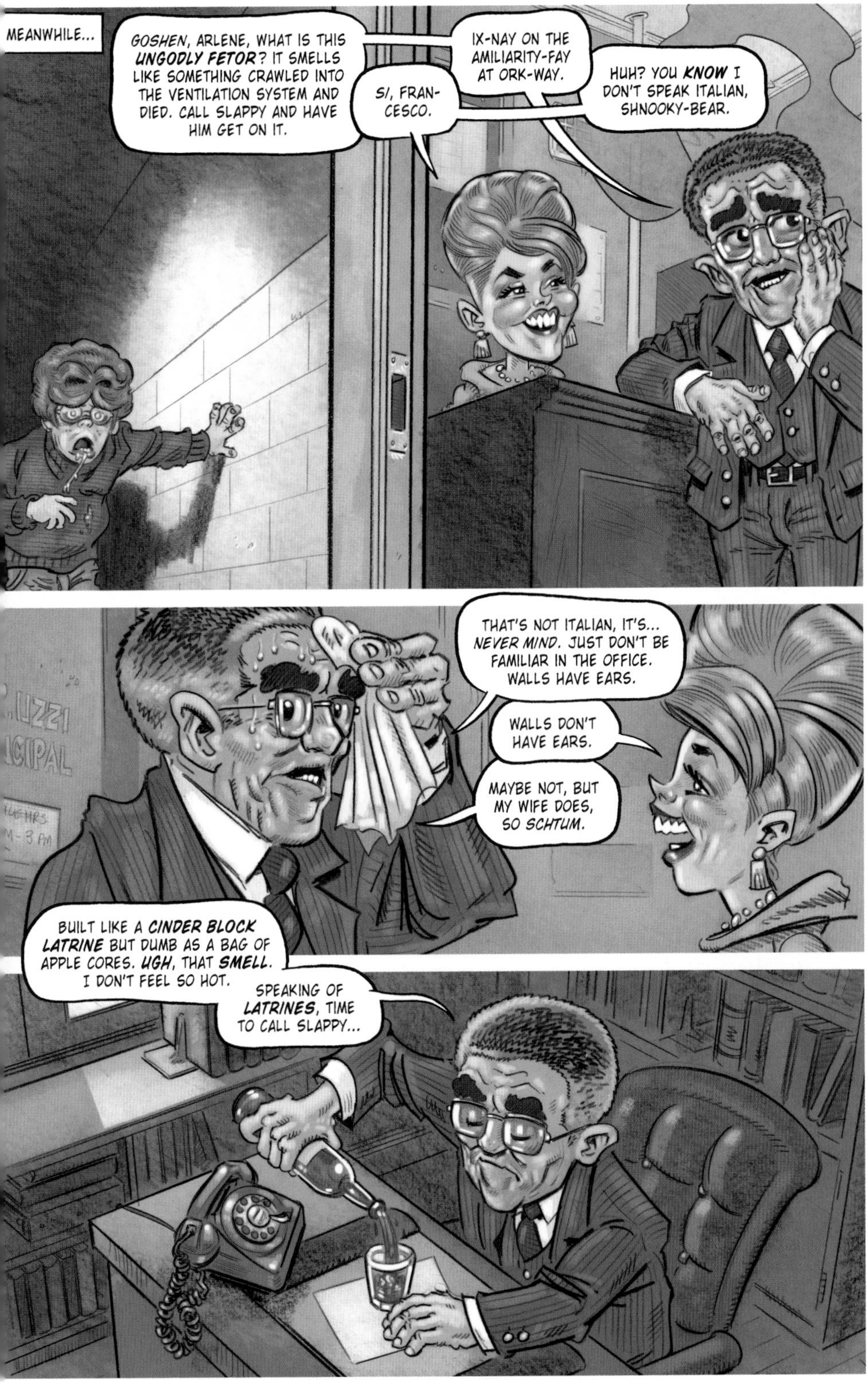
MEANWHILE...
GOSHEN, ARLENE, WHAT IS THIS **UNGODLY FETOR**? IT SMELLS LIKE SOMETHING CRAWLED INTO THE VENTILATION SYSTEM AND DIED. CALL SLAPPY AND HAVE HIM GET ON IT.
IX-NAY ON THE AMILIARITY-FAY AT ORK-WAY.
SÍ, FRANCESCO.
HUH? YOU **KNOW** I DON'T SPEAK ITALIAN, SHNOOKY-BEAR.
THAT'S NOT ITALIAN, IT'S... *NEVER MIND*. JUST DON'T BE FAMILIAR IN THE OFFICE. WALLS HAVE EARS.
WALLS DON'T HAVE EARS.
MAYBE NOT, BUT MY WIFE DOES, SO *SCHTUM*.
BUILT LIKE A ***CINDER BLOCK LATRINE*** BUT DUMB AS A BAG OF APPLE CORES. ***UGH***, THAT ***SMELL***. I DON'T FEEL SO HOT.
SPEAKING OF ***LATRINES***, TIME TO CALL SLAPPY...

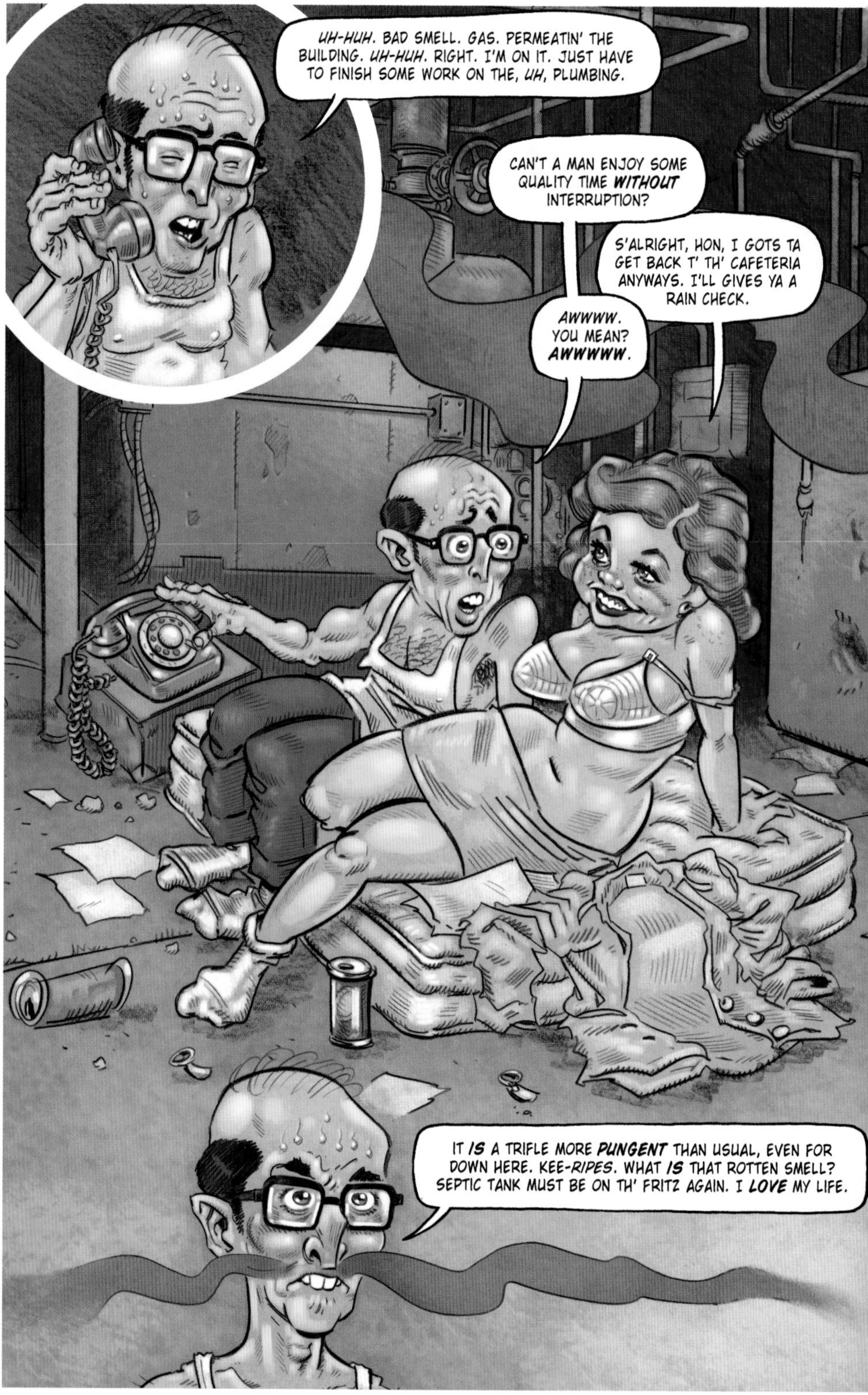
UH-HUH. BAD SMELL. GAS. PERMEATIN' THE BUILDING. UH-HUH. RIGHT. I'M ON IT. JUST HAVE TO FINISH SOME WORK ON THE, UH, PLUMBING.
CAN'T A MAN ENJOY SOME QUALITY TIME WITHOUT INTERRUPTION?
S'ALRIGHT, HON, I GOTS TA GET BACK T' TH' CAFETERIA ANYWAYS. I'LL GIVES YA A RAIN CHECK.
AWWWW. YOU MEAN? AWWWWW.
IT IS A TRIFLE MORE PUNGENT THAN USUAL, EVEN FOR DOWN HERE. KEE-RIPES. WHAT IS THAT ROTTEN SMELL? SEPTIC TANK MUST BE ON TH' FRITZ AGAIN. I LOVE MY LIFE.

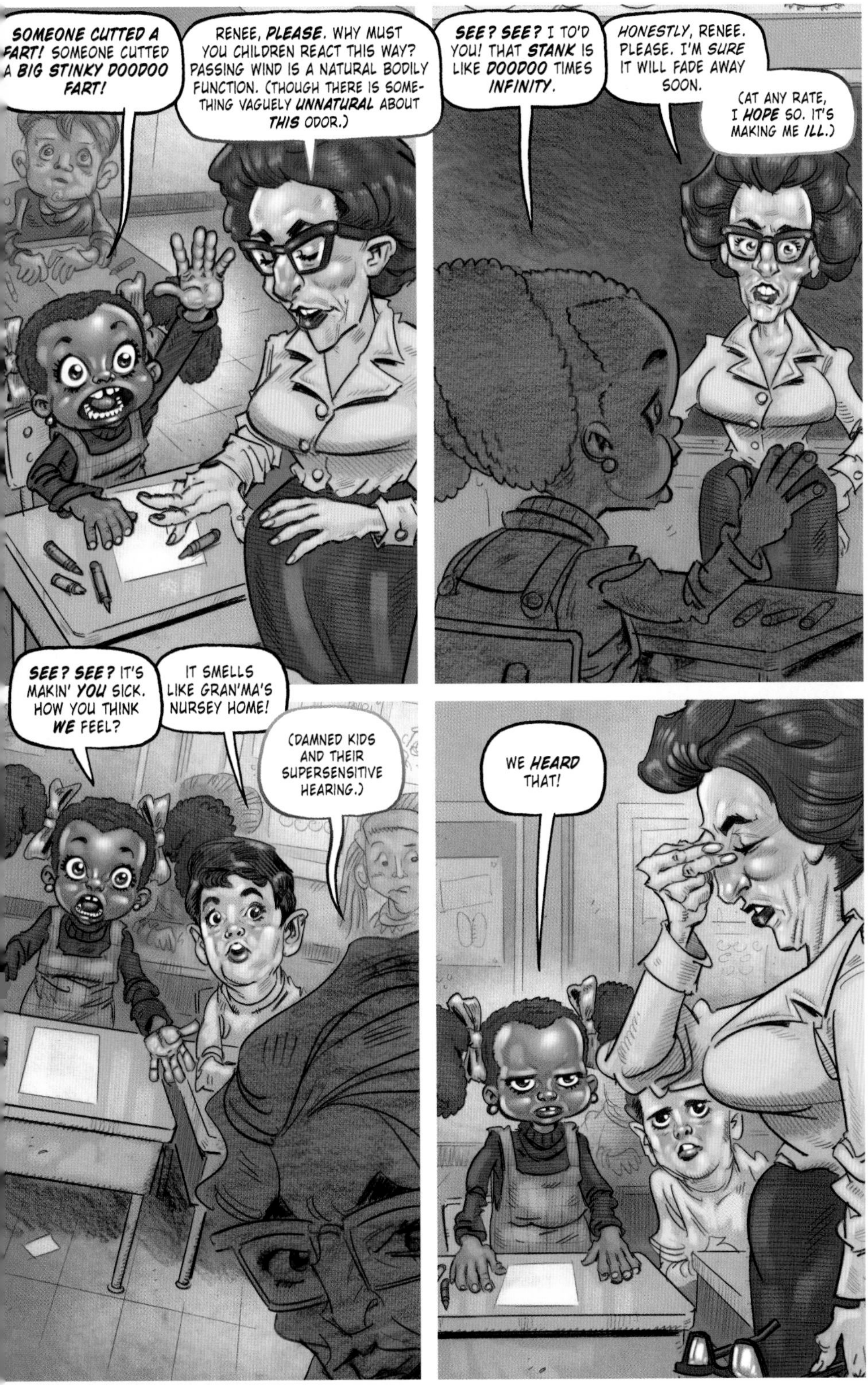
SOMEONE CUTTED A FART! SOMEONE CUTTED A BIG STINKY DOODOO FART!
RENEE, PLEASE. WHY MUST YOU CHILDREN REACT THIS WAY? PASSING WIND IS A NATURAL BODILY FUNCTION. (THOUGH THERE IS SOMETHING VAGUELY UNNATURAL ABOUT THIS ODOR.)
SEE? SEE? I TO'D YOU! THAT STANK IS LIKE DOODOO TIMES INFINITY.
HONESTLY, RENEE. PLEASE. I'M SURE IT WILL FADE AWAY SOON.
(AT ANY RATE, I HOPE SO. IT'S MAKING ME ILL.)
SEE? SEE? IT'S MAKIN' YOU SICK. HOW YOU THINK WE FEEL?
IT SMELLS LIKE GRAN'MA'S NURSEY HOME!
(DAMNED KIDS AND THEIR SUPERSENSITIVE HEARING.)
WE HEARD THAT!

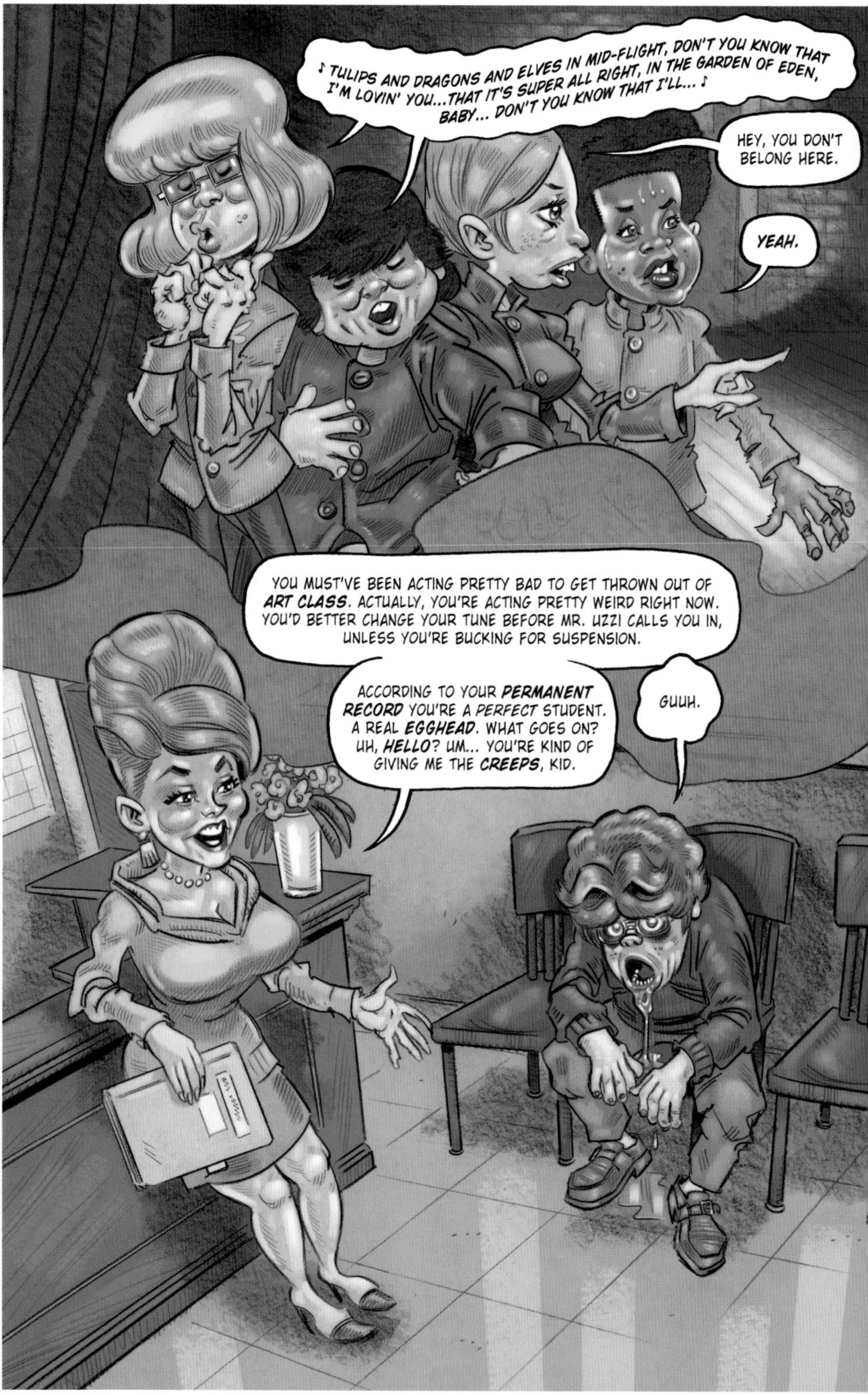
♪ TULIPS AND DRAGONS AND ELVES IN MID-FLIGHT, DON'T YOU KNOW THAT I'M LOVIN' YOU...THAT IT'S SUPER ALL RIGHT, IN THE GARDEN OF EDEN, BABY... DON'T YOU KNOW THAT I'LL... ♪
HEY, YOU DON'T BELONG HERE.
YEAH.
YOU MUST'VE BEEN ACTING PRETTY BAD TO GET THROWN OUT OF ART CLASS. ACTUALLY, YOU'RE ACTING PRETTY WEIRD RIGHT NOW. YOU'D BETTER CHANGE YOUR TUNE BEFORE MR. UZZI CALLS YOU IN, UNLESS YOU'RE BUCKING FOR SUSPENSION.
ACCORDING TO YOUR PERMANENT RECORD YOU'RE A PERFECT STUDENT. A REAL EGGHEAD. WHAT GOES ON? UH, HELLO? UM... YOU'RE KIND OF GIVING ME THE CREEPS, KID.
GUUH.

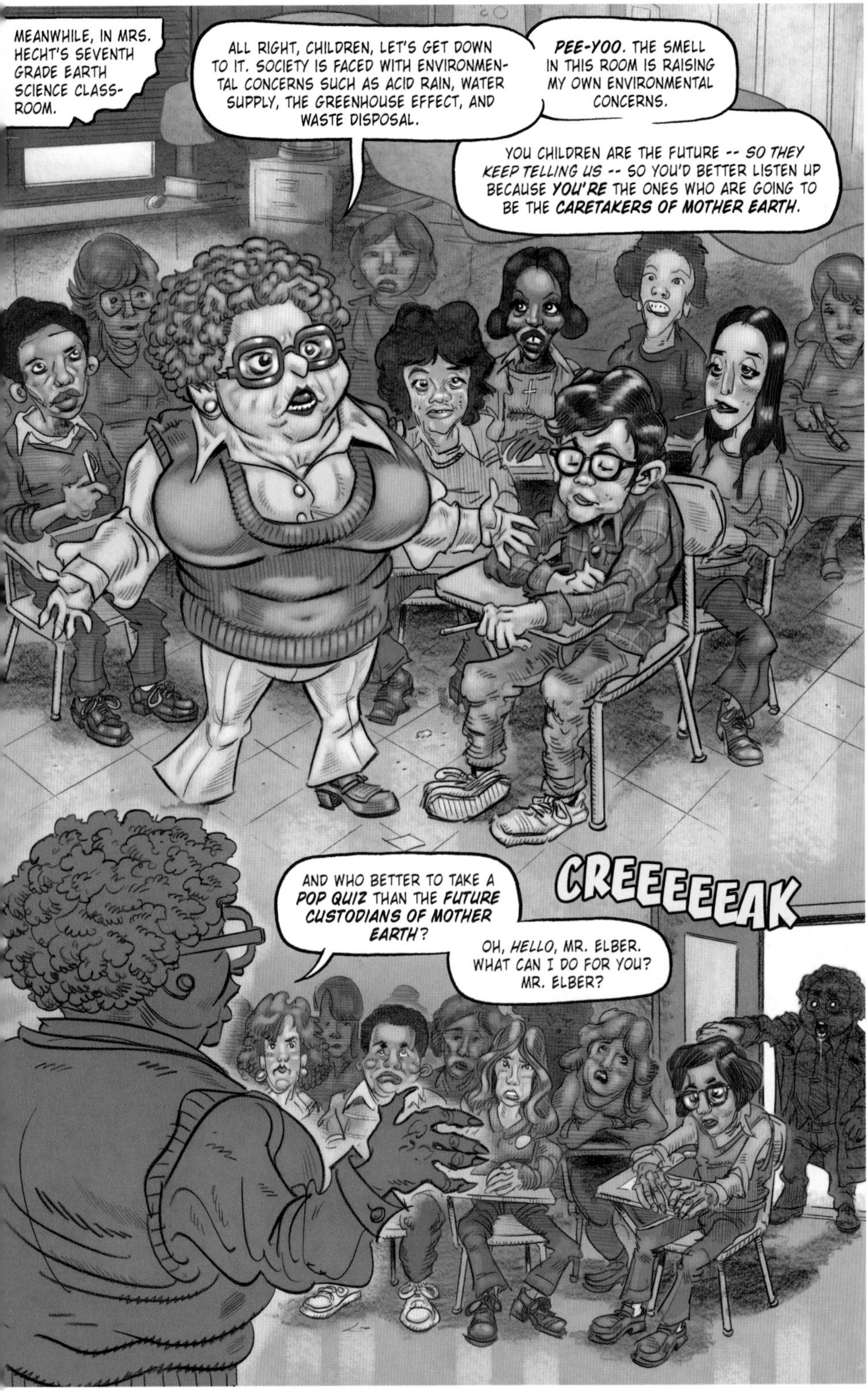
MEANWHILE, IN MRS. HECHT'S SEVENTH GRADE EARTH SCIENCE CLASS-ROOM.
ALL RIGHT, CHILDREN, LET'S GET DOWN TO IT. SOCIETY IS FACED WITH ENVIRONMENTAL CONCERNS SUCH AS ACID RAIN, WATER SUPPLY, THE GREENHOUSE EFFECT, AND WASTE DISPOSAL.
PEE-YOO. THE SMELL IN THIS ROOM IS RAISING MY OWN ENVIRONMENTAL CONCERNS.
YOU CHILDREN ARE THE FUTURE -- SO THEY KEEP TELLING US -- SO YOU'D BETTER LISTEN UP BECAUSE YOU'RE THE ONES WHO ARE GOING TO BE THE CARETAKERS OF MOTHER EARTH.
AND WHO BETTER TO TAKE A POP QUIZ THAN THE FUTURE CUSTODIANS OF MOTHER EARTH?
CREEEEEEAK
OH, HELLO, MR. ELBER. WHAT CAN I DO FOR YOU? MR. ELBER?

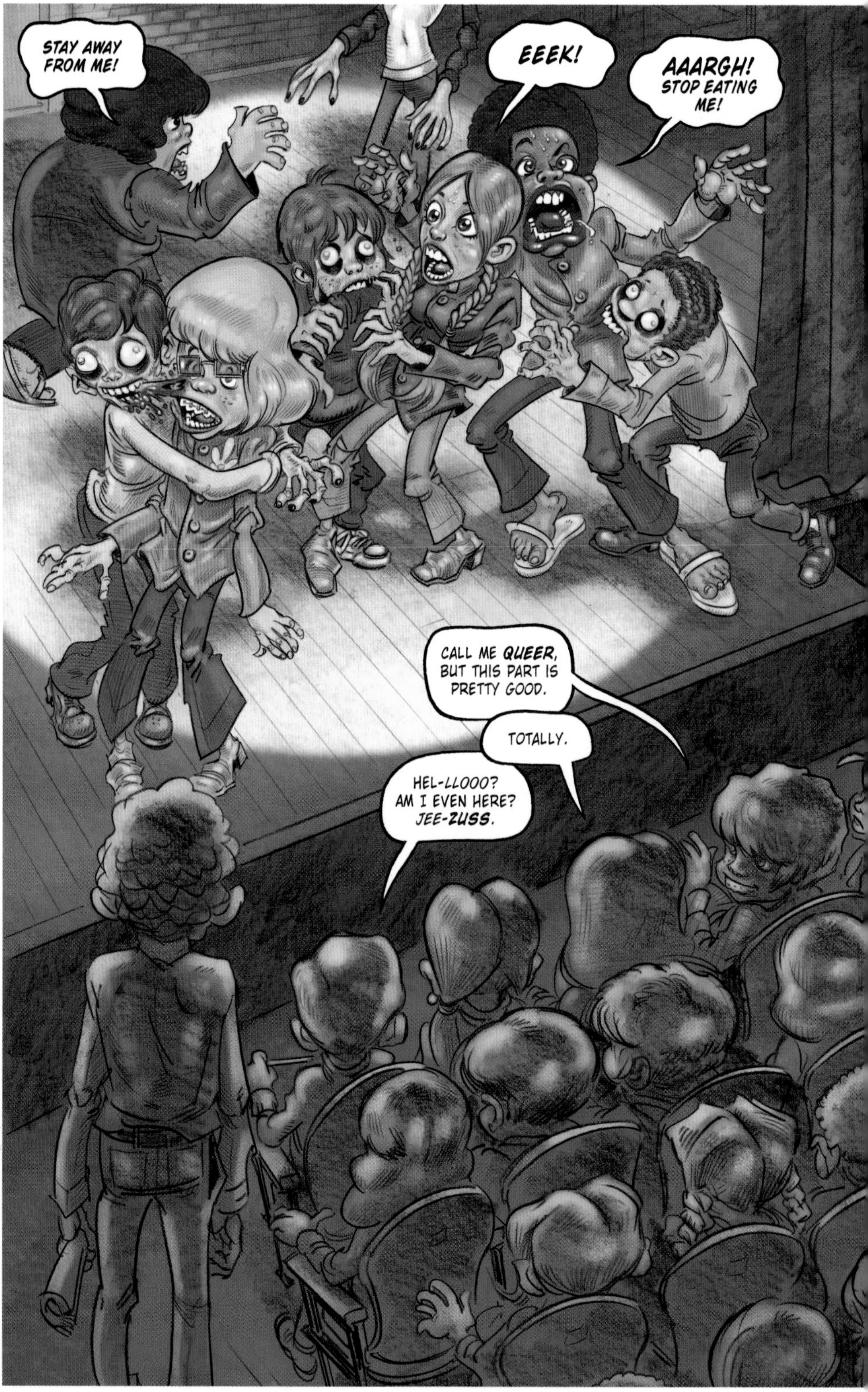
STAY AWAY FROM ME!
EEEK!
AAARGH! STOP EATING ME!
CALL ME QUEER, BUT THIS PART IS PRETTY GOOD.
TOTALLY.
HEL-LLOOO? AM I EVEN HERE? JEE-ZUSS.

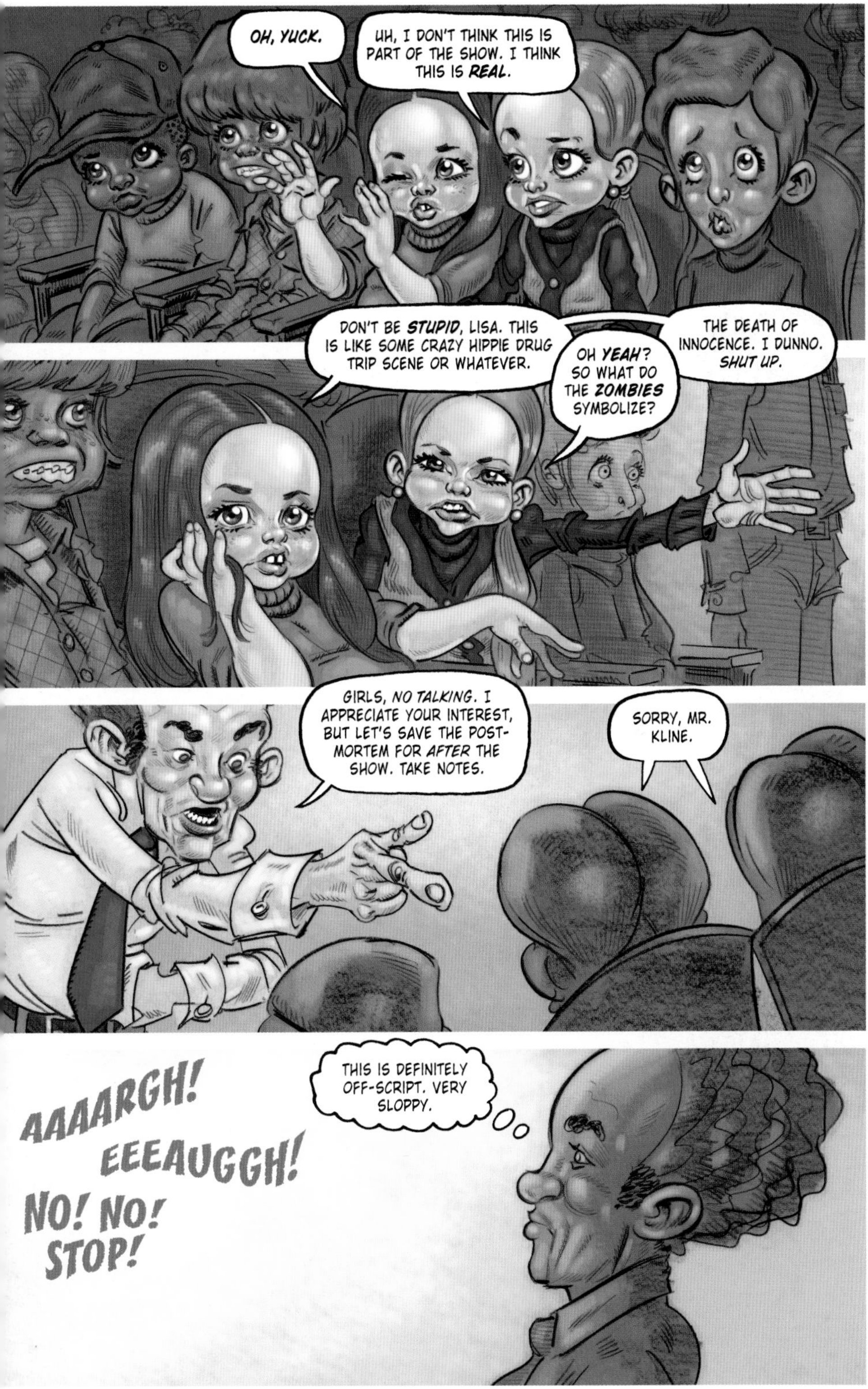
OH, YUCK.
UH, I DON'T THINK THIS IS PART OF THE SHOW. I THINK THIS IS REAL.
DON'T BE STUPID, LISA. THIS IS LIKE SOME CRAZY HIPPIE DRUG TRIP SCENE OR WHATEVER.
OH YEAH? SO WHAT DO THE ZOMBIES SYMBOLIZE?
THE DEATH OF INNOCENCE. I DUNNO. SHUT UP.
GIRLS, NO TALKING. I APPRECIATE YOUR INTEREST, BUT LET'S SAVE THE POST-MORTEM FOR AFTER THE SHOW. TAKE NOTES.
SORRY, MR. KLINE.
AAAARGH!
EEEAUGGH!
NO! NO! STOP!
THIS IS DEFINITELY OFF-SCRIPT. VERY SLOPPY.

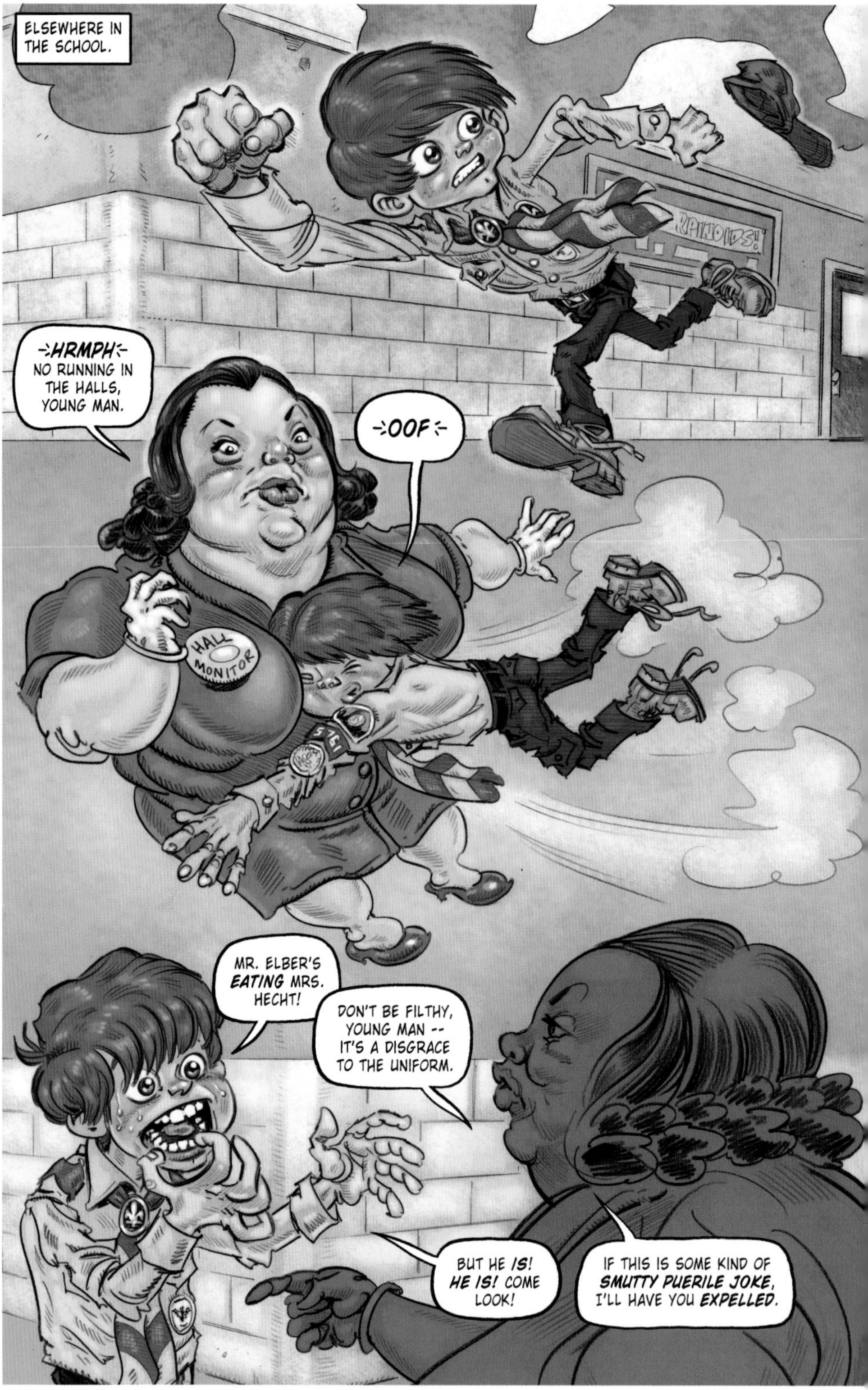
ELSEWHERE IN THE SCHOOL.
RPINOIDS!
-HRMPH- NO RUNNING IN THE HALLS, YOUNG MAN.
-OOF-
HALL MONITOR
MR. ELBER'S EATING MRS. HECHT!
DON'T BE FILTHY, YOUNG MAN -- IT'S A DISGRACE TO THE UNIFORM.
BUT HE IS! HE IS! COME LOOK!
IF THIS IS SOME KIND OF SMUTTY PUERILE JOKE, I'LL HAVE YOU EXPELLED.

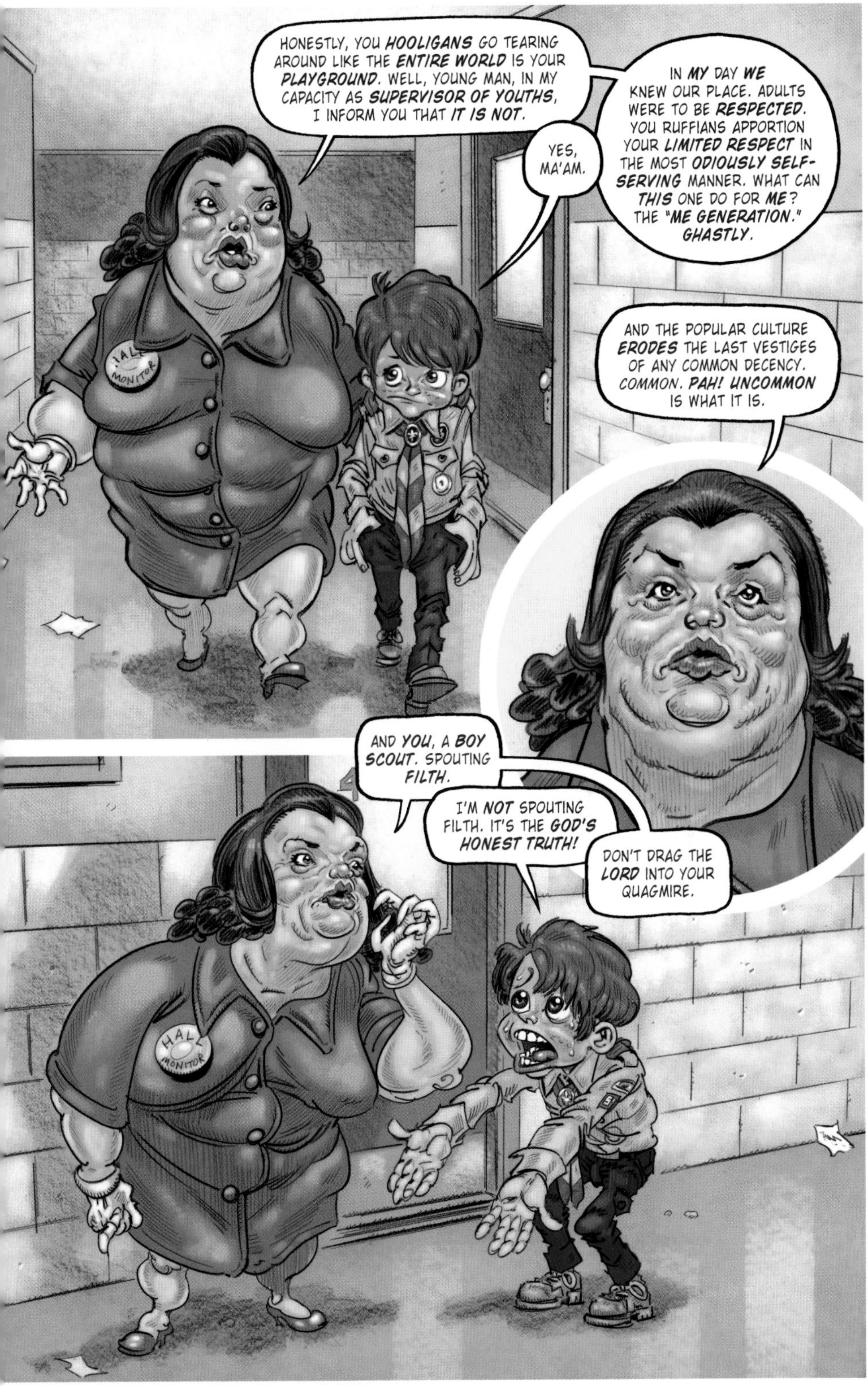
HONESTLY, YOU HOOLIGANS GO TEARING AROUND LIKE THE ENTIRE WORLD IS YOUR PLAYGROUND. WELL, YOUNG MAN, IN MY CAPACITY AS SUPERVISOR OF YOUTHS, I INFORM YOU THAT IT IS NOT.
YES, MA'AM.
IN MY DAY WE KNEW OUR PLACE. ADULTS WERE TO BE RESPECTED. YOU RUFFIANS APPORTION YOUR LIMITED RESPECT IN THE MOST ODIOUSLY SELF-SERVING MANNER. WHAT CAN THIS ONE DO FOR ME? THE "ME GENERATION." GHASTLY.
HALL MONITOR
AND THE POPULAR CULTURE ERODES THE LAST VESTIGES OF ANY COMMON DECENCY. COMMON. PAH! UNCOMMON IS WHAT IT IS.
AND YOU, A BOY SCOUT. SPOUTING FILTH.
I'M NOT SPOUTING FILTH. IT'S THE GOD'S HONEST TRUTH!
DON'T DRAG THE LORD INTO YOUR QUAGMIRE.
HALL MONITOR

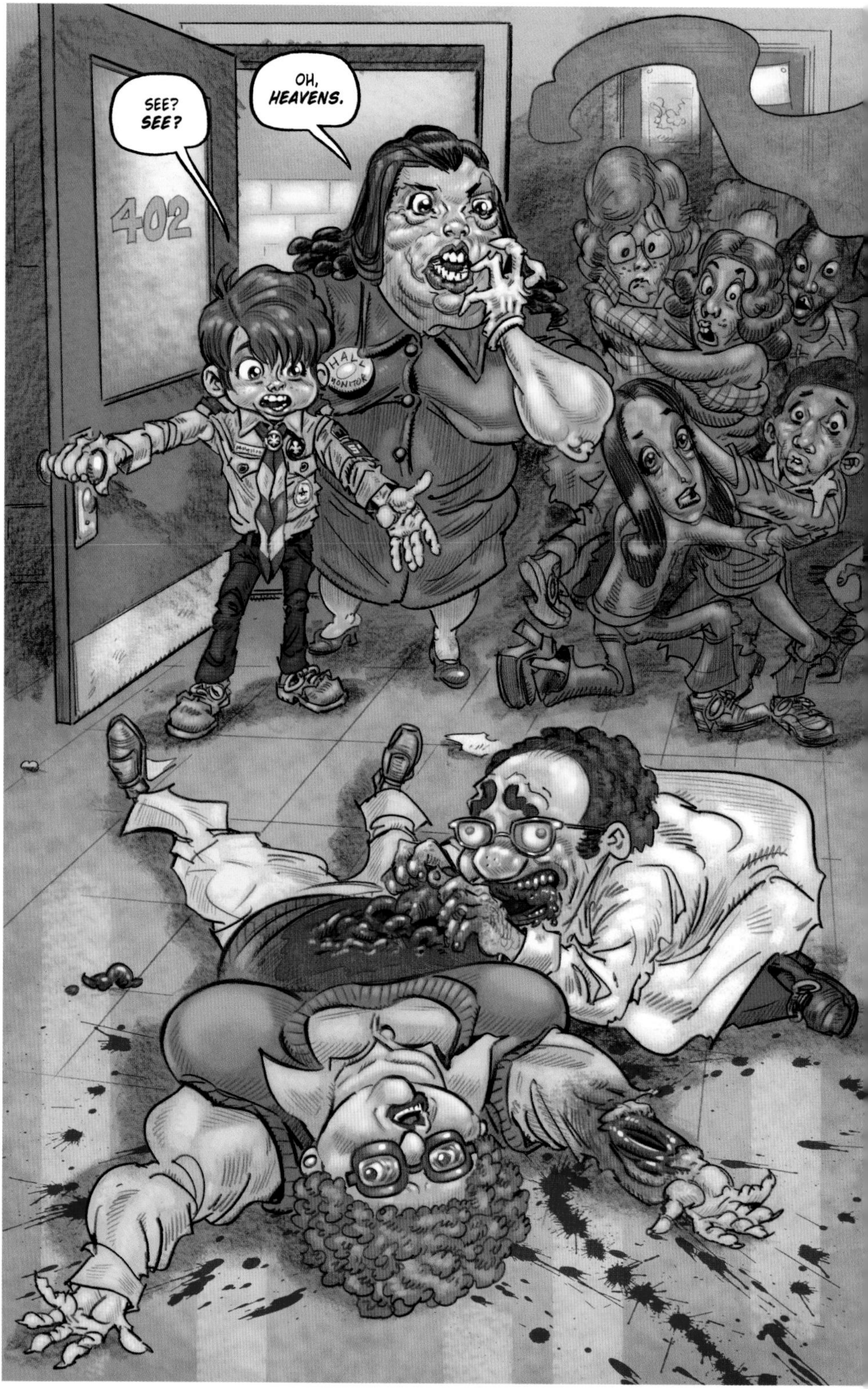
SEE? SEE?
OH, HEAVENS.
402
HALL MONITOR

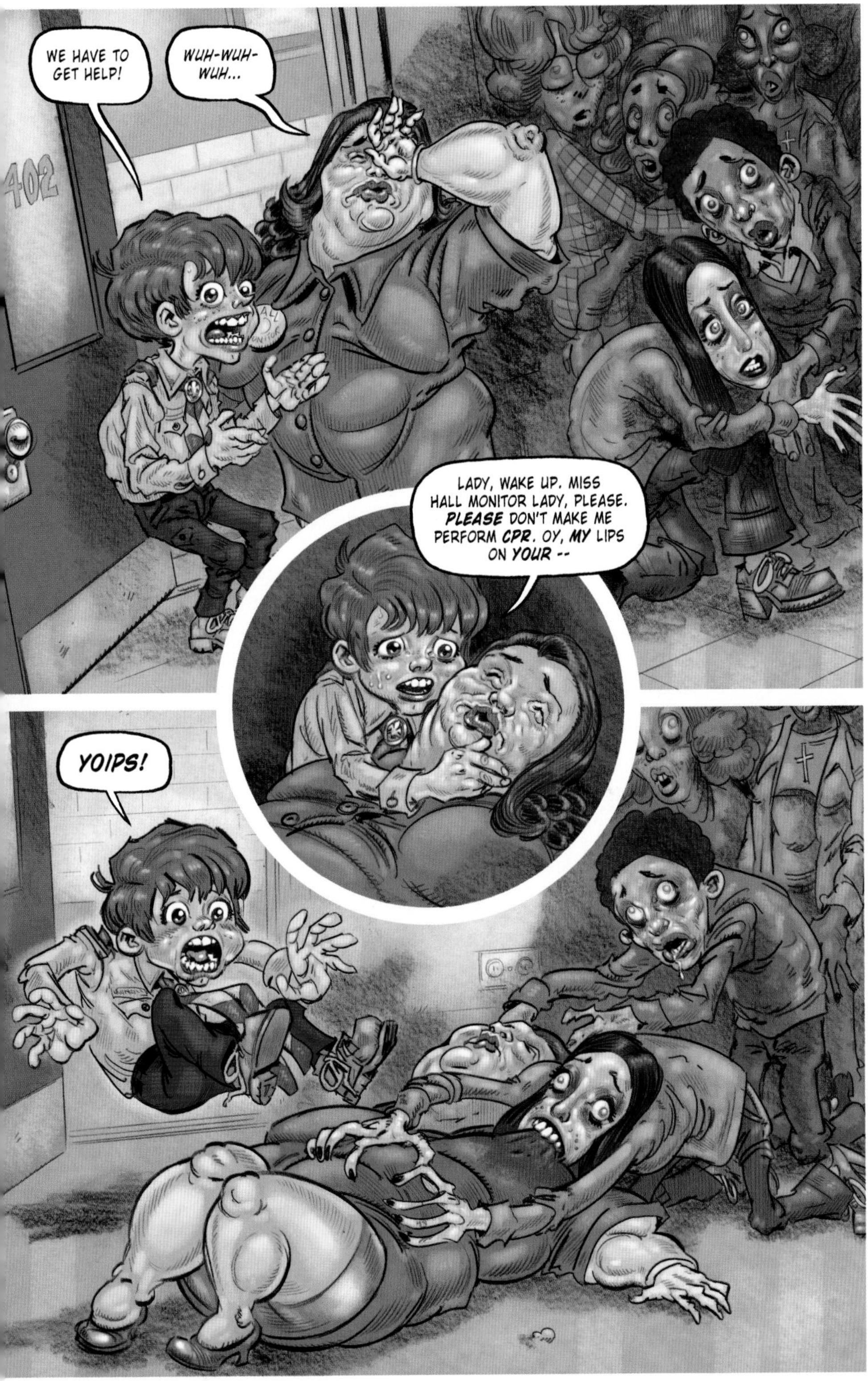
WE HAVE TO GET HELP!
WUH-WUH-WUH...
LADY, WAKE UP. MISS HALL MONITOR LADY, PLEASE. PLEASE DON'T MAKE ME PERFORM CPR. OY, MY LIPS ON YOUR --
YOIPS!
402

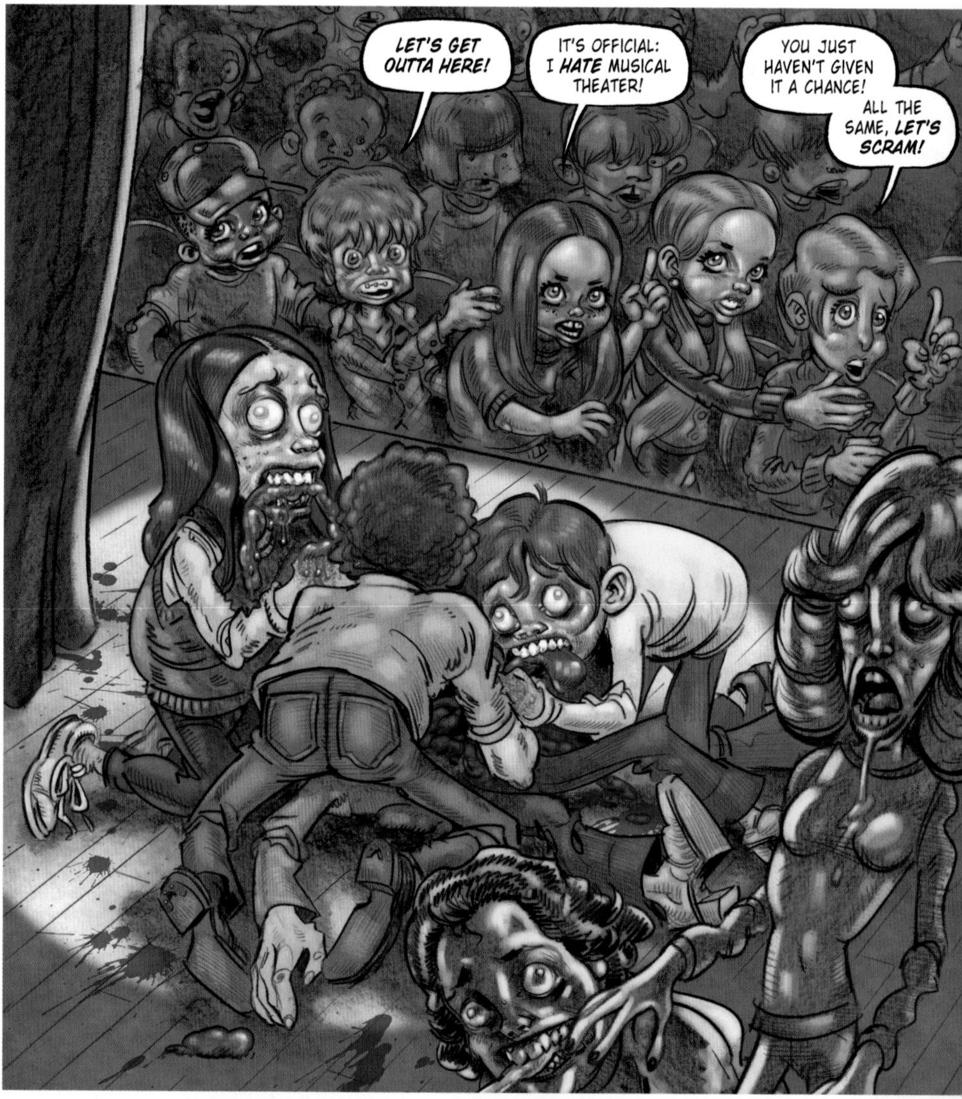
LET'S GET OUTTA HERE!
IT'S OFFICIAL: I HATE MUSICAL THEATER!
YOU JUST HAVEN'T GIVEN IT A CHANCE!
ALL THE SAME, LET'S SCRAM!

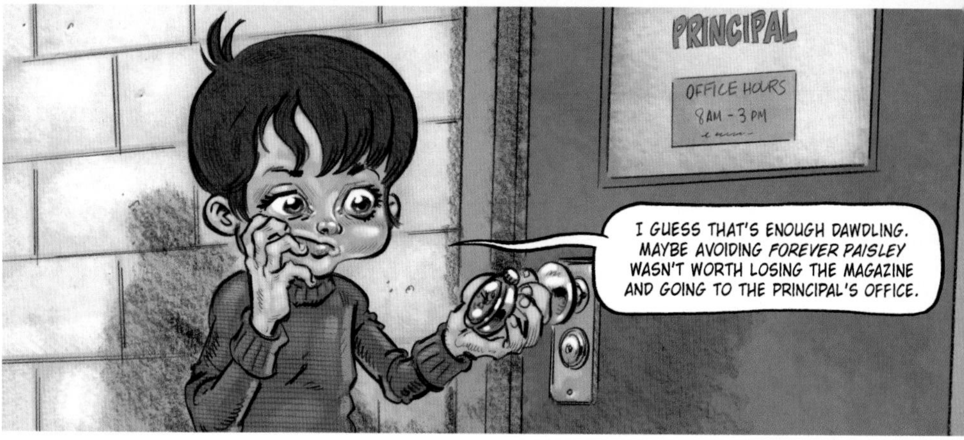
PRINCIPAL
OFFICE HOURS
8AM - 3 PM
I GUESS THAT'S ENOUGH DAWDLING. MAYBE AVOIDING FOREVER PAISLEY WASN'T WORTH LOSING THE MAGAZINE AND GOING TO THE PRINCIPAL'S OFFICE.

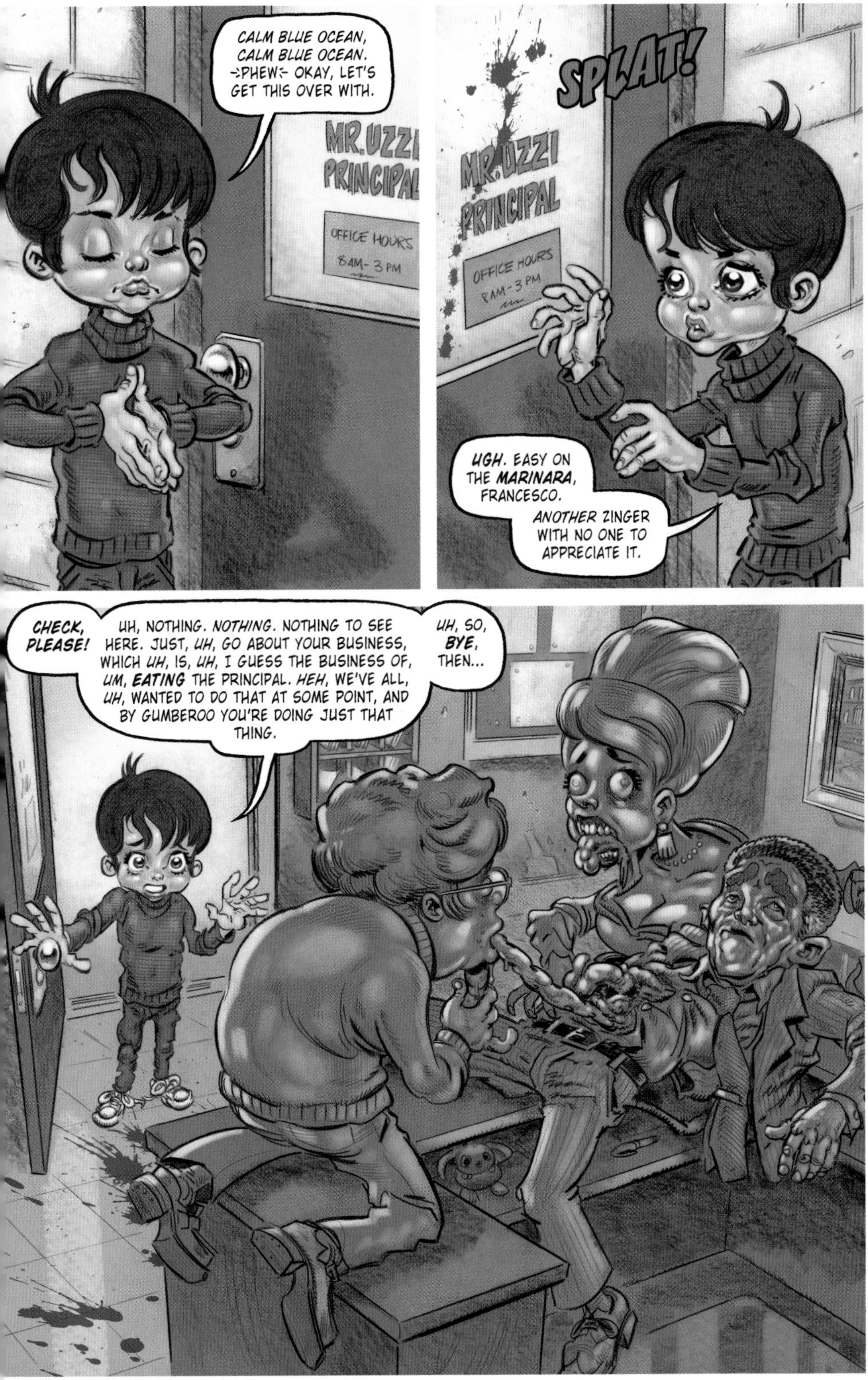
CALM BLUE OCEAN, CALM BLUE OCEAN. -PHEW- OKAY, LET'S GET THIS OVER WITH.
MR. UZZI PRINCIPAL
OFFICE HOURS 8AM-3PM
SPLAT!
MR. UZZI PRINCIPAL
OFFICE HOURS 8AM-3PM
UGH. EASY ON THE MARINARA, FRANCESCO.
ANOTHER ZINGER WITH NO ONE TO APPRECIATE IT.
CHECK, PLEASE!
UH, NOTHING. NOTHING. NOTHING TO SEE HERE. JUST, UH, GO ABOUT YOUR BUSINESS, WHICH UH, IS, UH, I GUESS THE BUSINESS OF, UM, EATING THE PRINCIPAL. HEH, WE'VE ALL, UH, WANTED TO DO THAT AT SOME POINT, AND BY GUMBEROO YOU'RE DOING JUST THAT THING.
UH, SO, BYE, THEN...

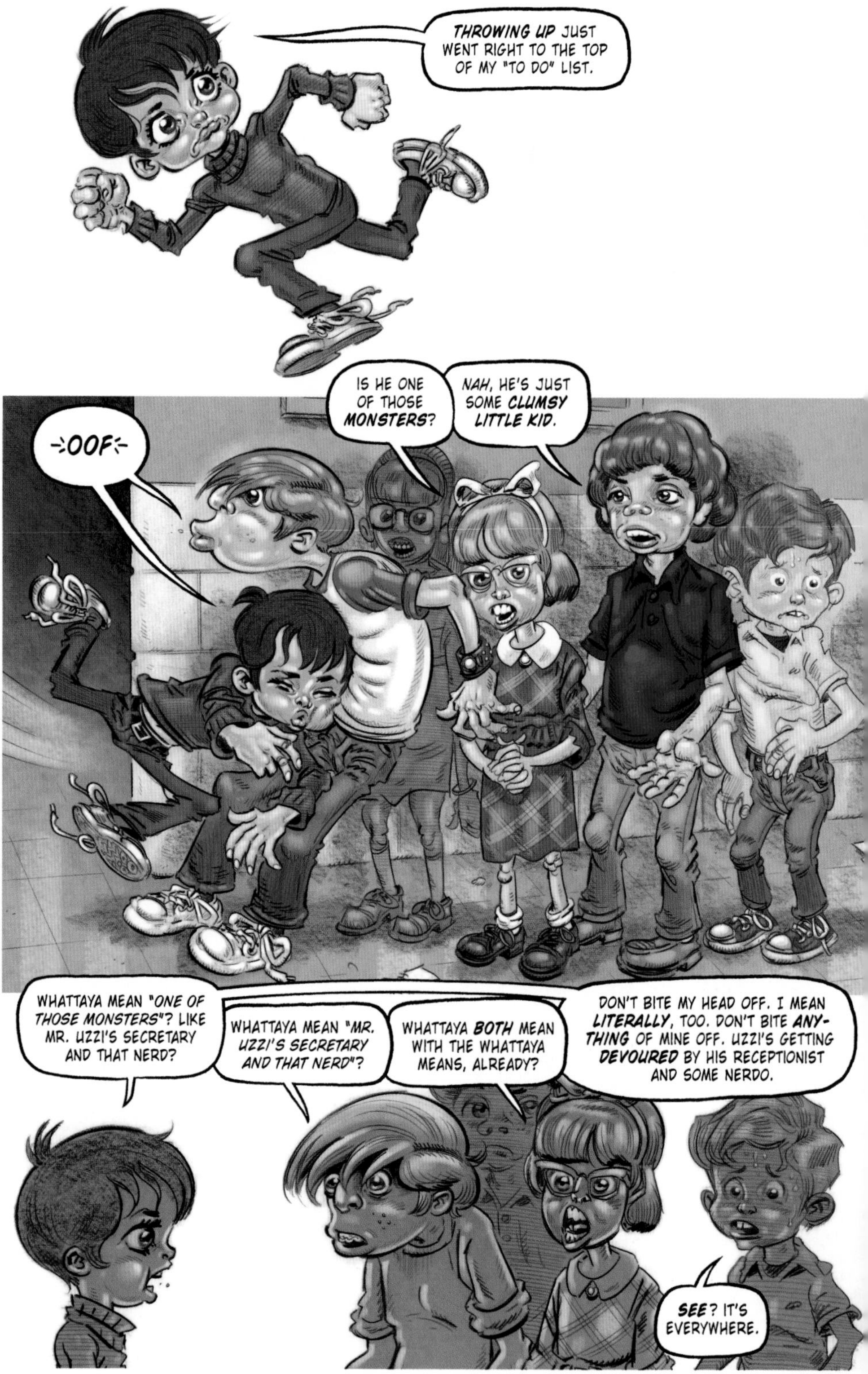
THROWING UP JUST WENT RIGHT TO THE TOP OF MY "TO DO" LIST.
OOF
IS HE ONE OF THOSE MONSTERS?
NAH, HE'S JUST SOME CLUMSY LITTLE KID.
WHATTAYA MEAN "ONE OF THOSE MONSTERS"? LIKE MR. UZZI'S SECRETARY AND THAT NERD?
WHATTAYA MEAN "MR. UZZI'S SECRETARY AND THAT NERD"?
WHATTAYA BOTH MEAN WITH THE WHATTAYA MEANS, ALREADY?
DON'T BITE MY HEAD OFF. I MEAN LITERALLY, TOO. DON'T BITE ANY-THING OF MINE OFF. UZZI'S GETTING DEVOURED BY HIS RECEPTIONIST AND SOME NERDO.
SEE? IT'S EVERYWHERE.

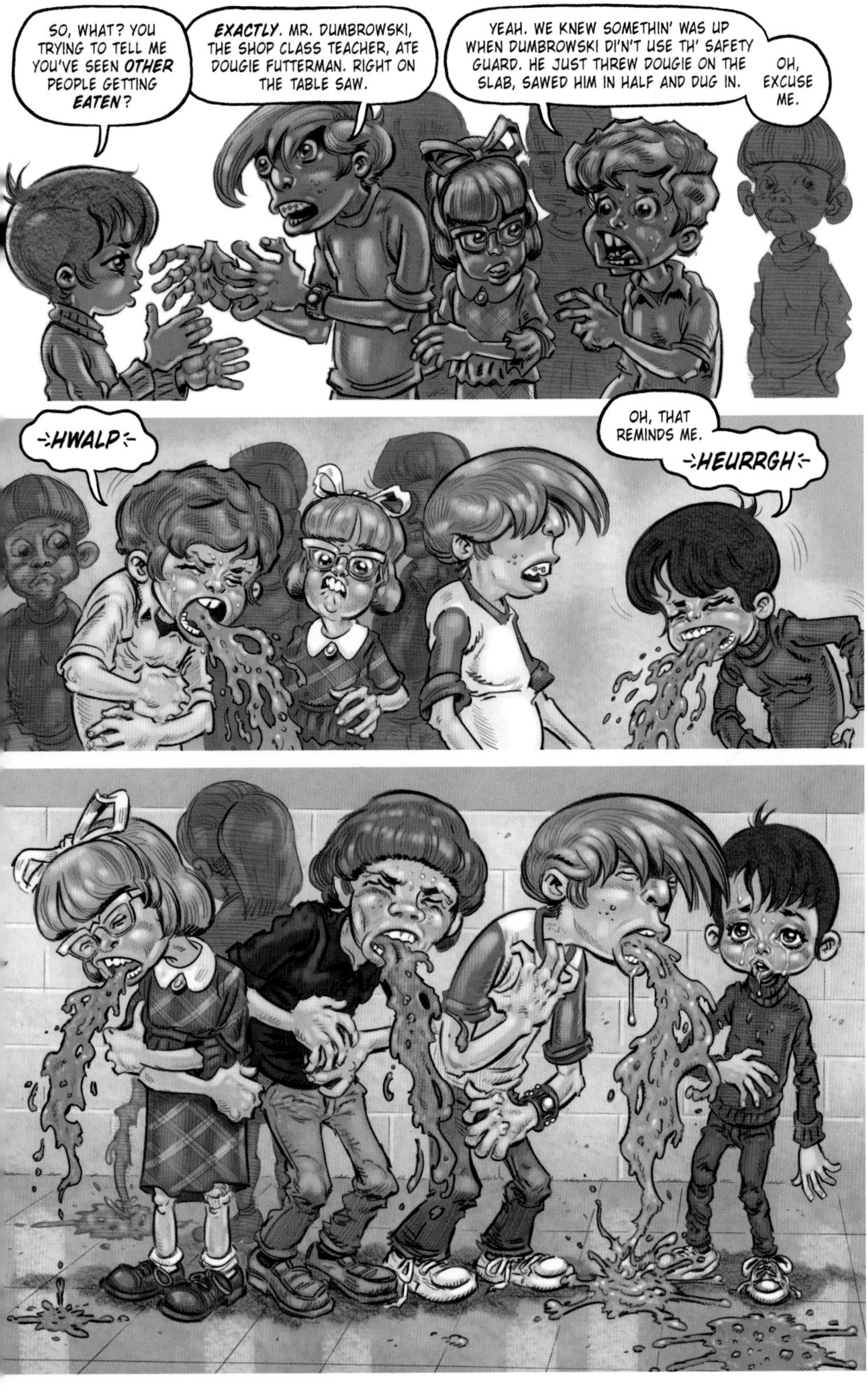
SO, WHAT? YOU TRYING TO TELL ME YOU'VE SEEN OTHER PEOPLE GETTING EATEN?
EXACTLY. MR. DUMBROWSKI, THE SHOP CLASS TEACHER, ATE DOUGIE FUTTERMAN. RIGHT ON THE TABLE SAW.
YEAH. WE KNEW SOMETHIN' WAS UP WHEN DUMBROWSKI DI'N'T USE TH' SAFETY GUARD. HE JUST THREW DOUGIE ON THE SLAB, SAWED HIM IN HALF AND DUG IN.
OH, EXCUSE ME.
HWALP
OH, THAT REMINDS ME.
HEURRGH

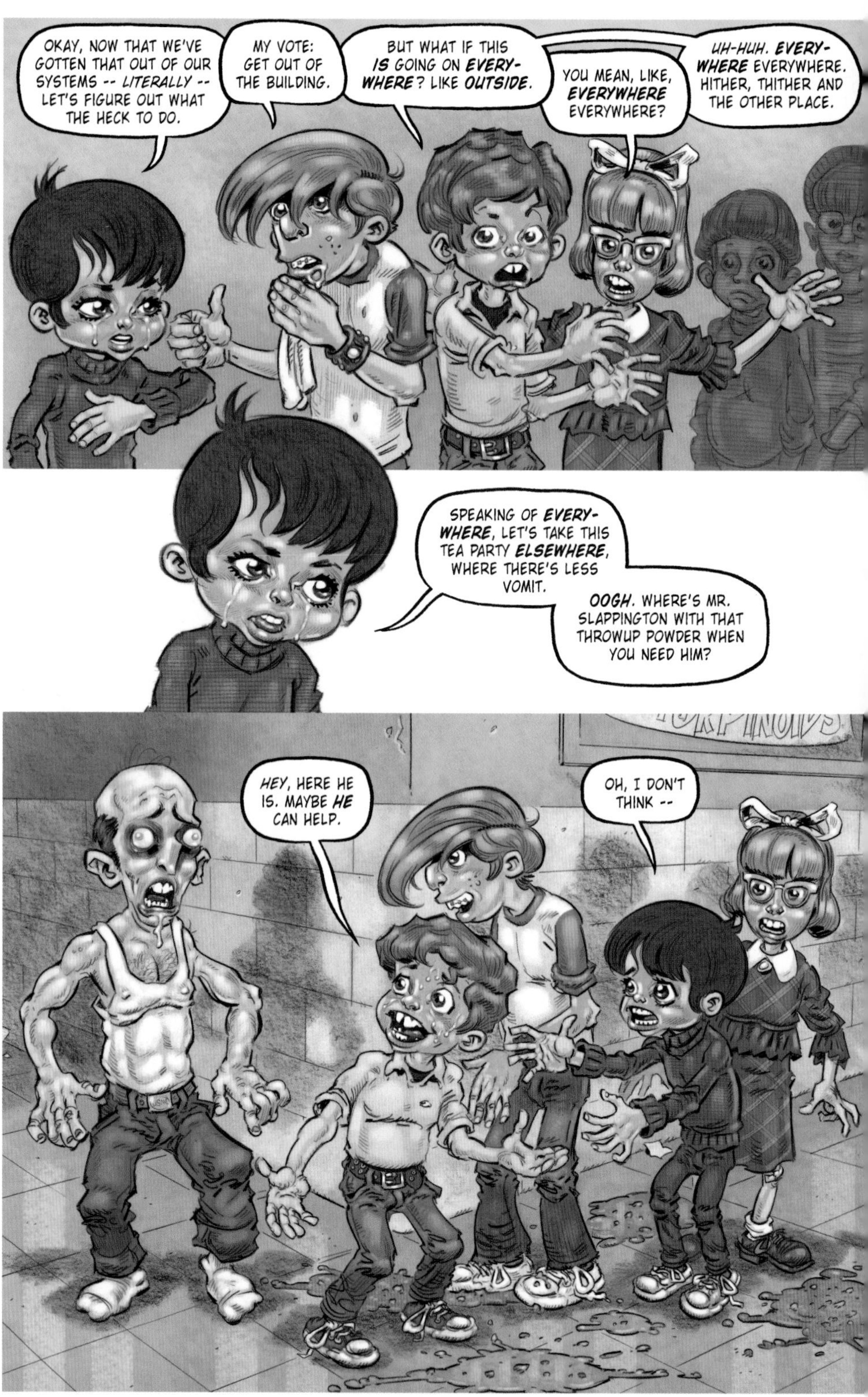
OKAY, NOW THAT WE'VE GOTTEN THAT OUT OF OUR SYSTEMS -- *LITERALLY* -- LET'S FIGURE OUT WHAT THE HECK TO DO.
MY VOTE: GET OUT OF THE BUILDING.
BUT WHAT IF THIS ***IS*** GOING ON ***EVERY-WHERE***? LIKE ***OUTSIDE***.
YOU MEAN, LIKE, ***EVERYWHERE*** EVERYWHERE?
UH-HUH. ***EVERY-WHERE*** EVERYWHERE. HITHER, THITHER AND THE OTHER PLACE.
SPEAKING OF ***EVERY-WHERE***, LET'S TAKE THIS TEA PARTY ***ELSEWHERE***, WHERE THERE'S LESS VOMIT.
OOGH. WHERE'S MR. SLAPPINGTON WITH THAT THROWUP POWDER WHEN YOU NEED HIM?
HEY, HERE HE IS. MAYBE ***HE*** CAN HELP.
OH, I DON'T THINK --

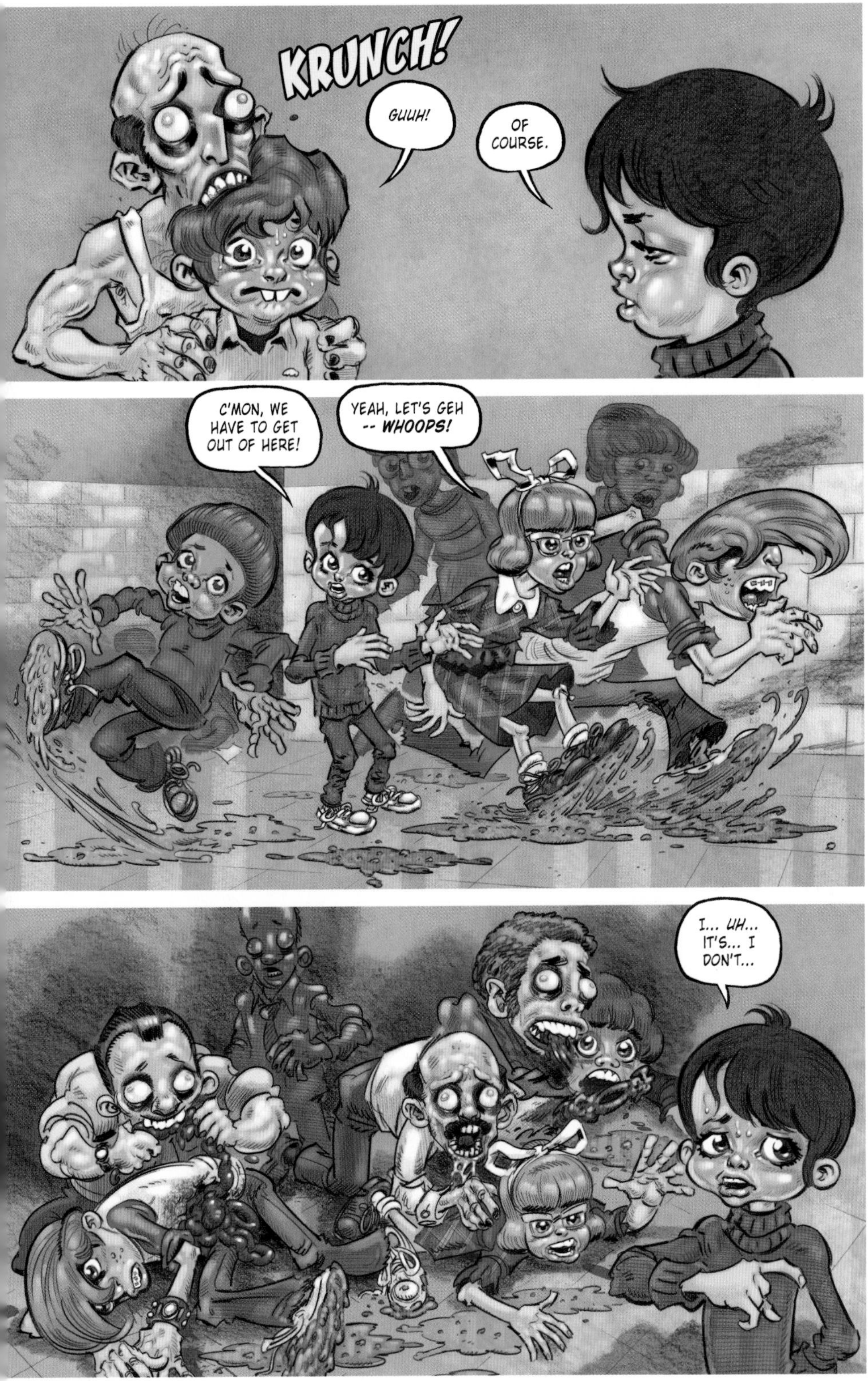
KRUNCH!
GUUH!
OF COURSE.
C'MON, WE HAVE TO GET OUT OF HERE!
YEAH, LET'S GEH -- WHOOPS!
I... UH... IT'S... I DON'T...

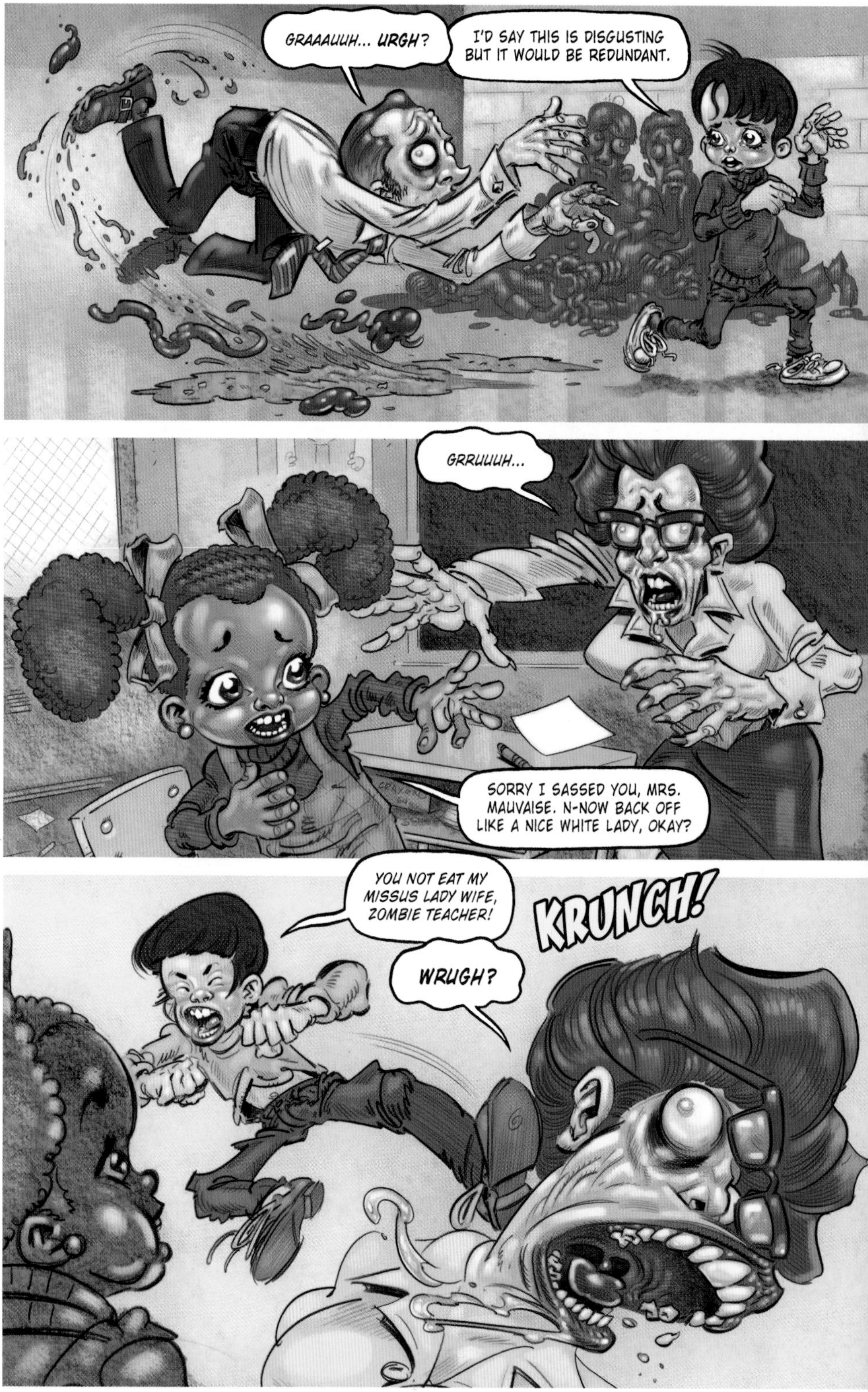
GRAAAUUH... URGH?
I'D SAY THIS IS DISGUSTING BUT IT WOULD BE REDUNDANT.
GRRUUUH...
SORRY I SASSED YOU, MRS. MAUVAISE. N-NOW BACK OFF LIKE A NICE WHITE LADY, OKAY?
YOU NOT EAT MY MISSUS LADY WIFE, ZOMBIE TEACHER!
KRUNCH!
WRUGH?

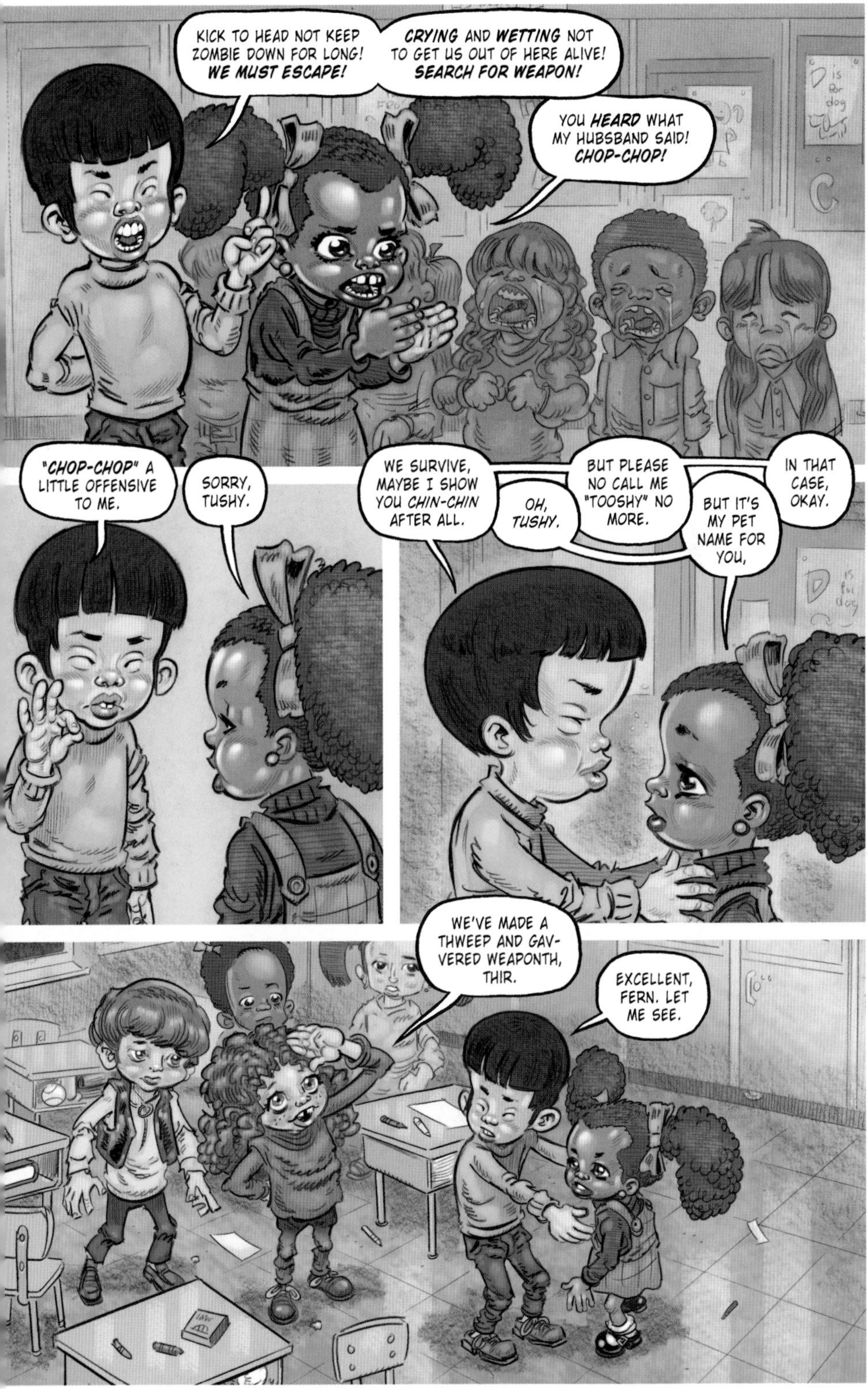
KICK TO HEAD NOT KEEP ZOMBIE DOWN FOR LONG! **WE MUST ESCAPE!**
CRYING AND ***WETTING*** NOT TO GET US OUT OF HERE ALIVE! ***SEARCH FOR WEAPON!***
YOU ***HEARD*** WHAT MY HUBSBAND SAID! ***CHOP-CHOP!***
"***CHOP-CHOP***" A LITTLE OFFENSIVE TO ME.
SORRY, TUSHY.
WE SURVIVE, MAYBE I SHOW YOU *CHIN-CHIN* AFTER ALL.
OH, *TUSHY.*
BUT PLEASE NO CALL ME "TOOSHY" NO MORE.
BUT IT'S MY PET NAME FOR YOU,
IN THAT CASE, OKAY.
WE'VE MADE A THWEEP AND GAV-VERED WEAPONTH, THIR.
EXCELLENT, FERN. LET ME SEE.

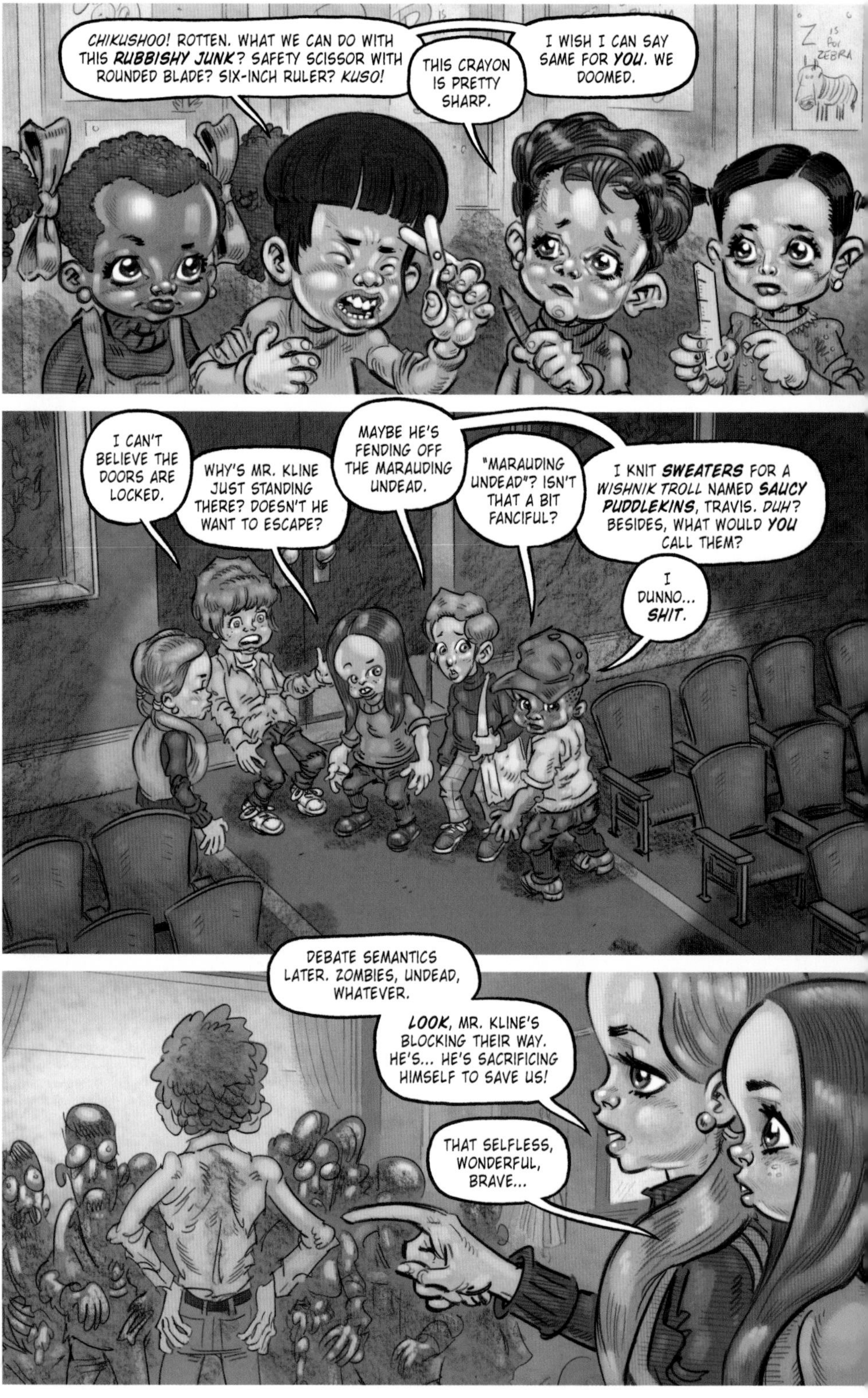
CHIKUSHOO! ROTTEN. WHAT WE CAN DO WITH THIS RUBBISHY JUNK? SAFETY SCISSOR WITH ROUNDED BLADE? SIX-INCH RULER? KUSO!
THIS CRAYON IS PRETTY SHARP.
I WISH I CAN SAY SAME FOR YOU. WE DOOMED.
Z IS FOR ZEBRA
I CAN'T BELIEVE THE DOORS ARE LOCKED.
WHY'S MR. KLINE JUST STANDING THERE? DOESN'T HE WANT TO ESCAPE?
MAYBE HE'S FENDING OFF THE MARAUDING UNDEAD.
"MARAUDING UNDEAD"? ISN'T THAT A BIT FANCIFUL?
I KNIT SWEATERS FOR A WISHNIK TROLL NAMED SAUCY PUDDLEKINS, TRAVIS. DUH? BESIDES, WHAT WOULD YOU CALL THEM?
I DUNNO... SHIT.
DEBATE SEMANTICS LATER. ZOMBIES, UNDEAD, WHATEVER.
LOOK, MR. KLINE'S BLOCKING THEIR WAY. HE'S... HE'S SACRIFICING HIMSELF TO SAVE US!
THAT SELFLESS, WONDERFUL, BRAVE...

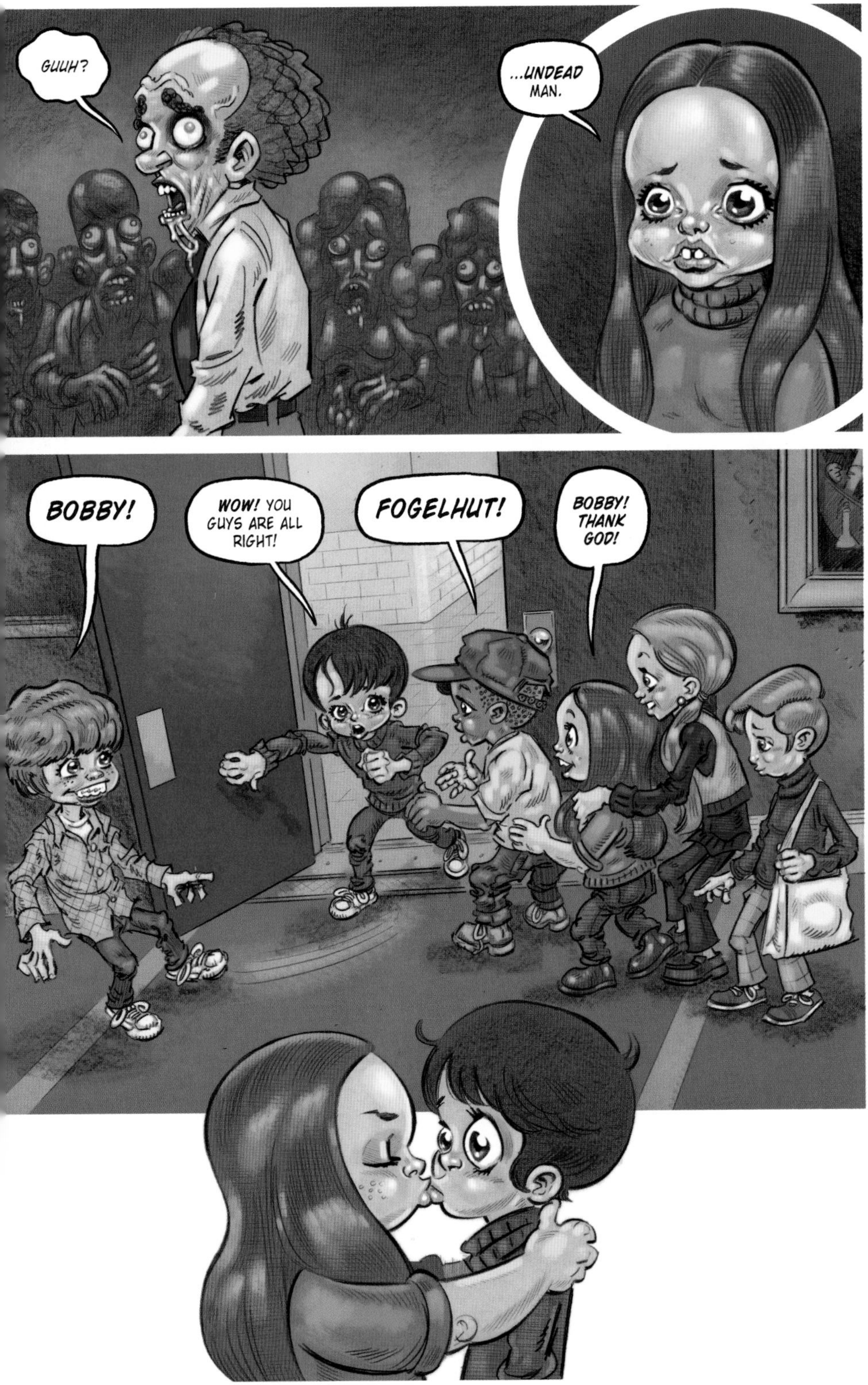
GUUH?
...UNDEAD MAN.
BOBBY!
WOW! YOU GUYS ARE ALL RIGHT!
FOGELHUT!
BOBBY! THANK GOD!

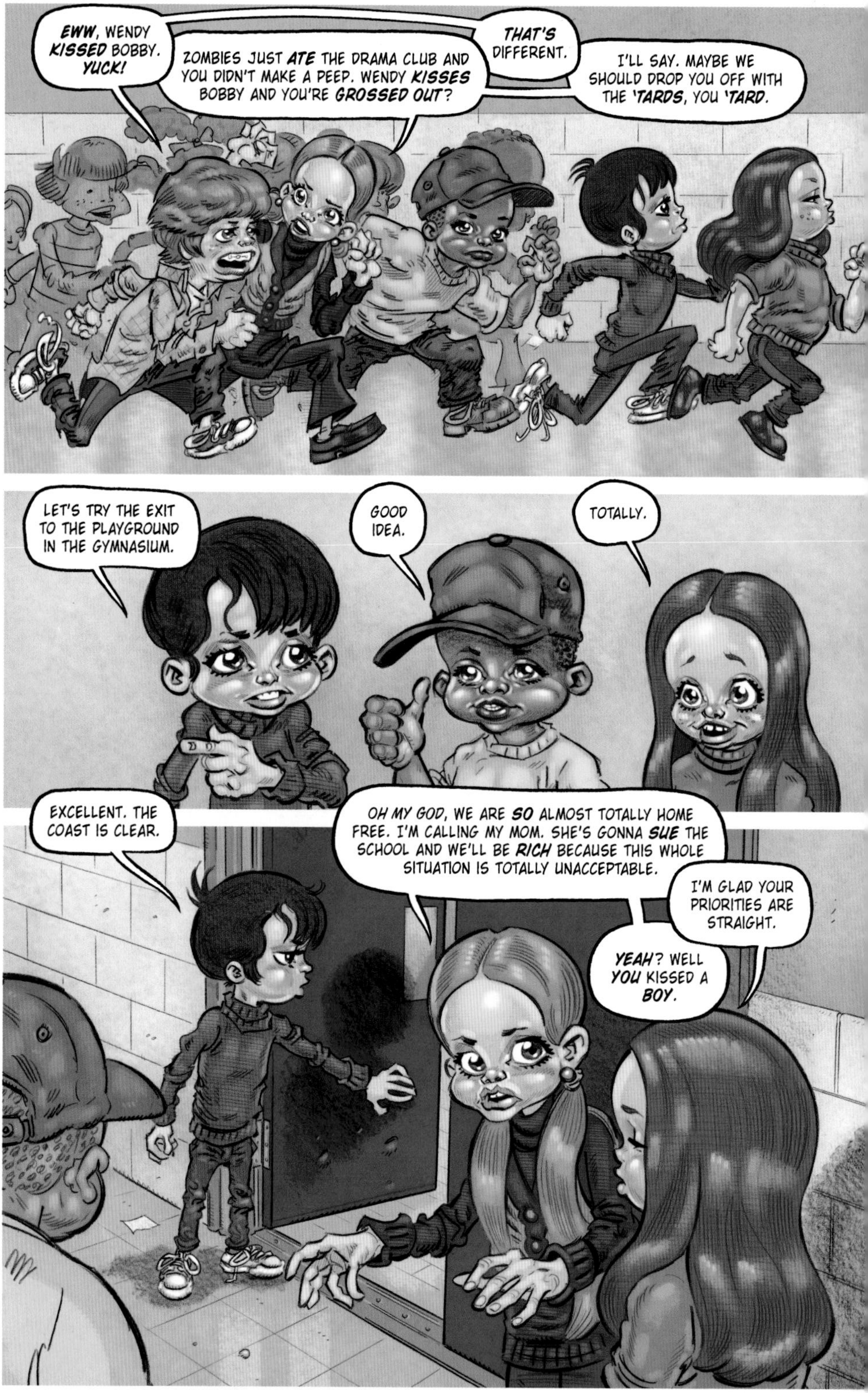
EWW, WENDY KISSED BOBBY. YUCK!
ZOMBIES JUST ATE THE DRAMA CLUB AND YOU DIDN'T MAKE A PEEP. WENDY KISSES BOBBY AND YOU'RE GROSSED OUT?
THAT'S DIFFERENT.
I'LL SAY. MAYBE WE SHOULD DROP YOU OFF WITH THE 'TARDS, YOU 'TARD.
LET'S TRY THE EXIT TO THE PLAYGROUND IN THE GYMNASIUM.
GOOD IDEA.
TOTALLY.
EXCELLENT. THE COAST IS CLEAR.
OH MY GOD, WE ARE SO ALMOST TOTALLY HOME FREE. I'M CALLING MY MOM. SHE'S GONNA SUE THE SCHOOL AND WE'LL BE RICH BECAUSE THIS WHOLE SITUATION IS TOTALLY UNACCEPTABLE.
I'M GLAD YOUR PRIORITIES ARE STRAIGHT.
YEAH? WELL YOU KISSED A BOY.

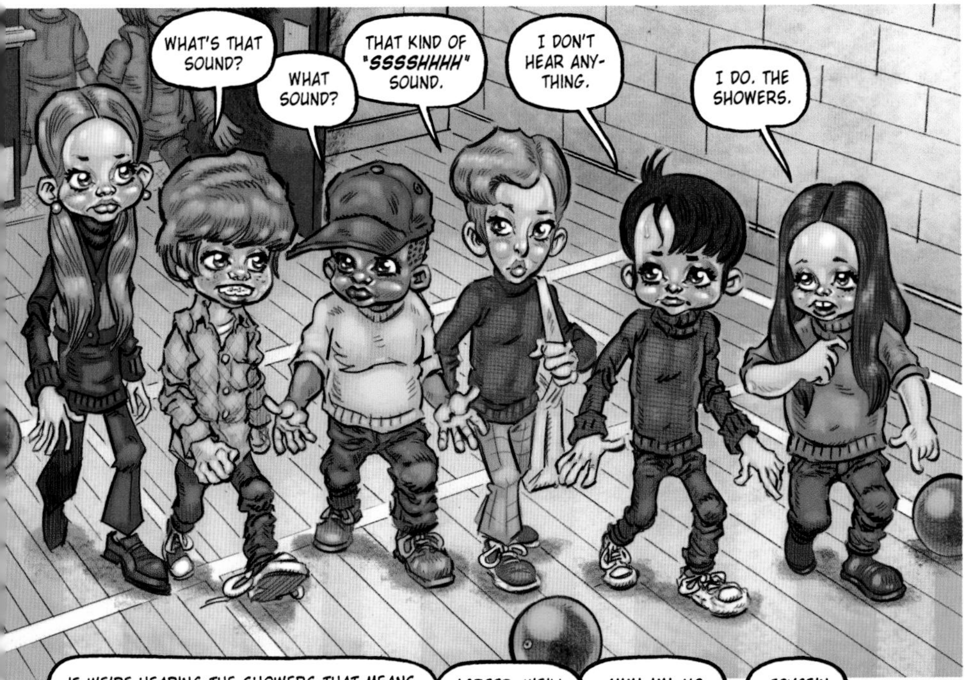
WHAT'S THAT SOUND?
WHAT SOUND?
THAT KIND OF "SSSSHHHH" SOUND.
I DON'T HEAR ANY-THING.
I DO. THE SHOWERS.

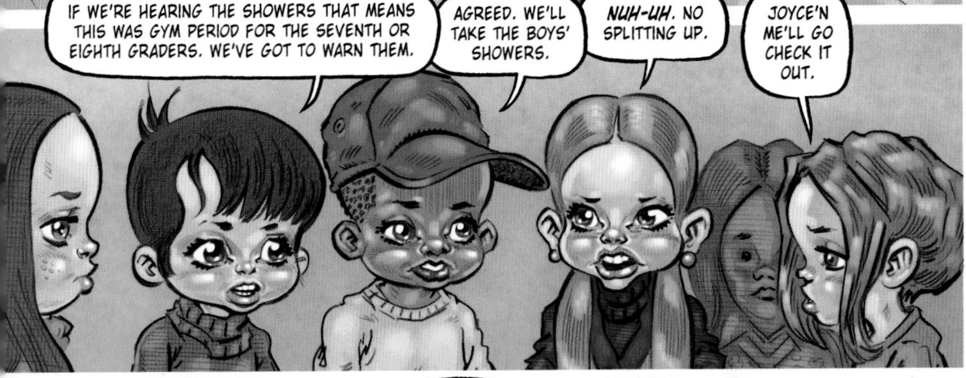
IF WE'RE HEARING THE SHOWERS THAT MEANS THIS WAS GYM PERIOD FOR THE SEVENTH OR EIGHTH GRADERS. WE'VE GOT TO WARN THEM.
AGREED. WE'LL TAKE THE BOYS' SHOWERS.
NUH-UH. NO SPLITTING UP.
JOYCE'N ME'LL GO CHECK IT OUT.

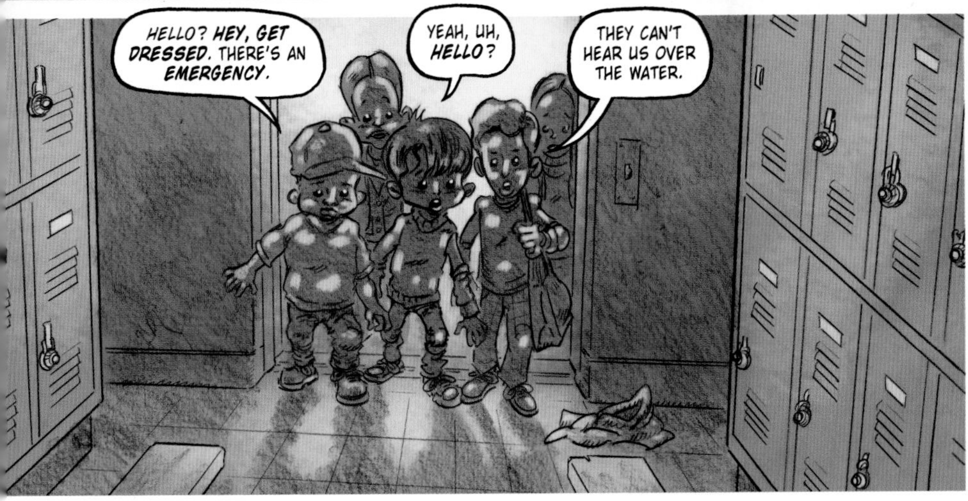
HELLO? HEY, GET DRESSED. THERE'S AN EMERGENCY.
YEAH, UH, HELLO?
THEY CAN'T HEAR US OVER THE WATER.

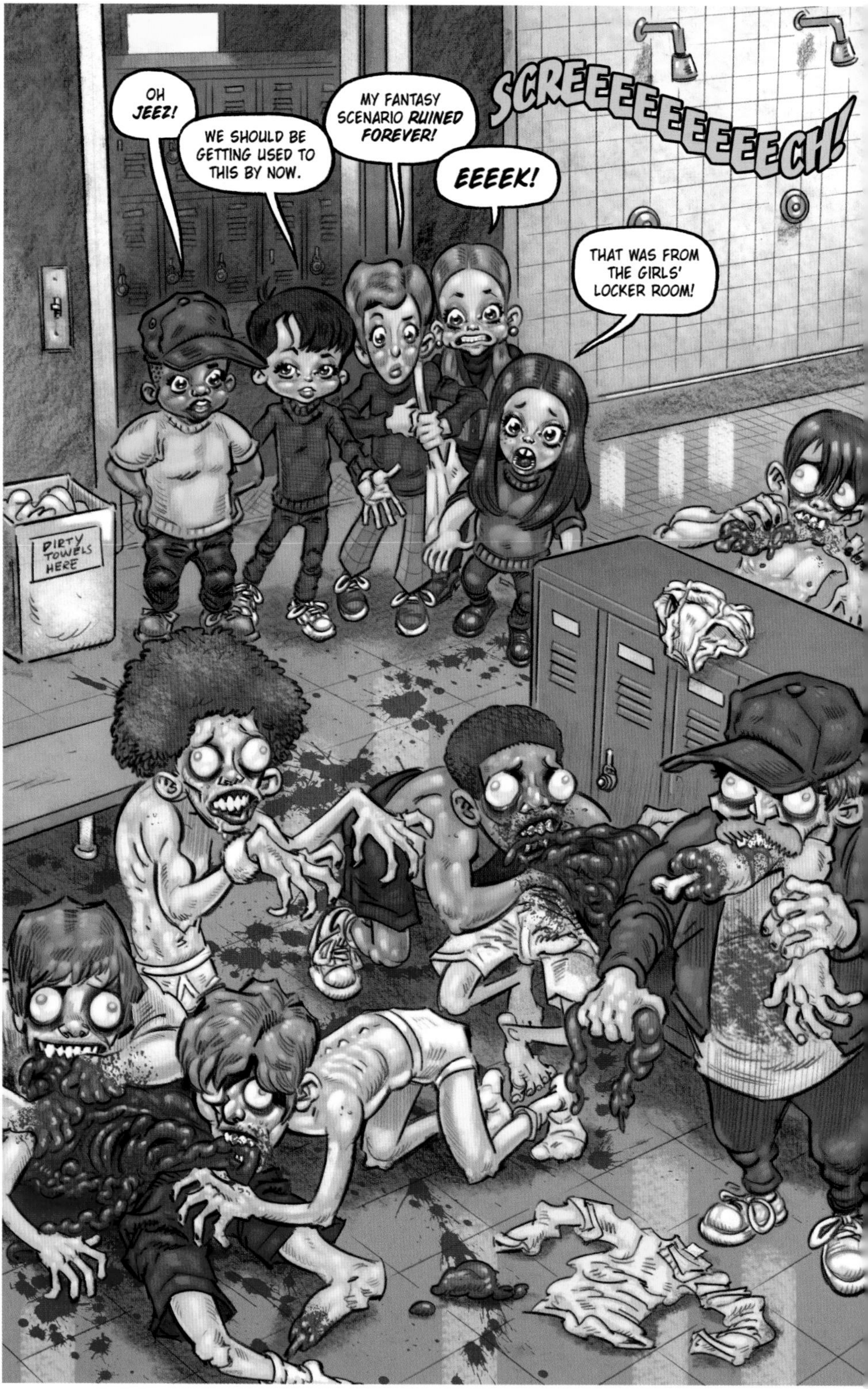
OH JEEZ!
WE SHOULD BE GETTING USED TO THIS BY NOW.
MY FANTASY SCENARIO RUINED FOREVER!
EEEEK!
SCREEEEEEEEEEECH!
THAT WAS FROM THE GIRLS' LOCKER ROOM!
DIRTY TOWELS HERE

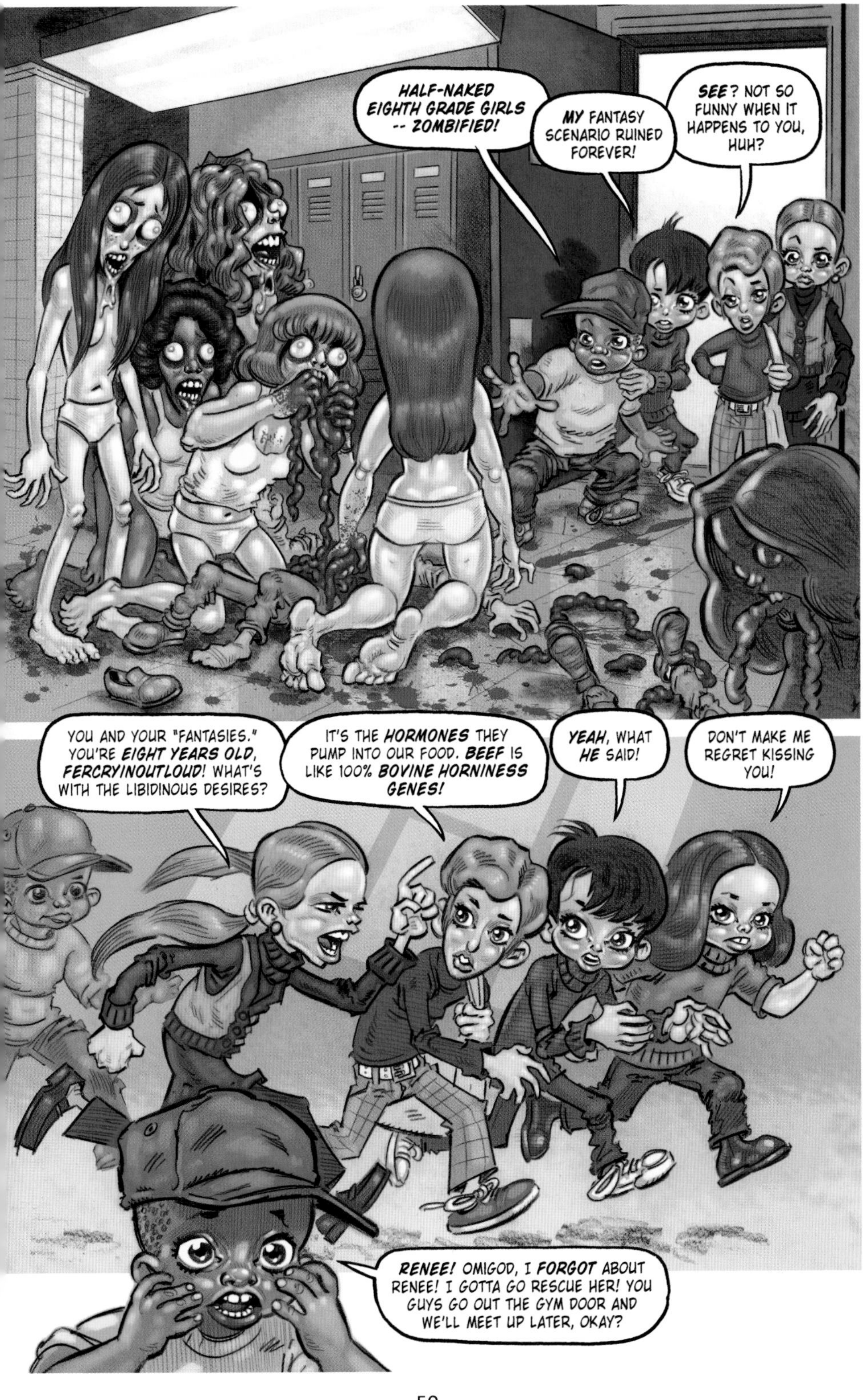
HALF-NAKED EIGHTH GRADE GIRLS -- ZOMBIFIED!
MY FANTASY SCENARIO RUINED FOREVER!
SEE? NOT SO FUNNY WHEN IT HAPPENS TO YOU, HUH?
YOU AND YOUR "FANTASIES." YOU'RE EIGHT YEARS OLD, FERCRYINOUTLOUD! WHAT'S WITH THE LIBIDINOUS DESIRES?
IT'S THE HORMONES THEY PUMP INTO OUR FOOD. BEEF IS LIKE 100% BOVINE HORNINESS GENES!
YEAH, WHAT HE SAID!
DON'T MAKE ME REGRET KISSING YOU!
RENEE! OMIGOD, I FORGOT ABOUT RENEE! I GOTTA GO RESCUE HER! YOU GUYS GO OUT THE GYM DOOR AND WE'LL MEET UP LATER, OKAY?

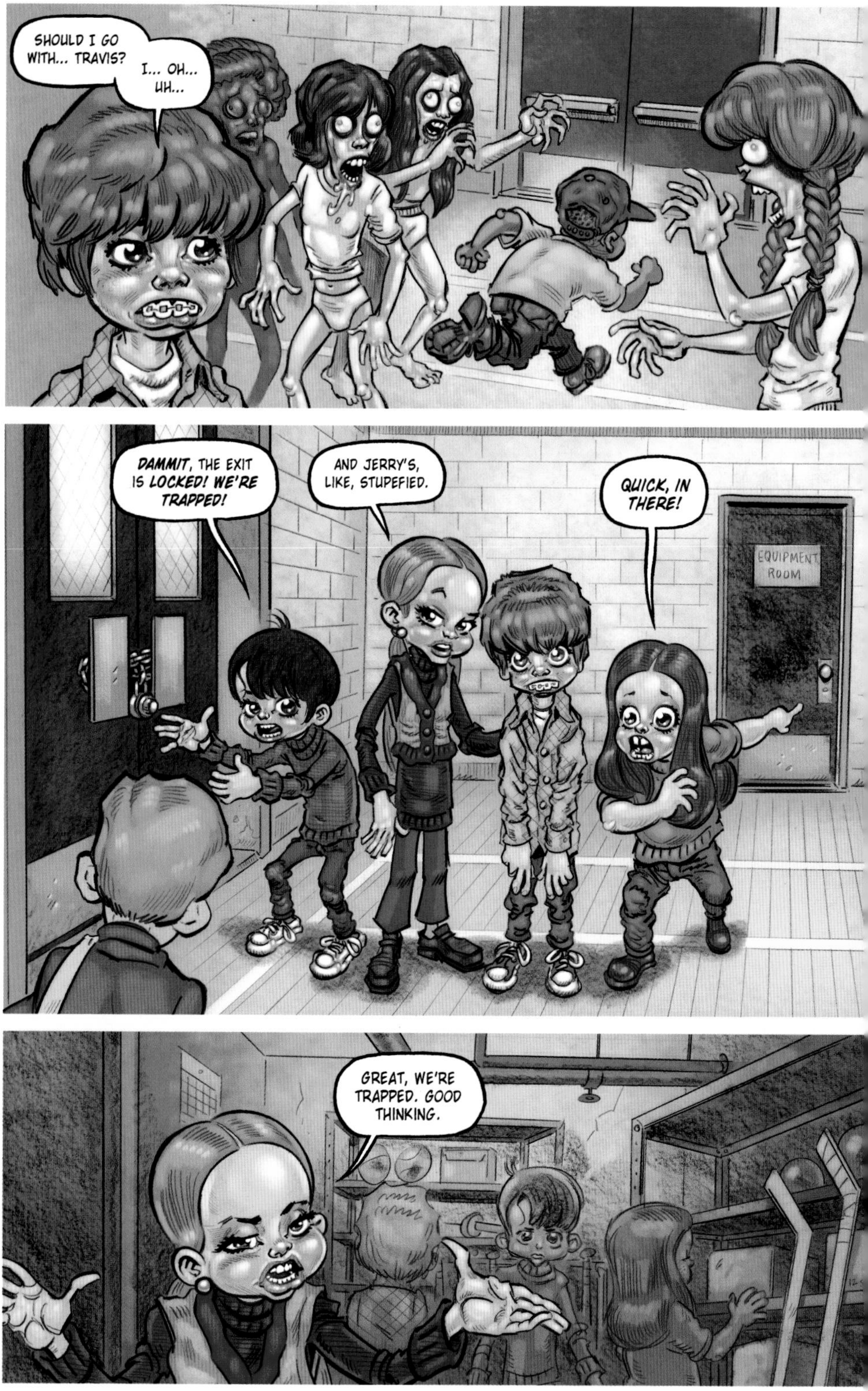
SHOULD I GO WITH... TRAVIS?
I... OH... UH...
DAMMIT, THE EXIT IS LOCKED! WE'RE TRAPPED!
AND JERRY'S, LIKE, STUPEFIED.
QUICK, IN THERE!
EQUIPMENT ROOM
GREAT, WE'RE TRAPPED. GOOD THINKING.

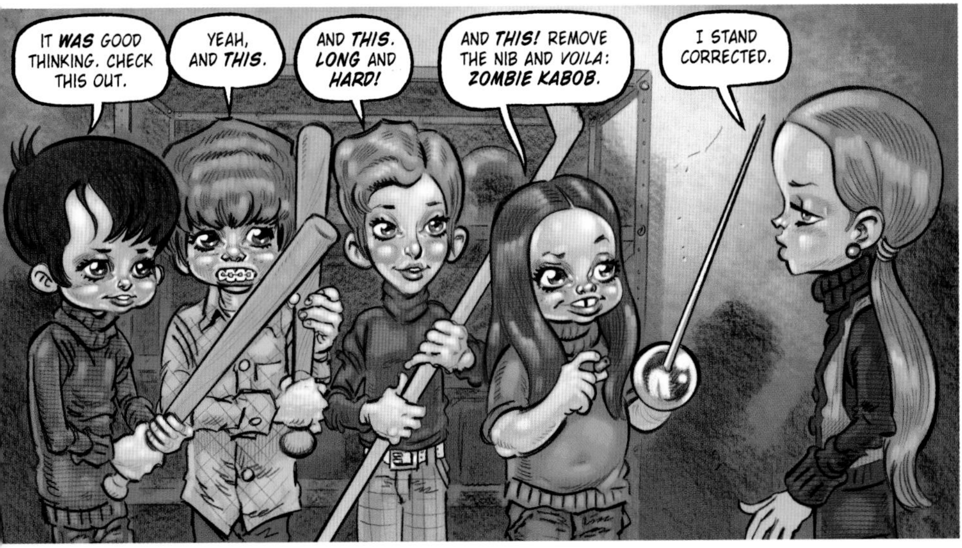
IT WAS GOOD THINKING. CHECK THIS OUT.
YEAH, AND THIS.
AND THIS. LONG AND HARD!
AND THIS! REMOVE THE NIB AND VOILA: ZOMBIE KABOB.
I STAND CORRECTED.

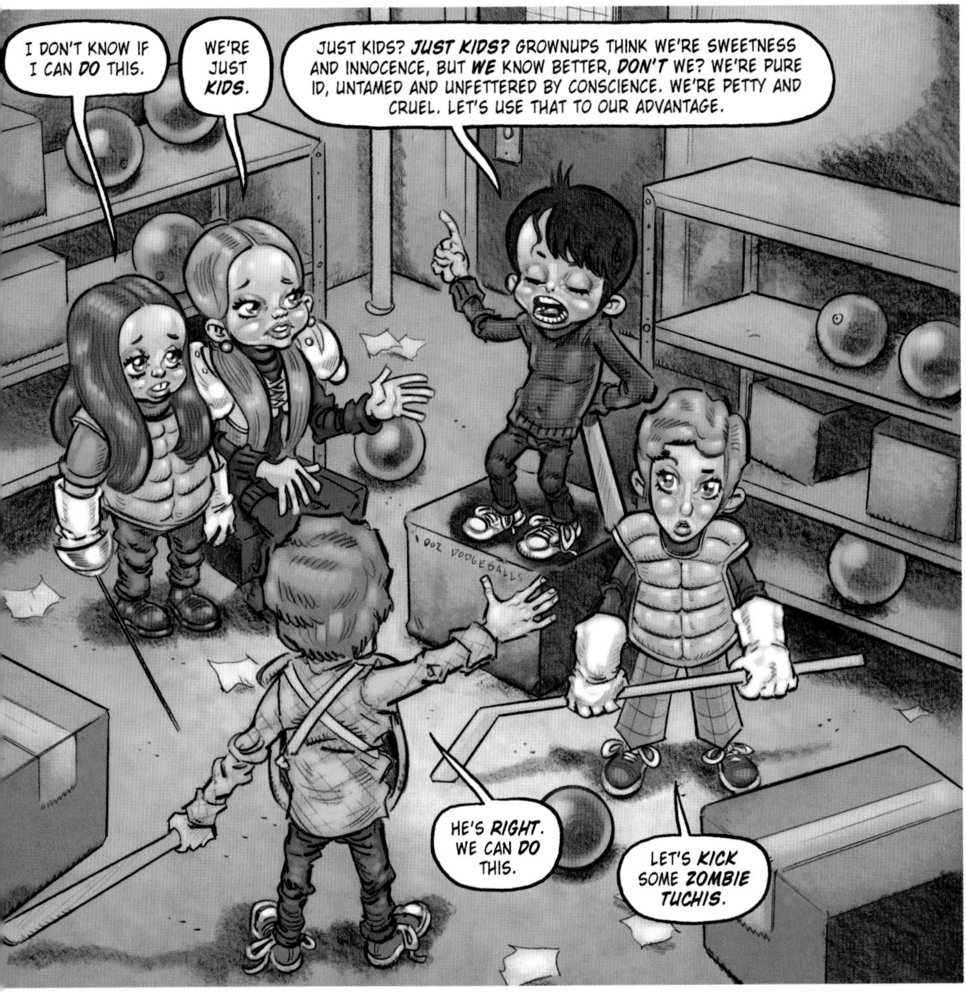
I DON'T KNOW IF I CAN DO THIS.
WE'RE JUST KIDS.
JUST KIDS? JUST KIDS? GROWNUPS THINK WE'RE SWEETNESS AND INNOCENCE, BUT WE KNOW BETTER, DON'T WE? WE'RE PURE ID, UNTAMED AND UNFETTERED BY CONSCIENCE. WE'RE PETTY AND CRUEL. LET'S USE THAT TO OUR ADVANTAGE.
HE'S RIGHT. WE CAN DO THIS.
LET'S KICK SOME ZOMBIE TUCHIS.

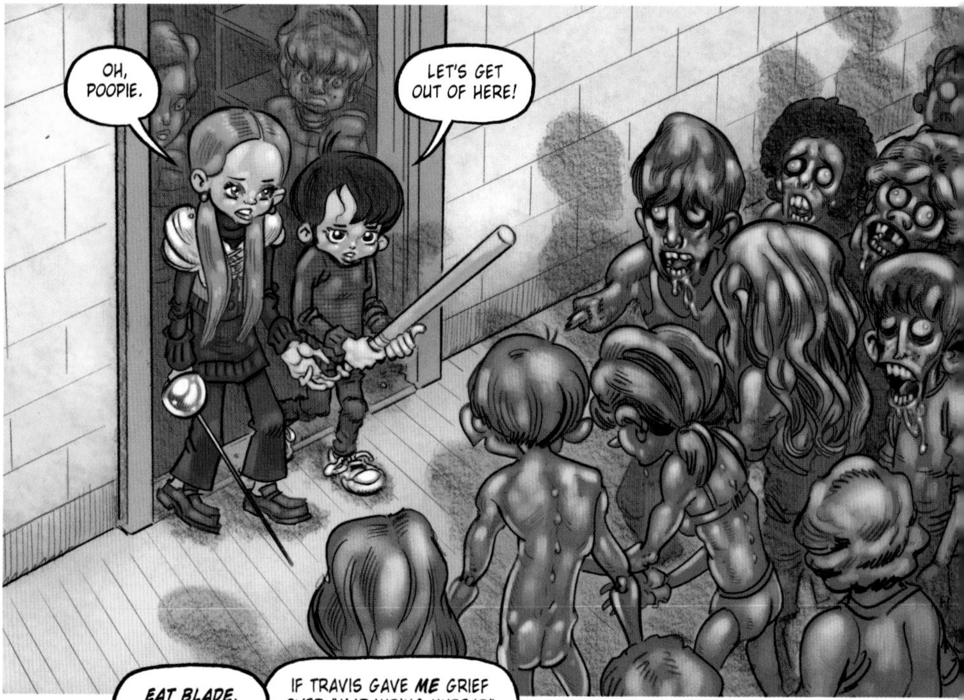
OH, POOPIE.
LET'S GET OUT OF HERE!

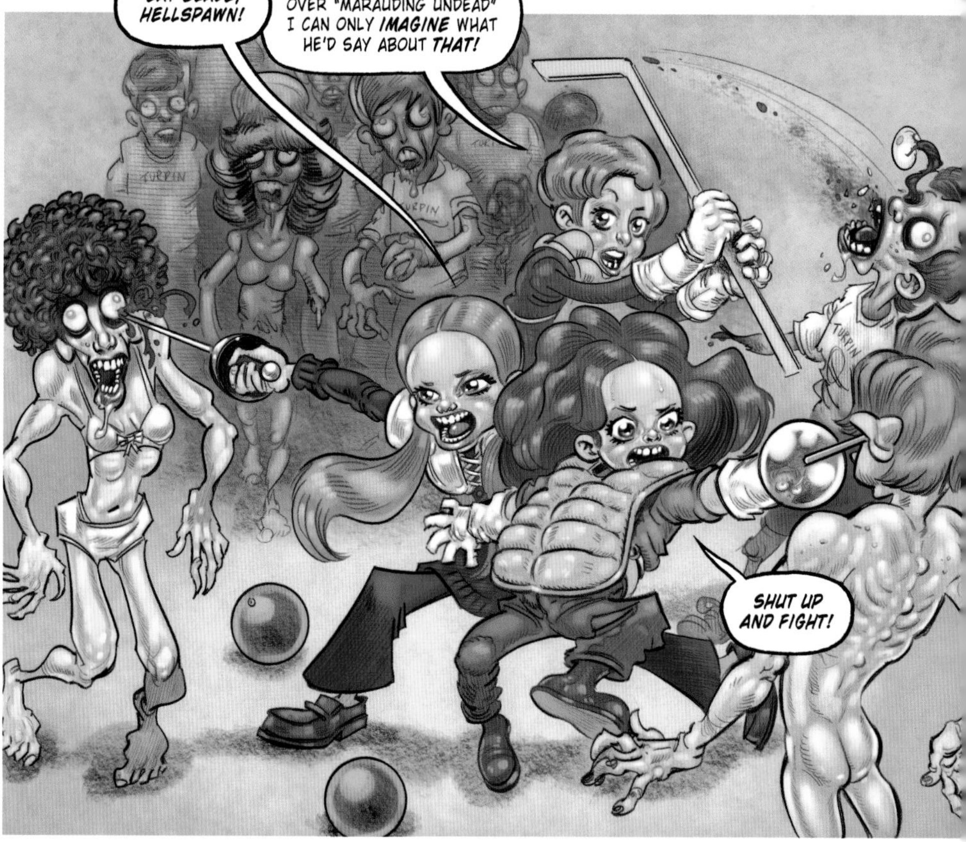
EAT BLADE, HELLSPAWN!
IF TRAVIS GAVE ME GRIEF OVER "MARAUDING UNDEAD" I CAN ONLY IMAGINE WHAT HE'D SAY ABOUT THAT!
TURPIN
TURPIN
TURPIN
TURPIN
SHUT UP AND FIGHT!

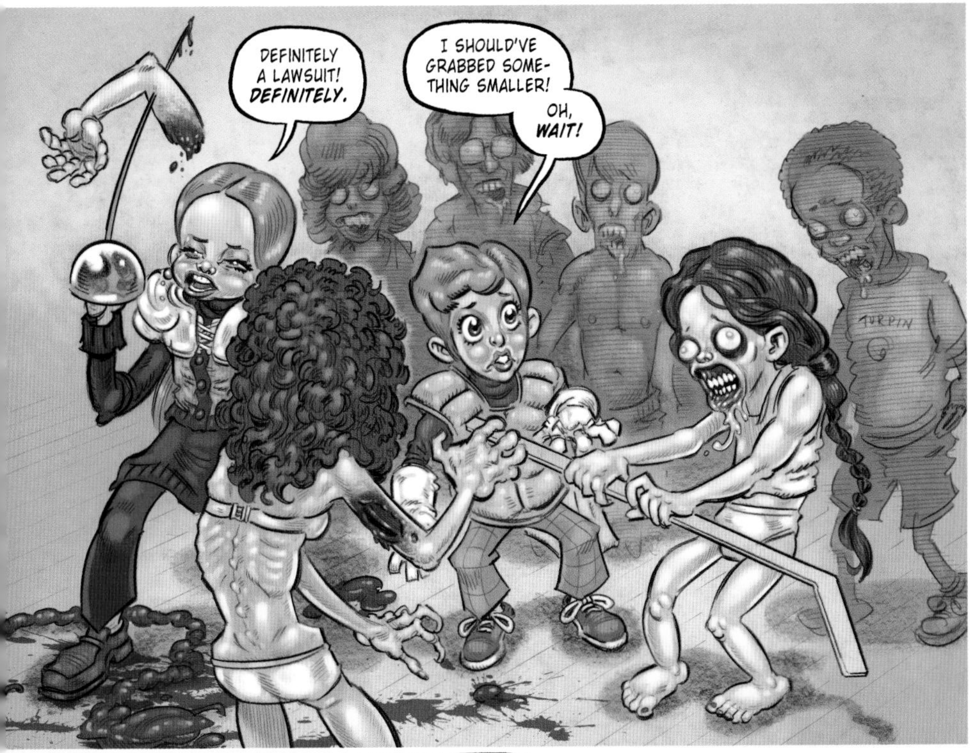
DEFINITELY A LAWSUIT! DEFINITELY.
I SHOULD'VE GRABBED SOMETHING SMALLER!
OH, WAIT!
TURPIN

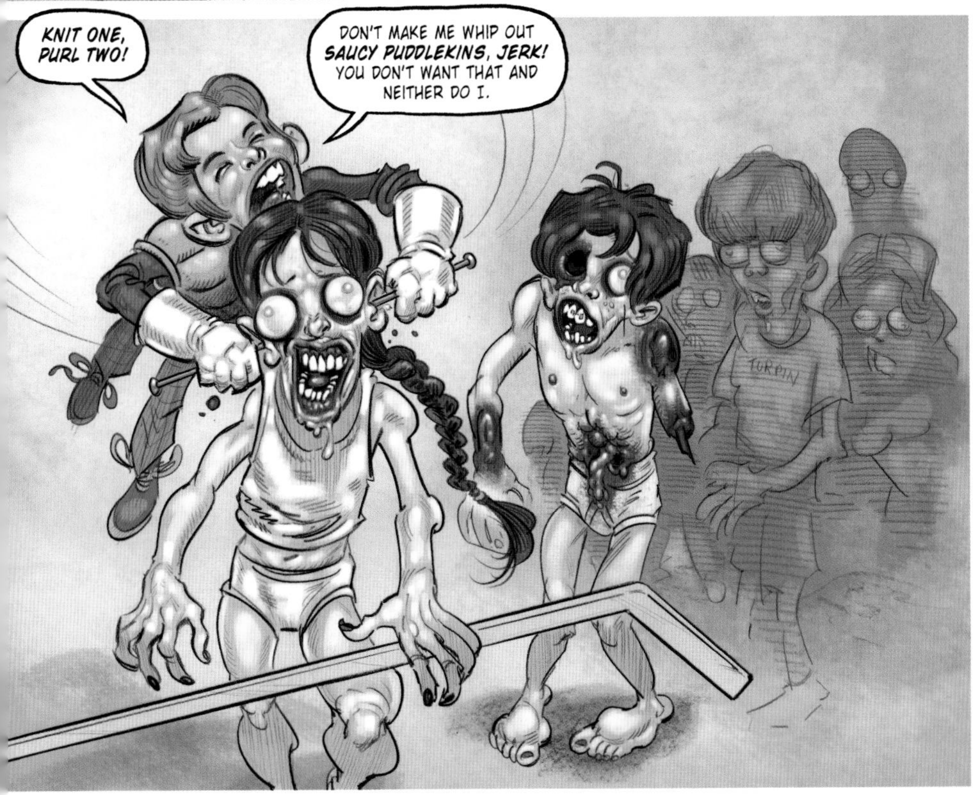
KNIT ONE, PURL TWO!
DON'T MAKE ME WHIP OUT SAUCY PUDDLEKINS, JERK! YOU DON'T WANT THAT AND NEITHER DO I.
TURPIN

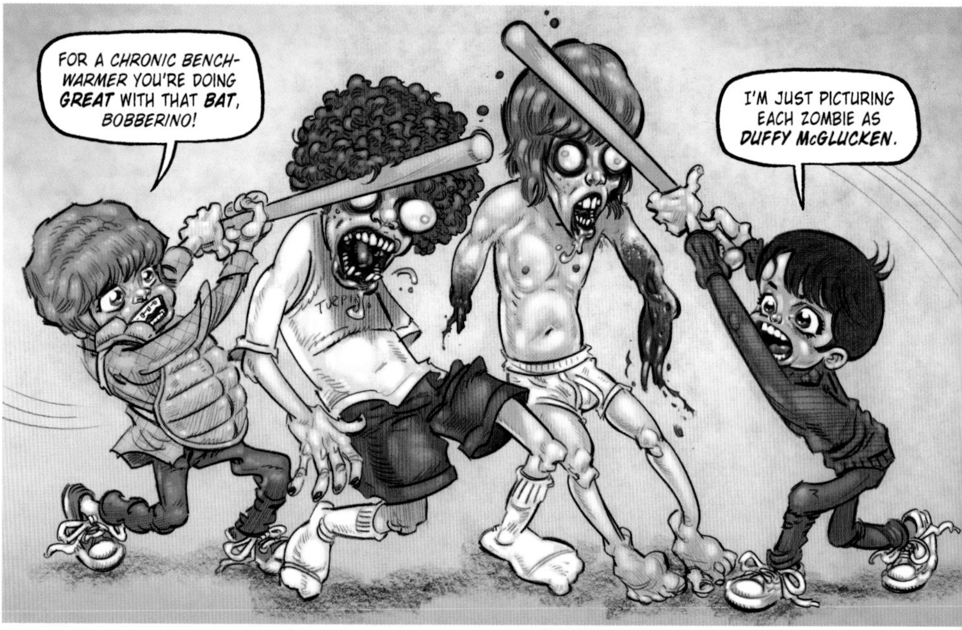
FOR A CHRONIC BENCH-WARMER YOU'RE DOING GREAT WITH THAT BAT, BOBBERINO!
I'M JUST PICTURING EACH ZOMBIE AS DUFFY McGLUCKEN.
TURPIN

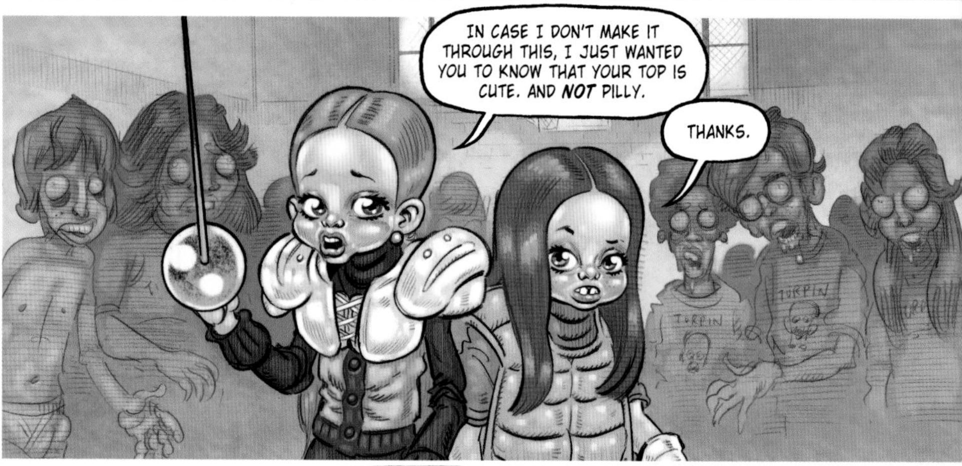
IN CASE I DON'T MAKE IT THROUGH THIS, I JUST WANTED YOU TO KNOW THAT YOUR TOP IS CUTE. AND NOT PILLY.
THANKS.
TURPIN
TURPIN

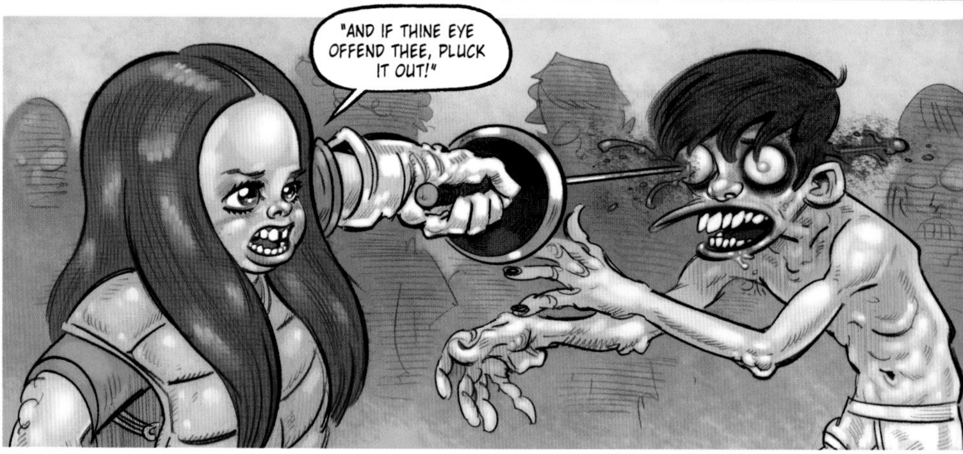
"AND IF THINE EYE OFFEND THEE, PLUCK IT OUT!"

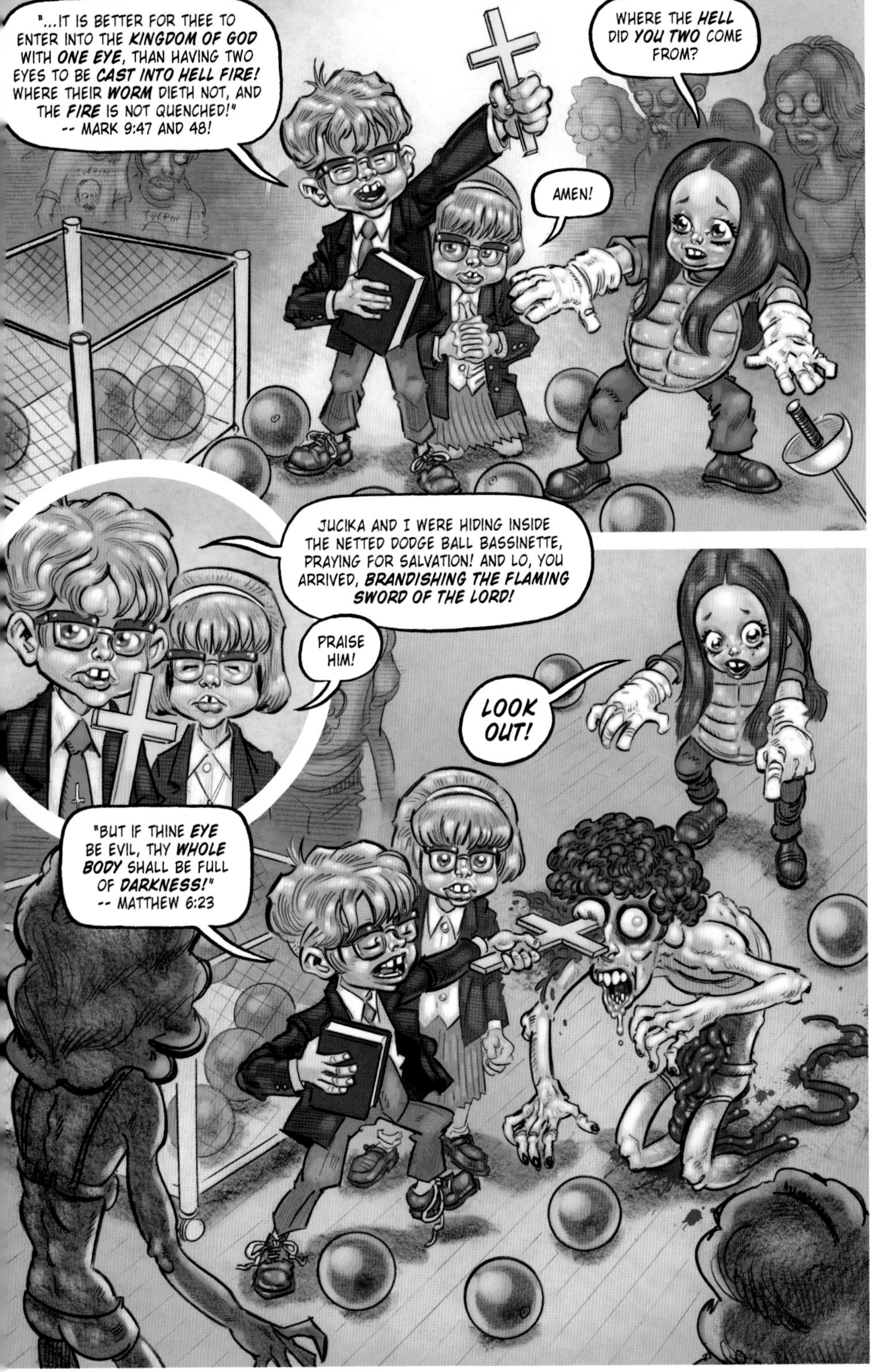
"...IT IS BETTER FOR THEE TO ENTER INTO THE KINGDOM OF GOD WITH ONE EYE, THAN HAVING TWO EYES TO BE CAST INTO HELL FIRE! WHERE THEIR WORM DIETH NOT, AND THE FIRE IS NOT QUENCHED!" -- MARK 9:47 AND 48!
WHERE THE HELL DID YOU TWO COME FROM?
AMEN!
JUCIKA AND I WERE HIDING INSIDE THE NETTED DODGE BALL BASSINETTE, PRAYING FOR SALVATION! AND LO, YOU ARRIVED, BRANDISHING THE FLAMING SWORD OF THE LORD!
PRAISE HIM!
LOOK OUT!
"BUT IF THINE EYE BE EVIL, THY WHOLE BODY SHALL BE FULL OF DARKNESS!" -- MATTHEW 6:23

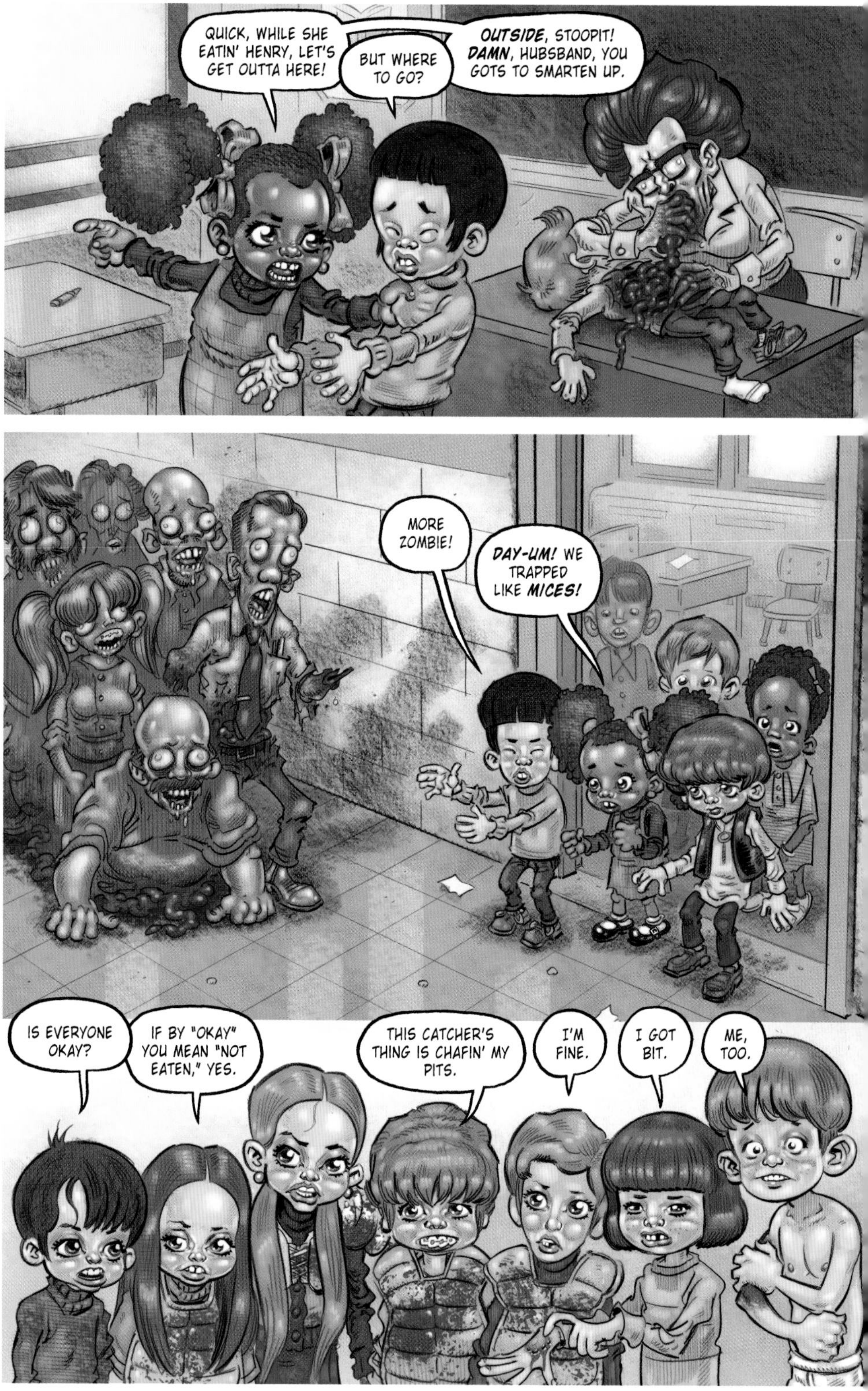
QUICK, WHILE SHE EATIN' HENRY, LET'S GET OUTTA HERE!
BUT WHERE TO GO?
OUTSIDE, STOOPIT! DAMN, HUBSBAND, YOU GOTS TO SMARTEN UP.
MORE ZOMBIE!
DAY-UM! WE TRAPPED LIKE MICES!
IS EVERYONE OKAY?
IF BY "OKAY" YOU MEAN "NOT EATEN," YES.
THIS CATCHER'S THING IS CHAFIN' MY PITS.
I'M FINE.
I GOT BIT.
ME, TOO.

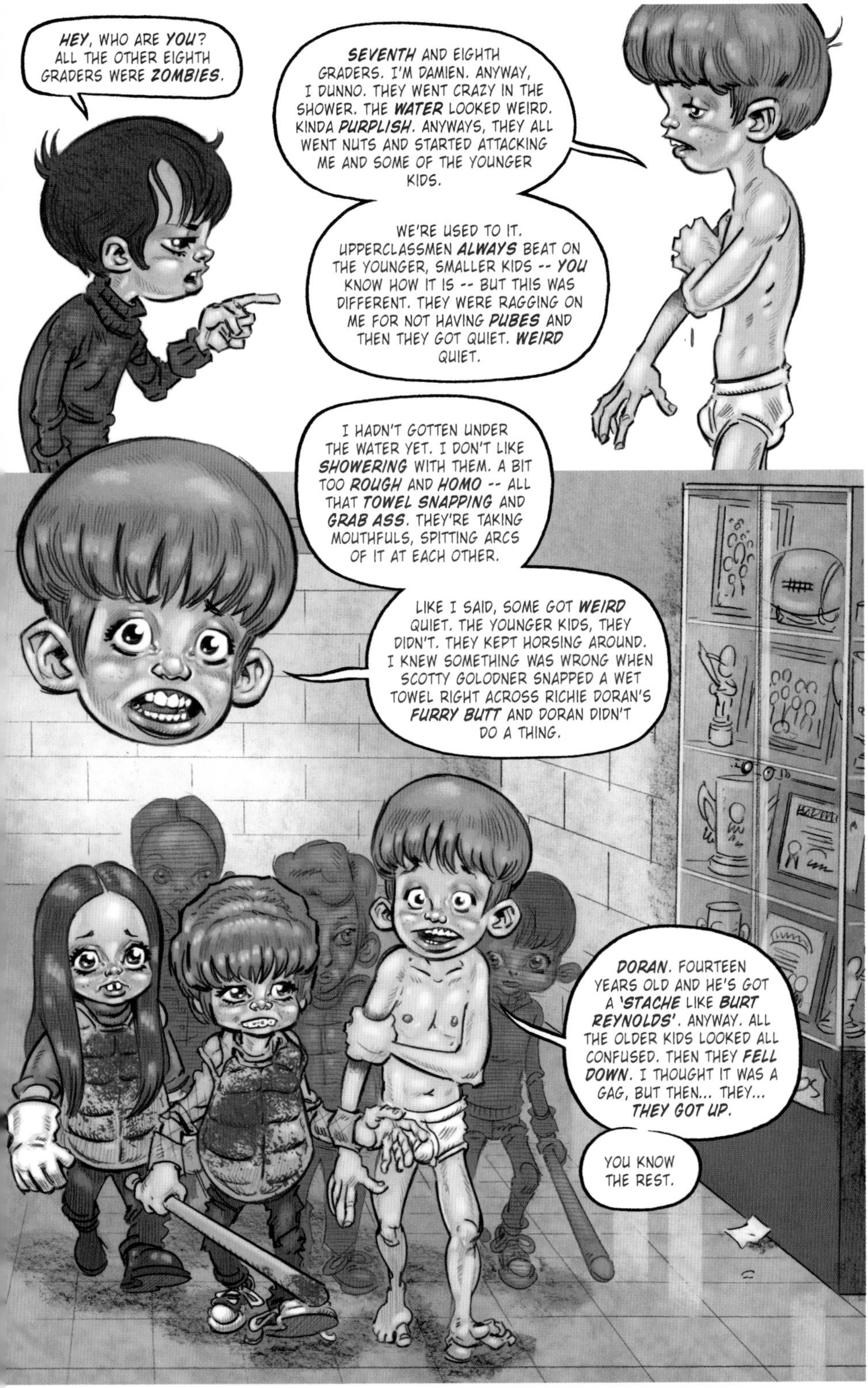
HEY, WHO ARE YOU? ALL THE OTHER EIGHTH GRADERS WERE ZOMBIES.
SEVENTH AND EIGHTH GRADERS. I'M DAMIEN. ANYWAY, I DUNNO. THEY WENT CRAZY IN THE SHOWER. THE WATER LOOKED WEIRD. KINDA PURPLISH. ANYWAYS, THEY ALL WENT NUTS AND STARTED ATTACKING ME AND SOME OF THE YOUNGER KIDS.
WE'RE USED TO IT. UPPERCLASSMEN ALWAYS BEAT ON THE YOUNGER, SMALLER KIDS -- YOU KNOW HOW IT IS -- BUT THIS WAS DIFFERENT. THEY WERE RAGGING ON ME FOR NOT HAVING PUBES AND THEN THEY GOT QUIET. WEIRD QUIET.
I HADN'T GOTTEN UNDER THE WATER YET. I DON'T LIKE SHOWERING WITH THEM. A BIT TOO ROUGH AND HOMO -- ALL THAT TOWEL SNAPPING AND GRAB ASS. THEY'RE TAKING MOUTHFULS, SPITTING ARCS OF IT AT EACH OTHER.
LIKE I SAID, SOME GOT WEIRD QUIET. THE YOUNGER KIDS, THEY DIDN'T. THEY KEPT HORSING AROUND. I KNEW SOMETHING WAS WRONG WHEN SCOTTY GOLODNER SNAPPED A WET TOWEL RIGHT ACROSS RICHIE DORAN'S FURRY BUTT AND DORAN DIDN'T DO A THING.
DORAN. FOURTEEN YEARS OLD AND HE'S GOT A 'STACHE LIKE BURT REYNOLDS'. ANYWAY. ALL THE OLDER KIDS LOOKED ALL CONFUSED. THEN THEY FELL DOWN. I THOUGHT IT WAS A GAG, BUT THEN... THEY... THEY GOT UP.
YOU KNOW THE REST.

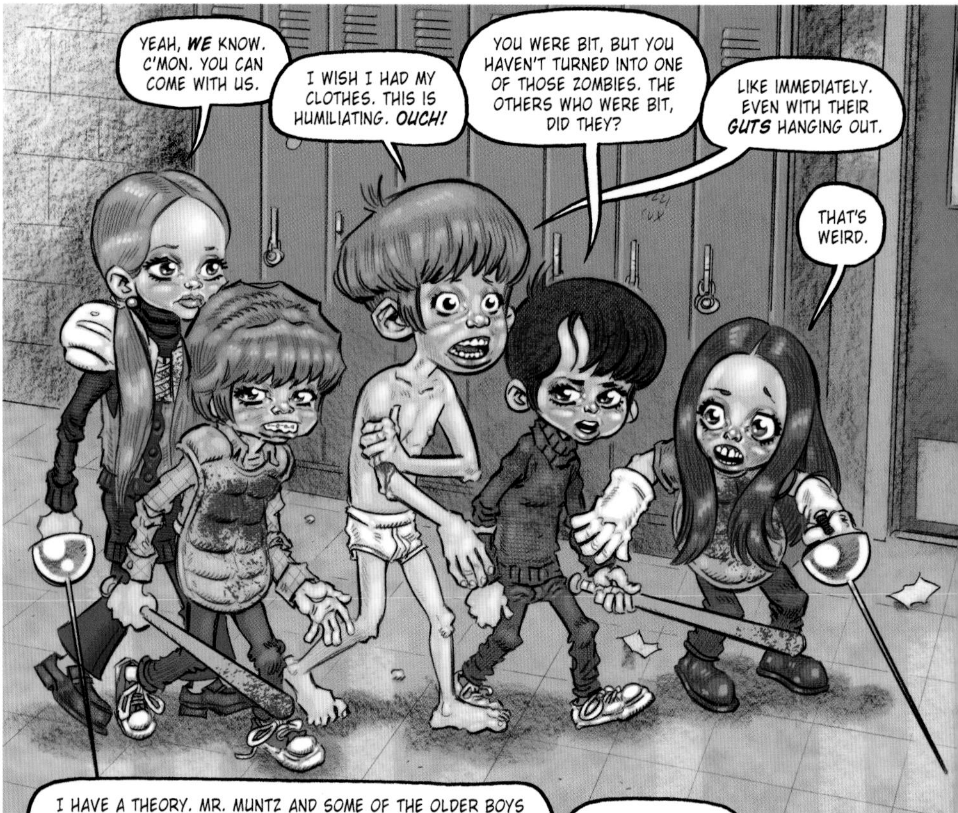

YEAH, **WE** KNOW. C'MON. YOU CAN COME WITH US.
I WISH I HAD MY CLOTHES. THIS IS HUMILIATING. ***OUCH!***
YOU WERE BIT, BUT YOU HAVEN'T TURNED INTO ONE OF THOSE ZOMBIES. THE OTHERS WHO WERE BIT, DID THEY?
LIKE IMMEDIATELY. EVEN WITH THEIR ***GUTS*** HANGING OUT.
THAT'S WEIRD.

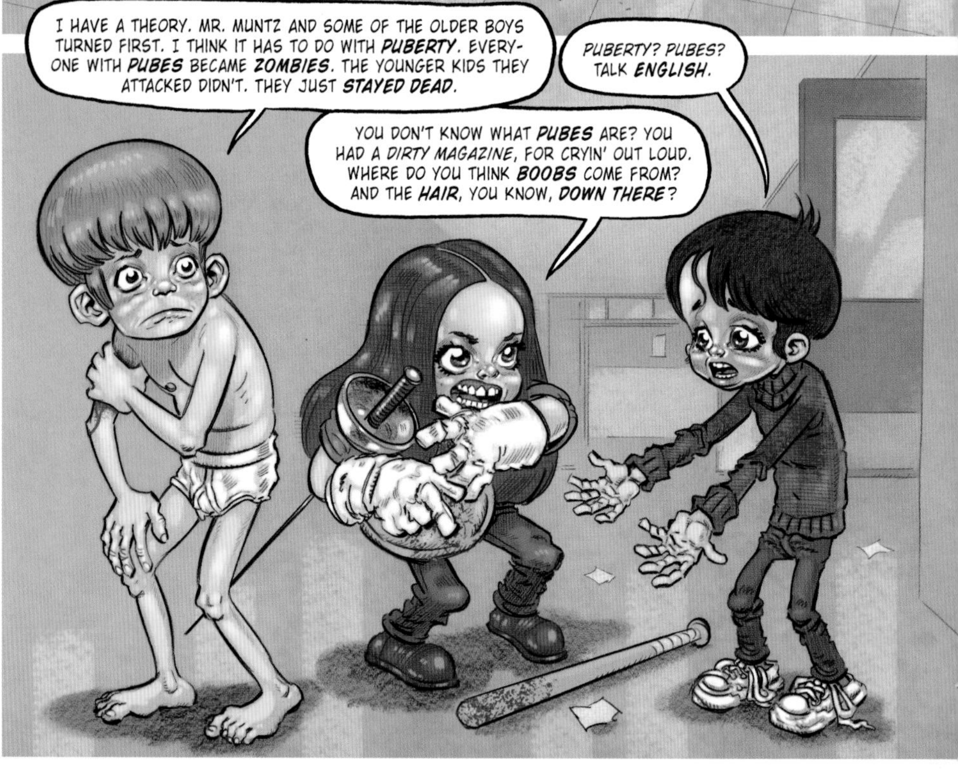

I HAVE A THEORY. MR. MUNTZ AND SOME OF THE OLDER BOYS TURNED FIRST. I THINK IT HAS TO DO WITH ***PUBERTY***. EVERYONE WITH ***PUBES*** BECAME ***ZOMBIES***. THE YOUNGER KIDS THEY ATTACKED DIDN'T. THEY JUST ***STAYED DEAD***.
PUBERTY? PUBES? TALK ***ENGLISH***.
YOU DON'T KNOW WHAT ***PUBES*** ARE? YOU HAD A *DIRTY MAGAZINE*, FOR CRYIN' OUT LOUD. WHERE DO YOU THINK ***BOOBS*** COME FROM? AND THE ***HAIR***, YOU KNOW, ***DOWN THERE***?

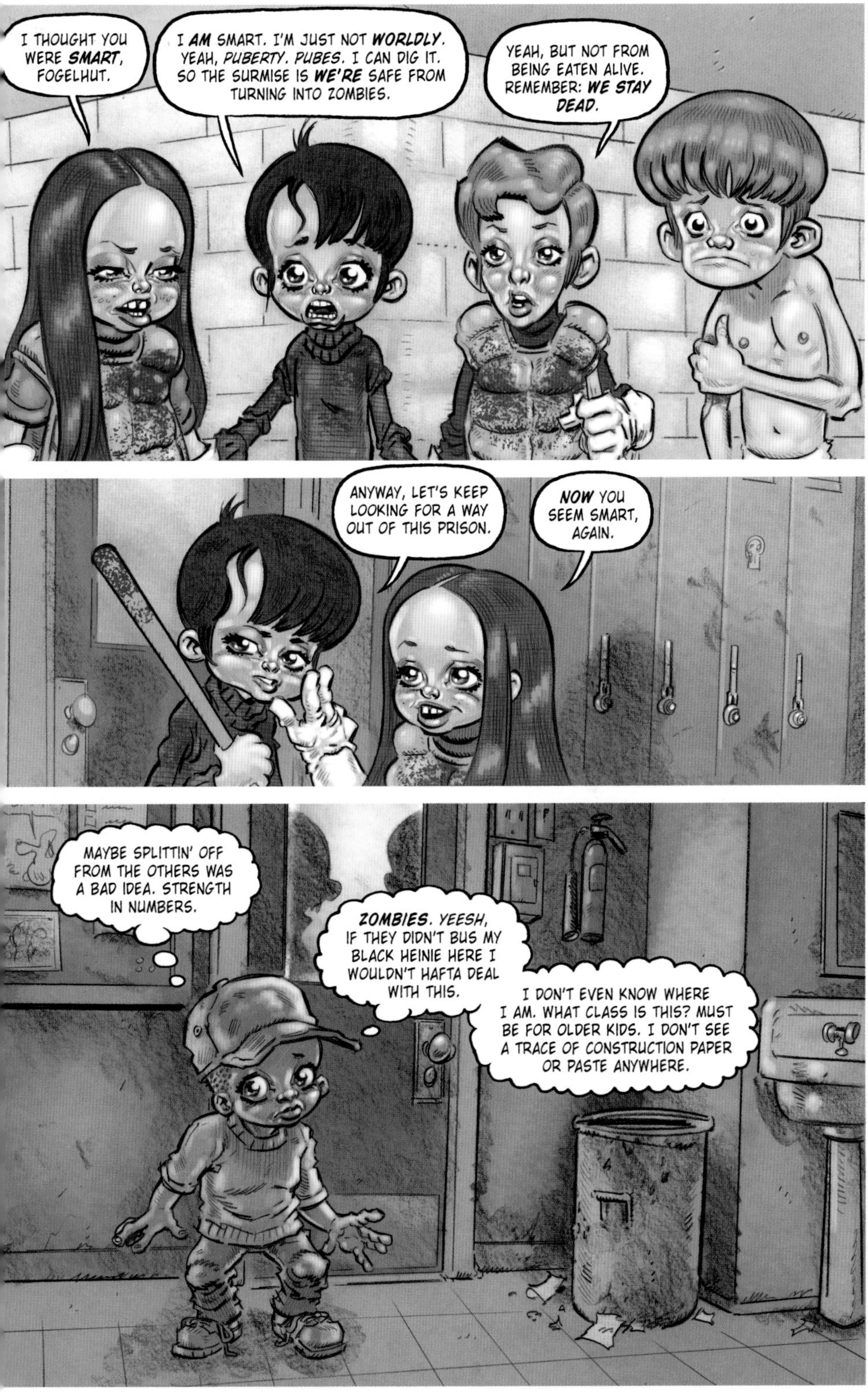
I THOUGHT YOU WERE SMART, FOGELHUT.
I AM SMART. I'M JUST NOT WORLDLY. YEAH, PUBERTY. PUBES. I CAN DIG IT. SO THE SURMISE IS WE'RE SAFE FROM TURNING INTO ZOMBIES.
YEAH, BUT NOT FROM BEING EATEN ALIVE. REMEMBER: WE STAY DEAD.
ANYWAY, LET'S KEEP LOOKING FOR A WAY OUT OF THIS PRISON.
NOW YOU SEEM SMART, AGAIN.
MAYBE SPLITTIN' OFF FROM THE OTHERS WAS A BAD IDEA. STRENGTH IN NUMBERS.
ZOMBIES. YEESH, IF THEY DIDN'T BUS MY BLACK HEINIE HERE I WOULDN'T HAFTA DEAL WITH THIS.
I DON'T EVEN KNOW WHERE I AM. WHAT CLASS IS THIS? MUST BE FOR OLDER KIDS. I DON'T SEE A TRACE OF CONSTRUCTION PAPER OR PASTE ANYWHERE.

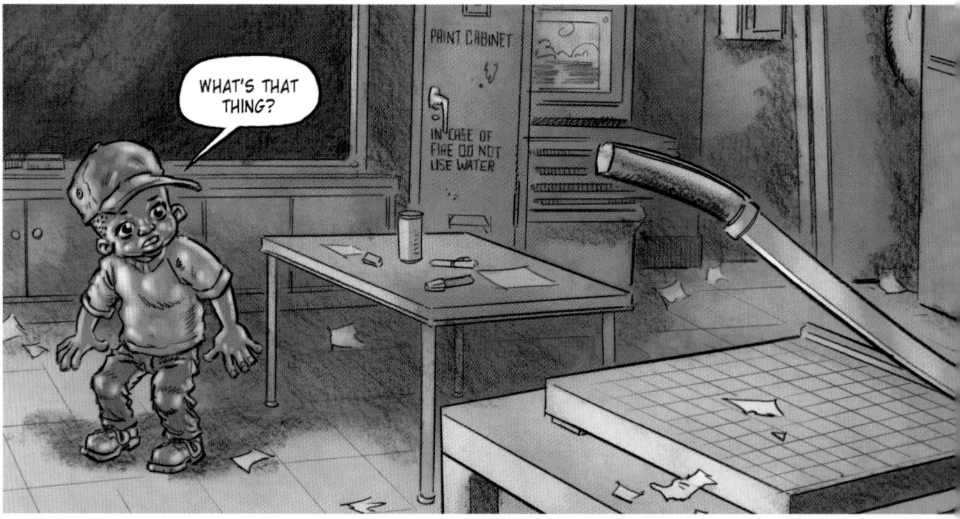
WHAT'S THAT THING?
PAINT CABINET
IN CASE OF FIRE DO NOT USE WATER

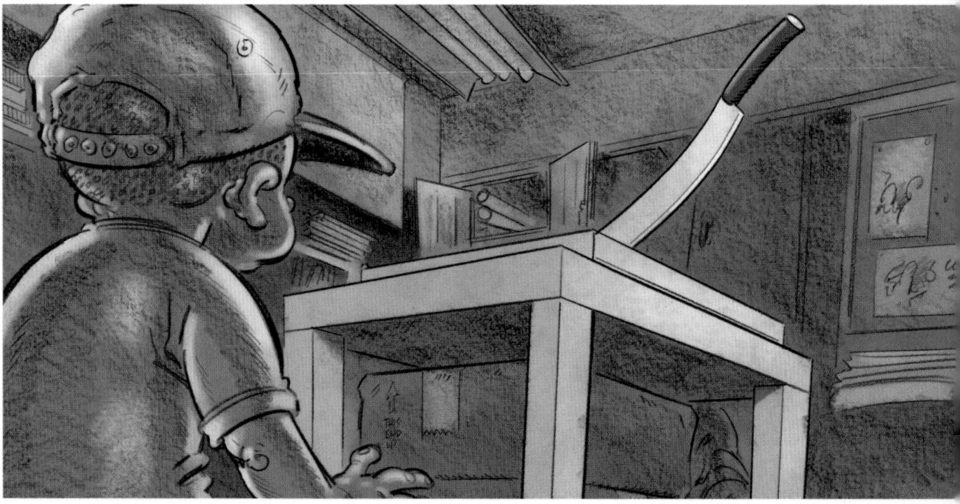

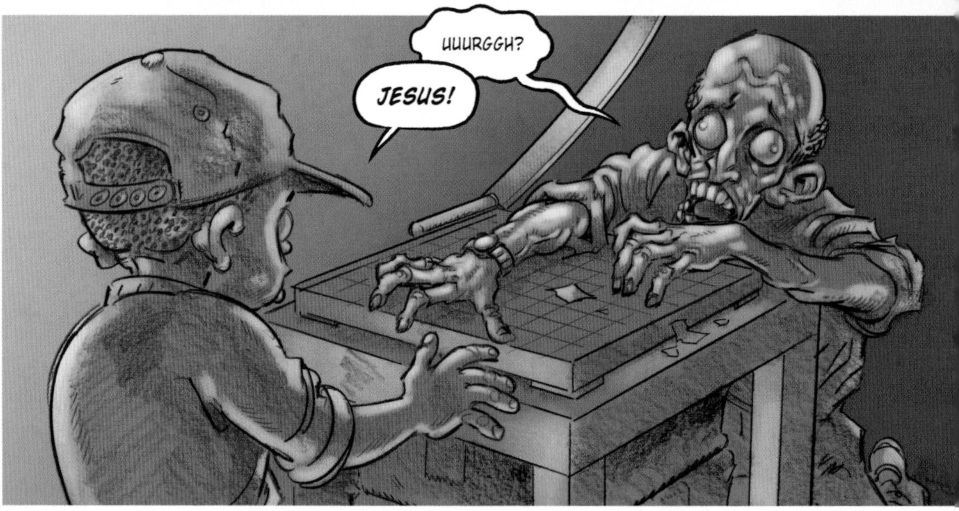
UUURGGH?
JESUS!

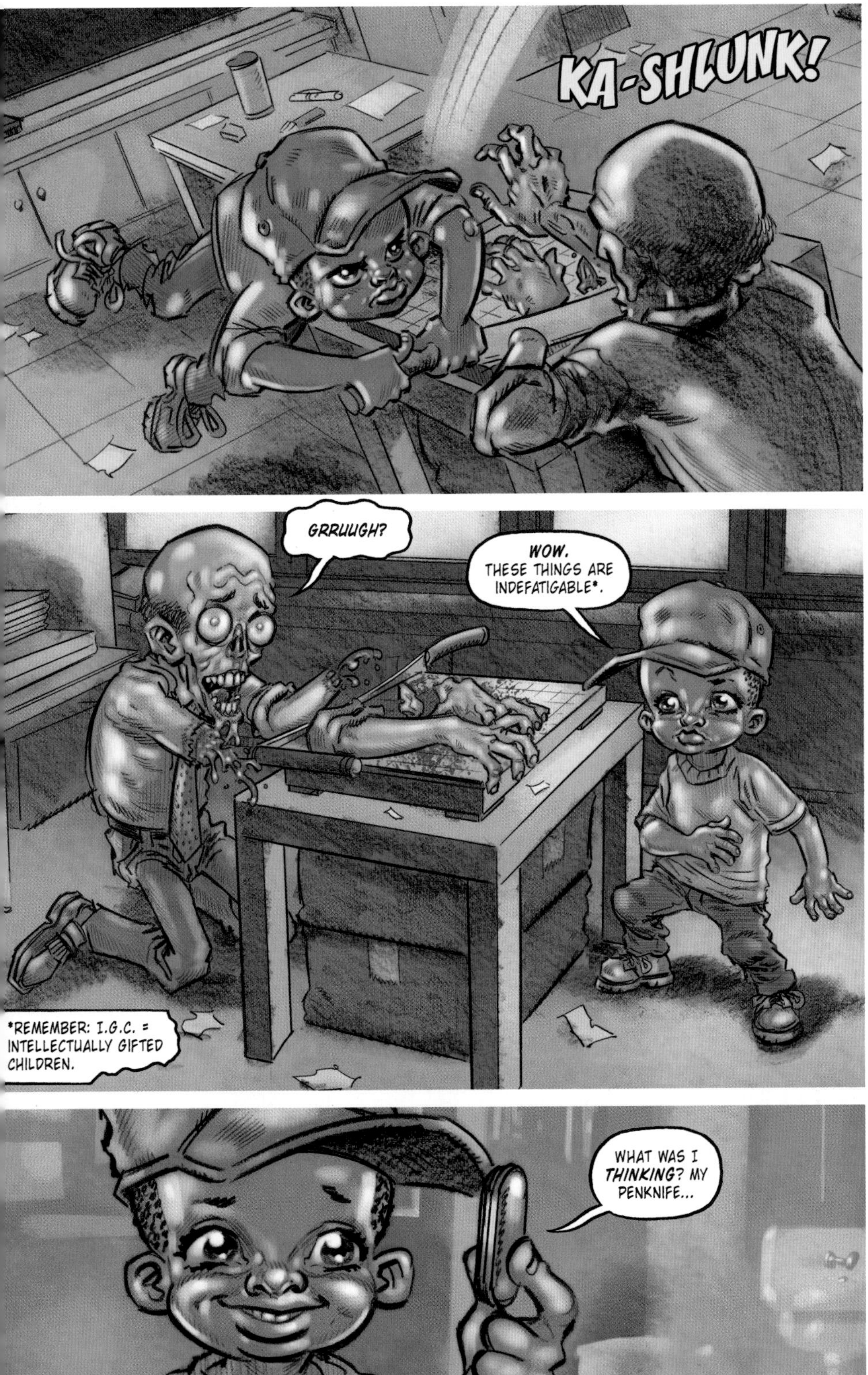
KA-SHLUNK!
GRRUUGH?
WOW. THESE THINGS ARE INDEFATIGABLE*.
*REMEMBER: I.G.C. = INTELLECTUALLY GIFTED CHILDREN.
WHAT WAS I THINKING? MY PENKNIFE...

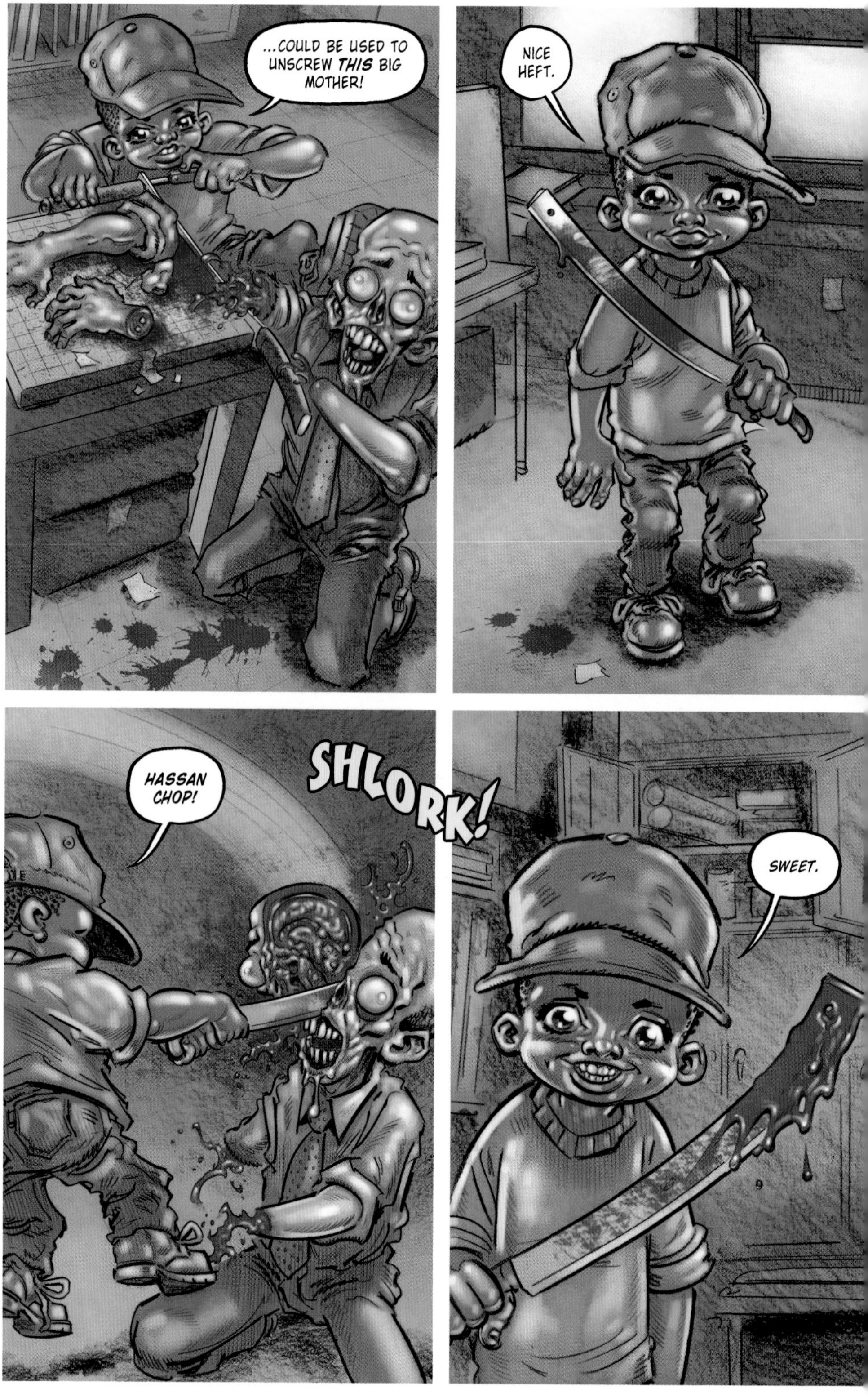
...COULD BE USED TO UNSCREW *THIS* BIG MOTHER!
NICE HEFT.
HASSAN CHOP!
SHLORK!
SWEET.

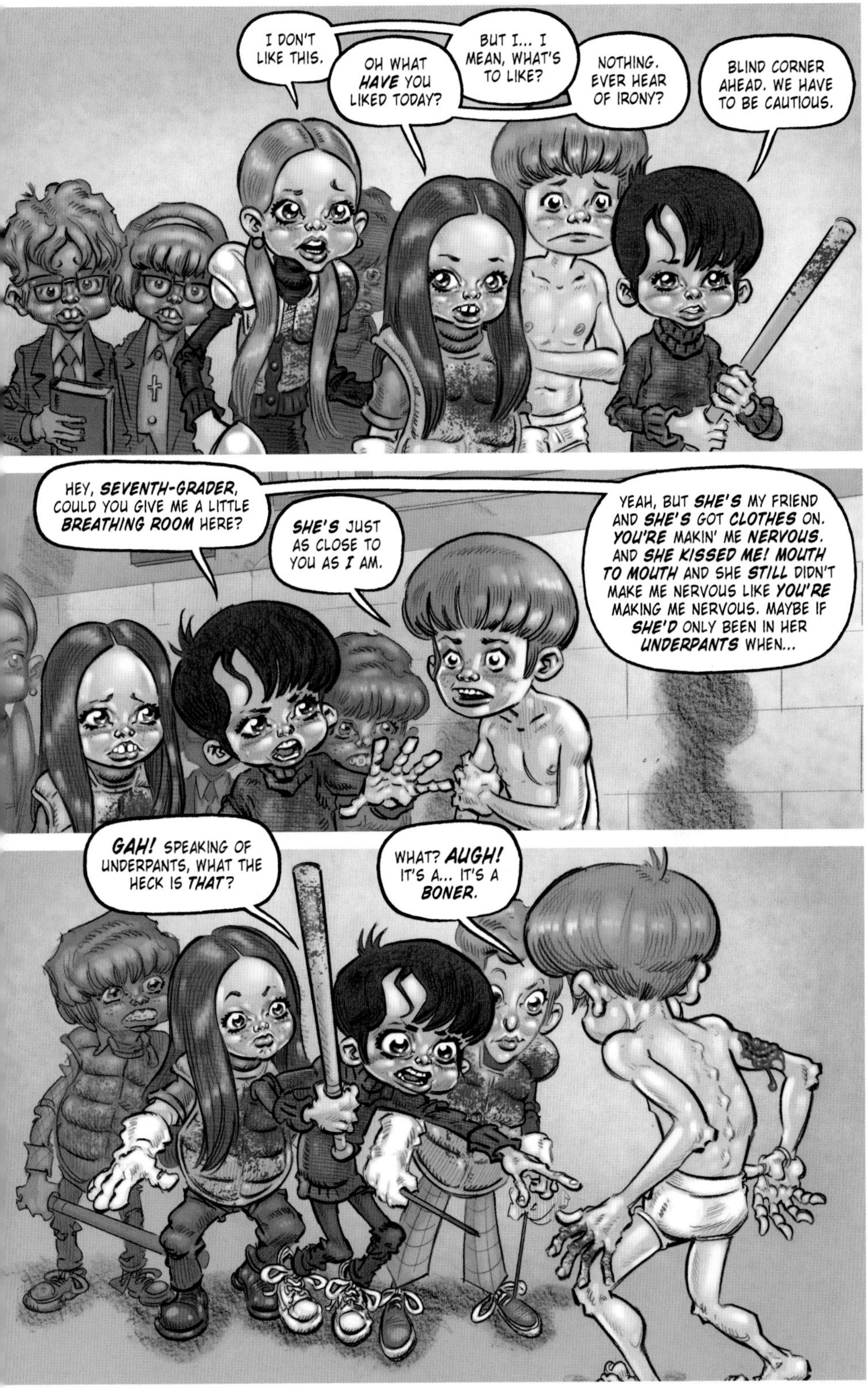
I DON'T LIKE THIS.
OH WHAT HAVE YOU LIKED TODAY?
BUT I... I MEAN, WHAT'S TO LIKE?
NOTHING. EVER HEAR OF IRONY?
BLIND CORNER AHEAD. WE HAVE TO BE CAUTIOUS.
HEY, SEVENTH-GRADER, COULD YOU GIVE ME A LITTLE BREATHING ROOM HERE?
SHE'S JUST AS CLOSE TO YOU AS I AM.
YEAH, BUT SHE'S MY FRIEND AND SHE'S GOT CLOTHES ON. YOU'RE MAKIN' ME NERVOUS. AND SHE KISSED ME! MOUTH TO MOUTH AND SHE STILL DIDN'T MAKE ME NERVOUS LIKE YOU'RE MAKING ME NERVOUS. MAYBE IF SHE'D ONLY BEEN IN HER UNDERPANTS WHEN...
GAH! SPEAKING OF UNDERPANTS, WHAT THE HECK IS THAT?
WHAT? AUGH! IT'S A... IT'S A BONER.

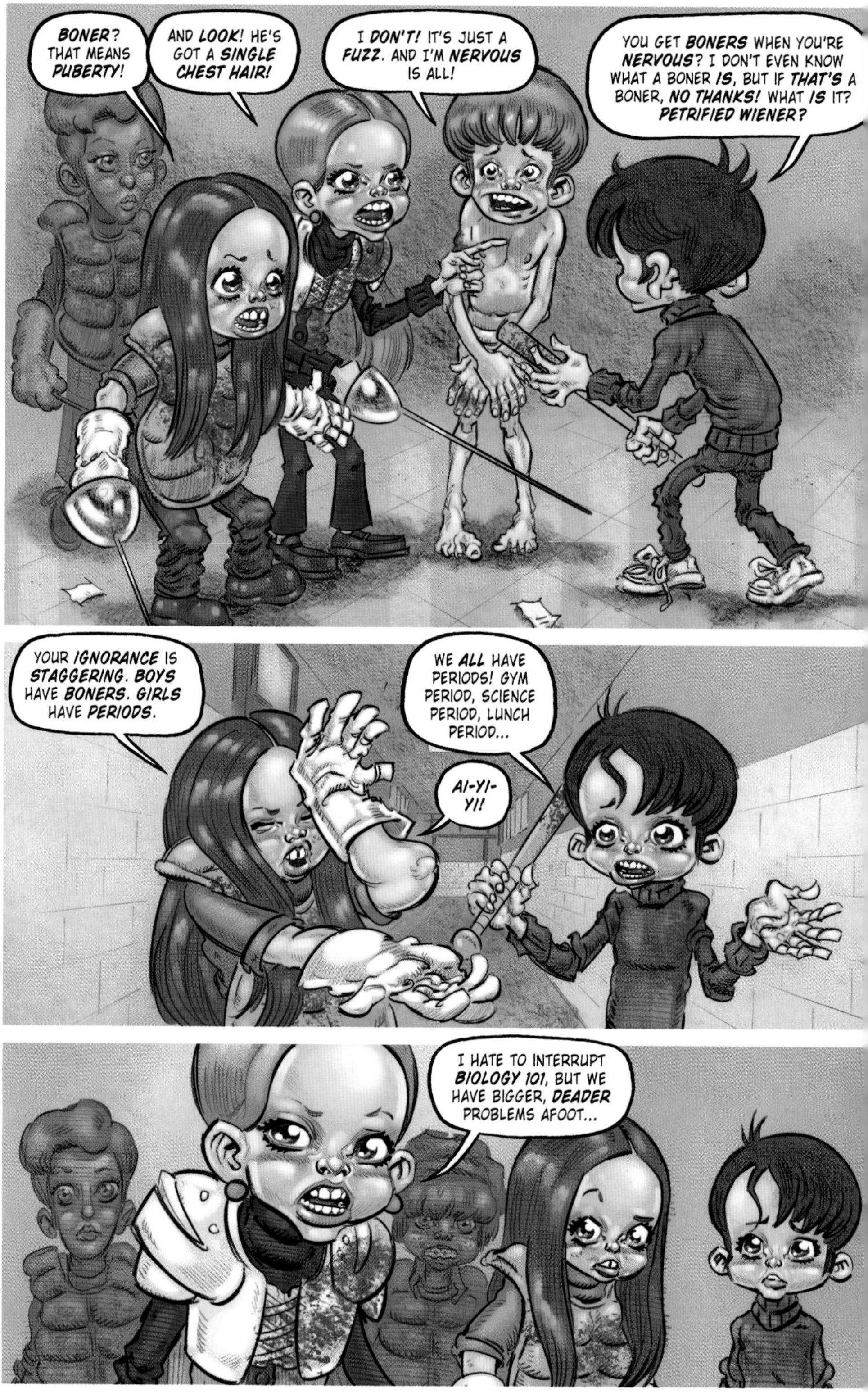
BONER? THAT MEANS PUBERTY!
AND LOOK! HE'S GOT A SINGLE CHEST HAIR!
I DON'T! IT'S JUST A FUZZ. AND I'M NERVOUS IS ALL!
YOU GET BONERS WHEN YOU'RE NERVOUS? I DON'T EVEN KNOW WHAT A BONER IS, BUT IF THAT'S A BONER, NO THANKS! WHAT IS IT? PETRIFIED WIENER?
YOUR IGNORANCE IS STAGGERING. BOYS HAVE BONERS. GIRLS HAVE PERIODS.
WE ALL HAVE PERIODS! GYM PERIOD, SCIENCE PERIOD, LUNCH PERIOD...
AI-YI-YI!
I HATE TO INTERRUPT BIOLOGY 101, BUT WE HAVE BIGGER, DEADER PROBLEMS AFOOT...

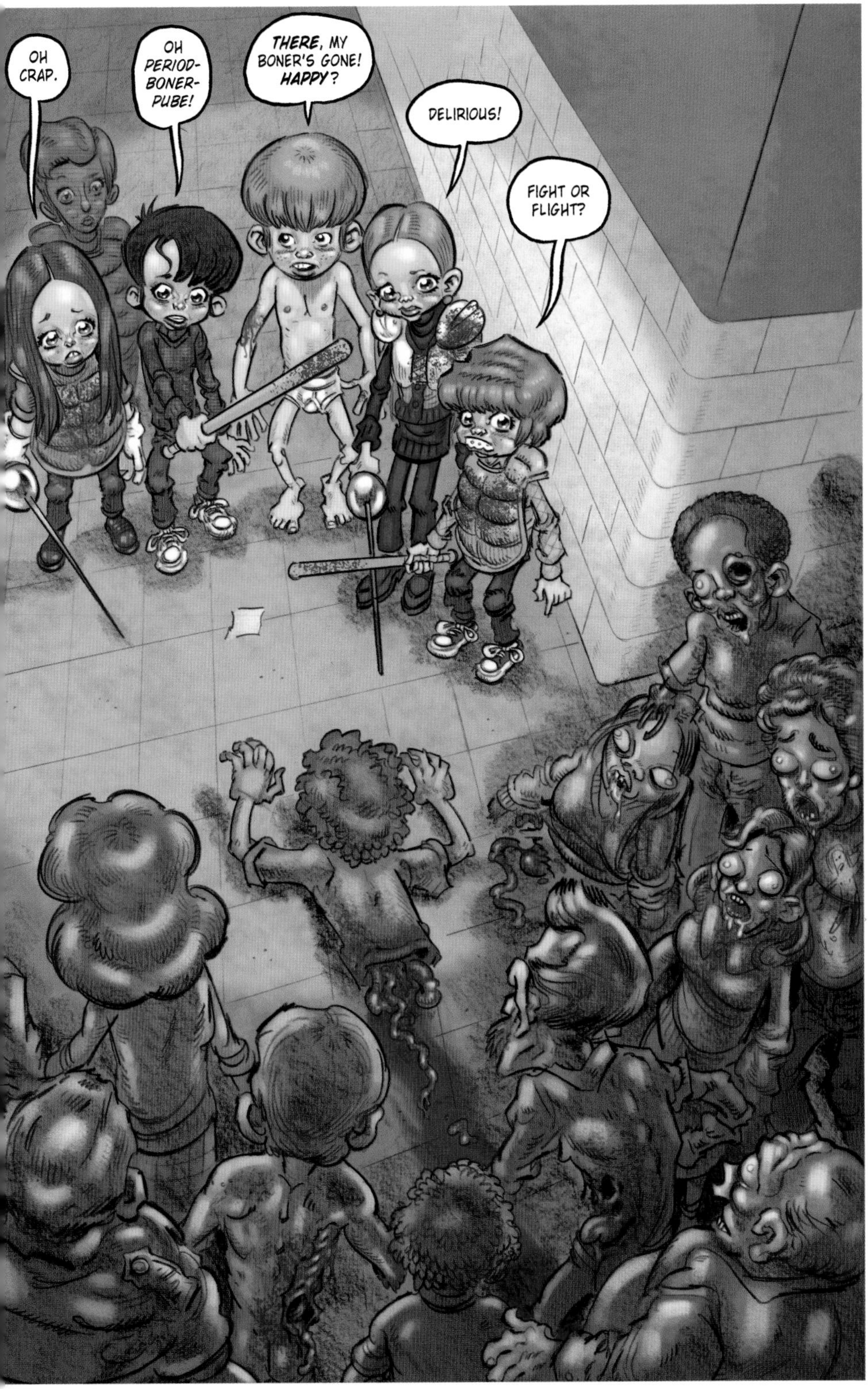
OH CRAP.
OH PERIOD-BONER-PUBE!
THERE, MY BONER'S GONE! HAPPY?
DELIRIOUS!
FIGHT OR FLIGHT?

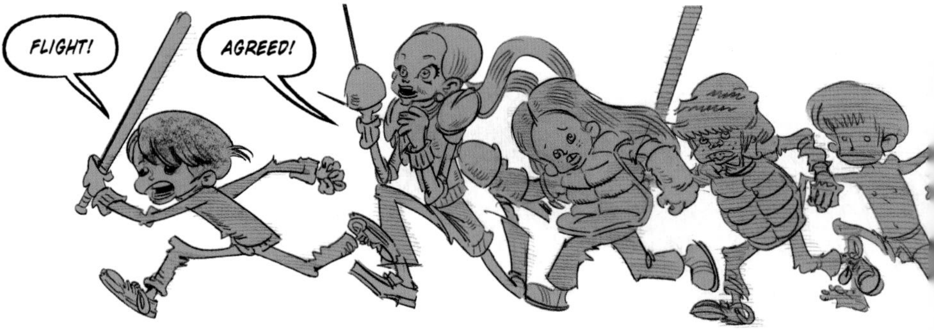
FLIGHT!
AGREED!

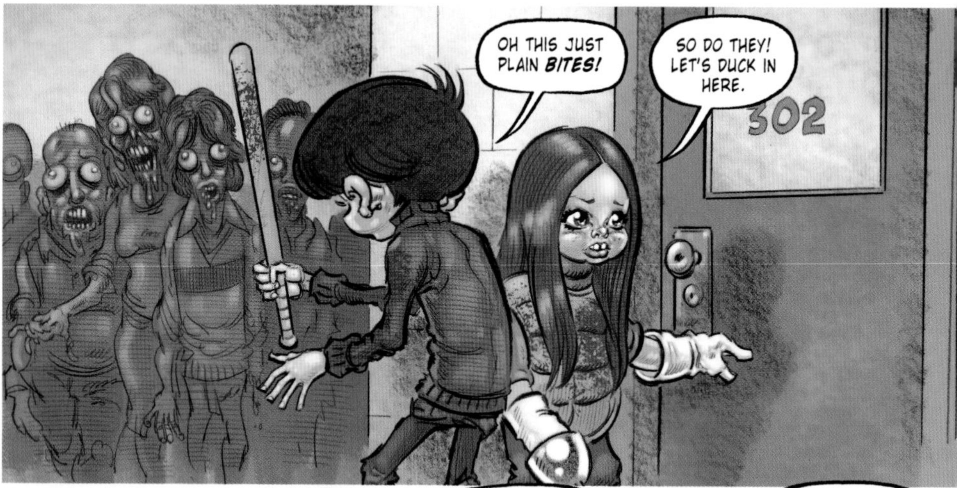
OH THIS JUST PLAIN BITES!
SO DO THEY! LET'S DUCK IN HERE.
302

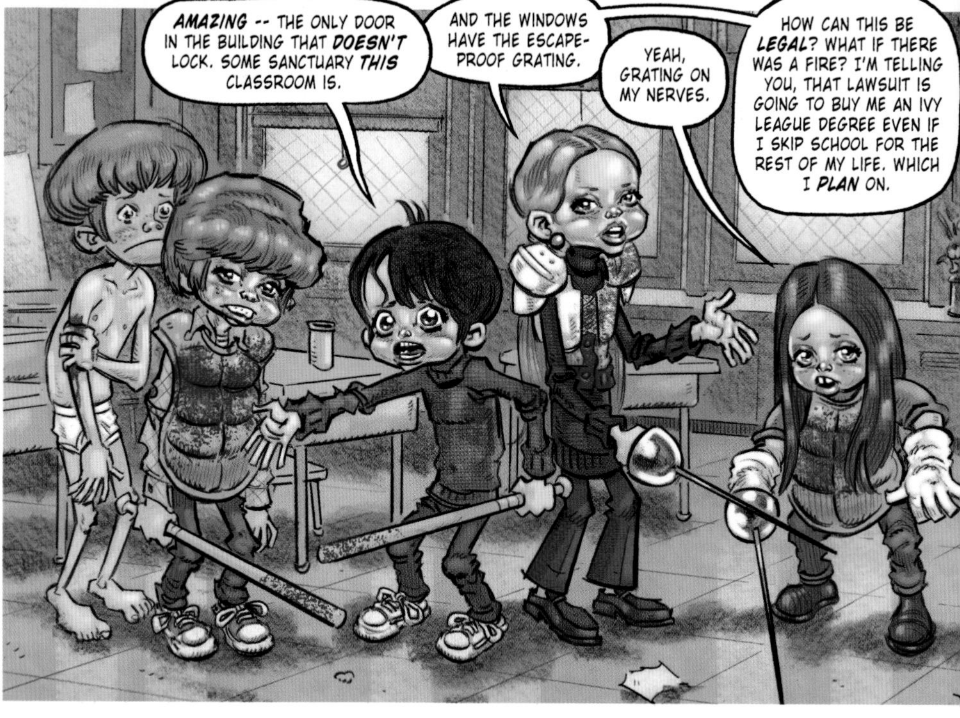
AMAZING -- THE ONLY DOOR IN THE BUILDING THAT DOESN'T LOCK. SOME SANCTUARY THIS CLASSROOM IS.
AND THE WINDOWS HAVE THE ESCAPE-PROOF GRATING.
YEAH, GRATING ON MY NERVES.
HOW CAN THIS BE LEGAL? WHAT IF THERE WAS A FIRE? I'M TELLING YOU, THAT LAWSUIT IS GOING TO BUY ME AN IVY LEAGUE DEGREE EVEN IF I SKIP SCHOOL FOR THE REST OF MY LIFE. WHICH I PLAN ON.

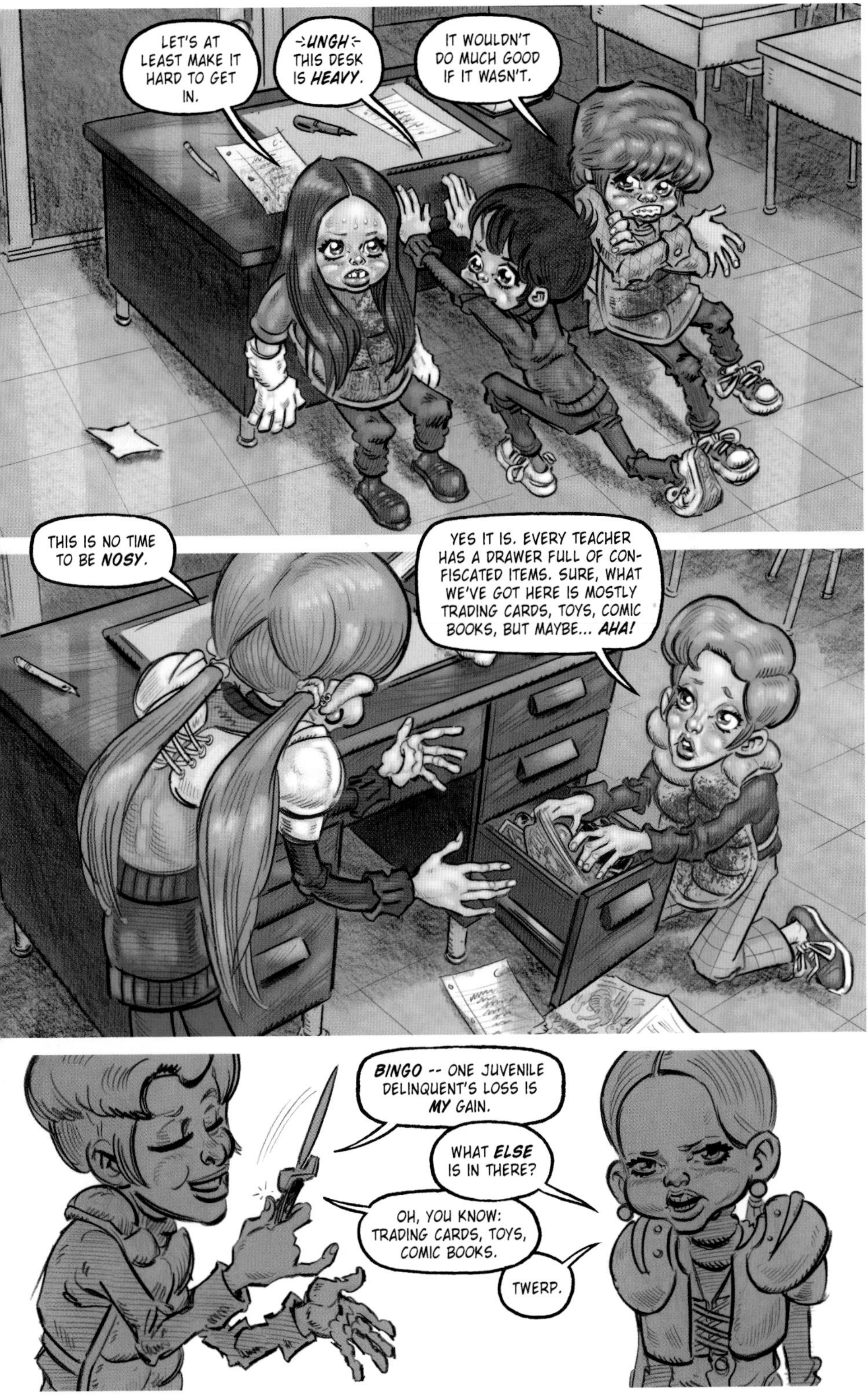
LET'S AT LEAST MAKE IT HARD TO GET IN.
-UNGH- THIS DESK IS HEAVY.
IT WOULDN'T DO MUCH GOOD IF IT WASN'T.
THIS IS NO TIME TO BE NOSY.
YES IT IS. EVERY TEACHER HAS A DRAWER FULL OF CONFISCATED ITEMS. SURE, WHAT WE'VE GOT HERE IS MOSTLY TRADING CARDS, TOYS, COMIC BOOKS, BUT MAYBE... AHA!
BINGO -- ONE JUVENILE DELINQUENT'S LOSS IS MY GAIN.
WHAT ELSE IS IN THERE?
OH, YOU KNOW: TRADING CARDS, TOYS, COMIC BOOKS.
TWERP.

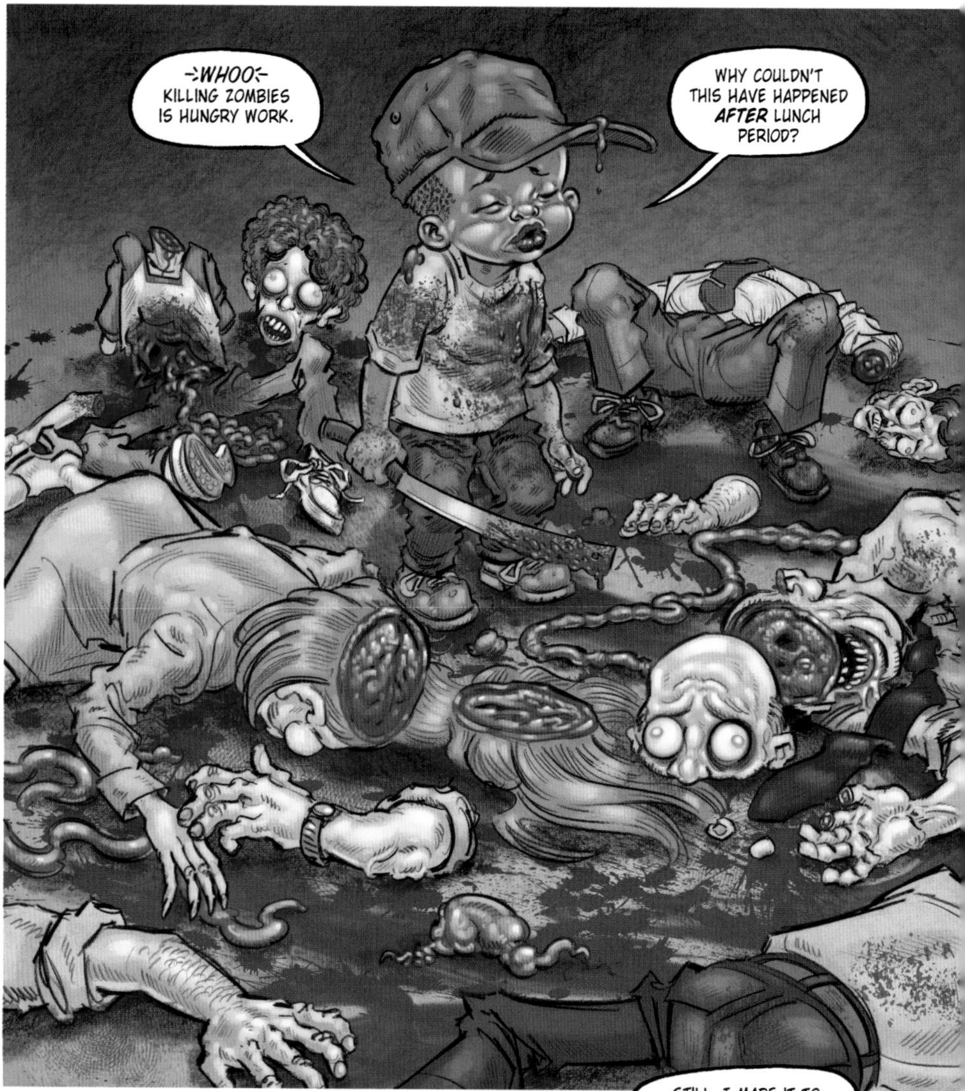

-WHOO- KILLING ZOMBIES IS HUNGRY WORK.
WHY COULDN'T THIS HAVE HAPPENED AFTER LUNCH PERIOD?

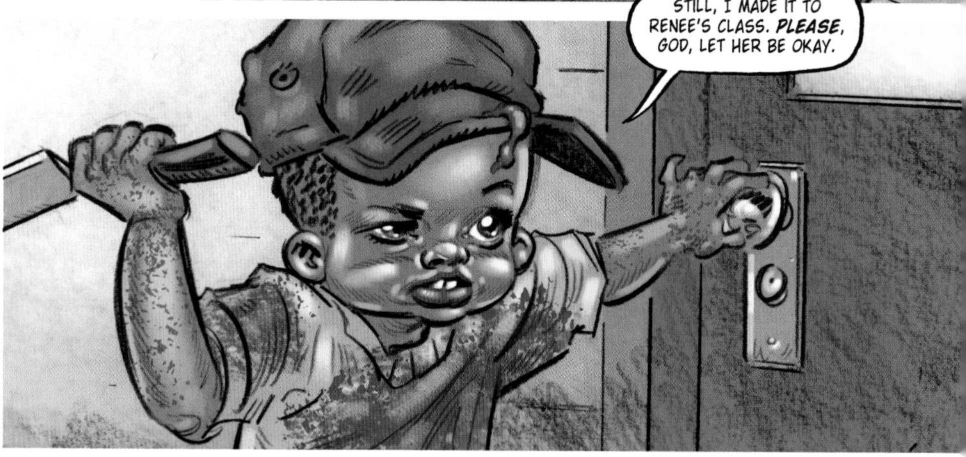

STILL, I MADE IT TO RENEE'S CLASS. PLEASE, GOD, LET HER BE OKAY.

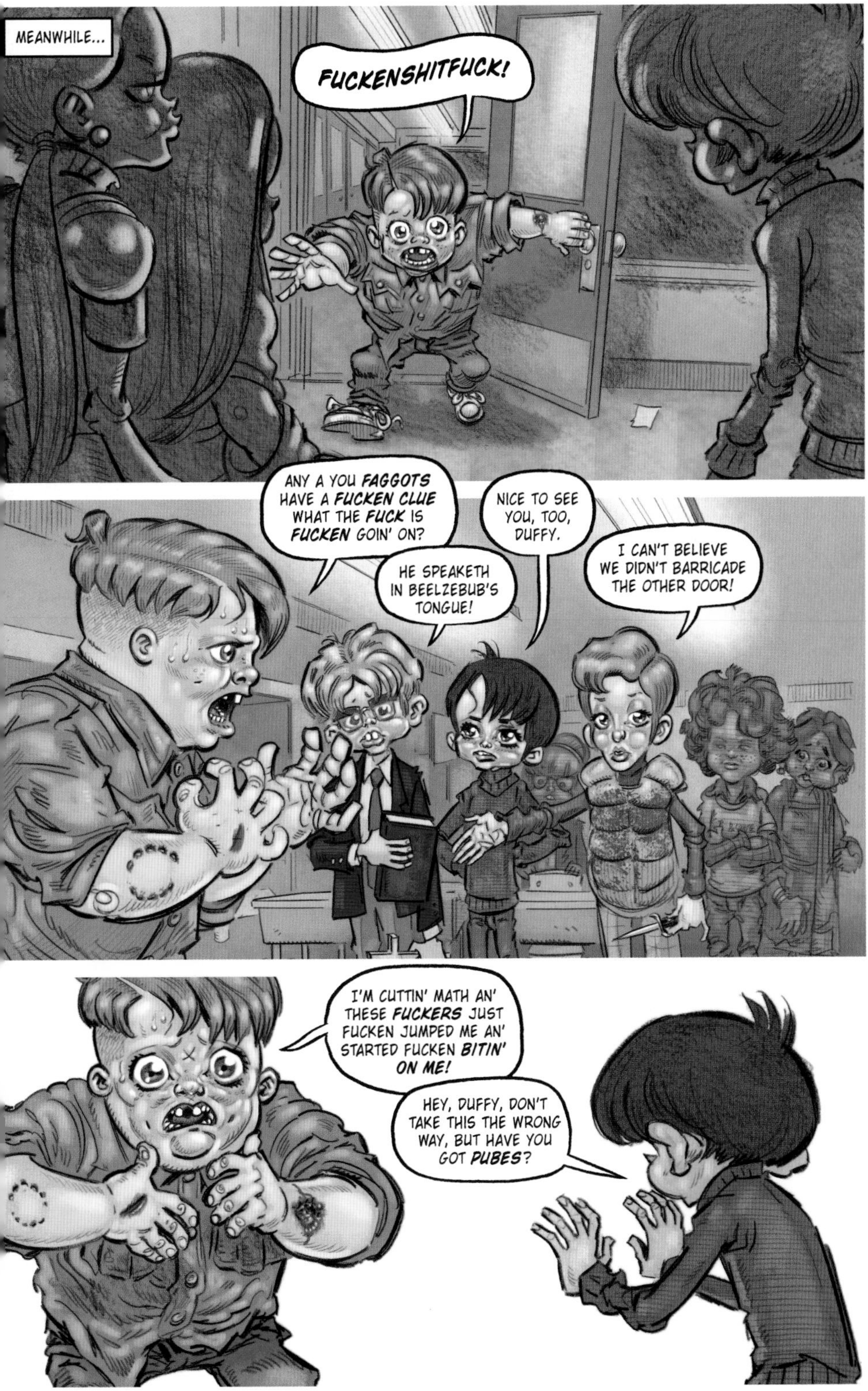
MEANWHILE...
FUCKENSHITFUCK!
ANY A YOU FAGGOTS HAVE A FUCKEN CLUE WHAT THE FUCK IS FUCKEN GOIN' ON?
HE SPEAKETH IN BEELZEBUB'S TONGUE!
NICE TO SEE YOU, TOO, DUFFY.
I CAN'T BELIEVE WE DIDN'T BARRICADE THE OTHER DOOR!
I'M CUTTIN' MATH AN' THESE FUCKERS JUST FUCKEN JUMPED ME AN' STARTED FUCKEN BITIN' ON ME!
HEY, DUFFY, DON'T TAKE THIS THE WRONG WAY, BUT HAVE YOU GOT PUBES?

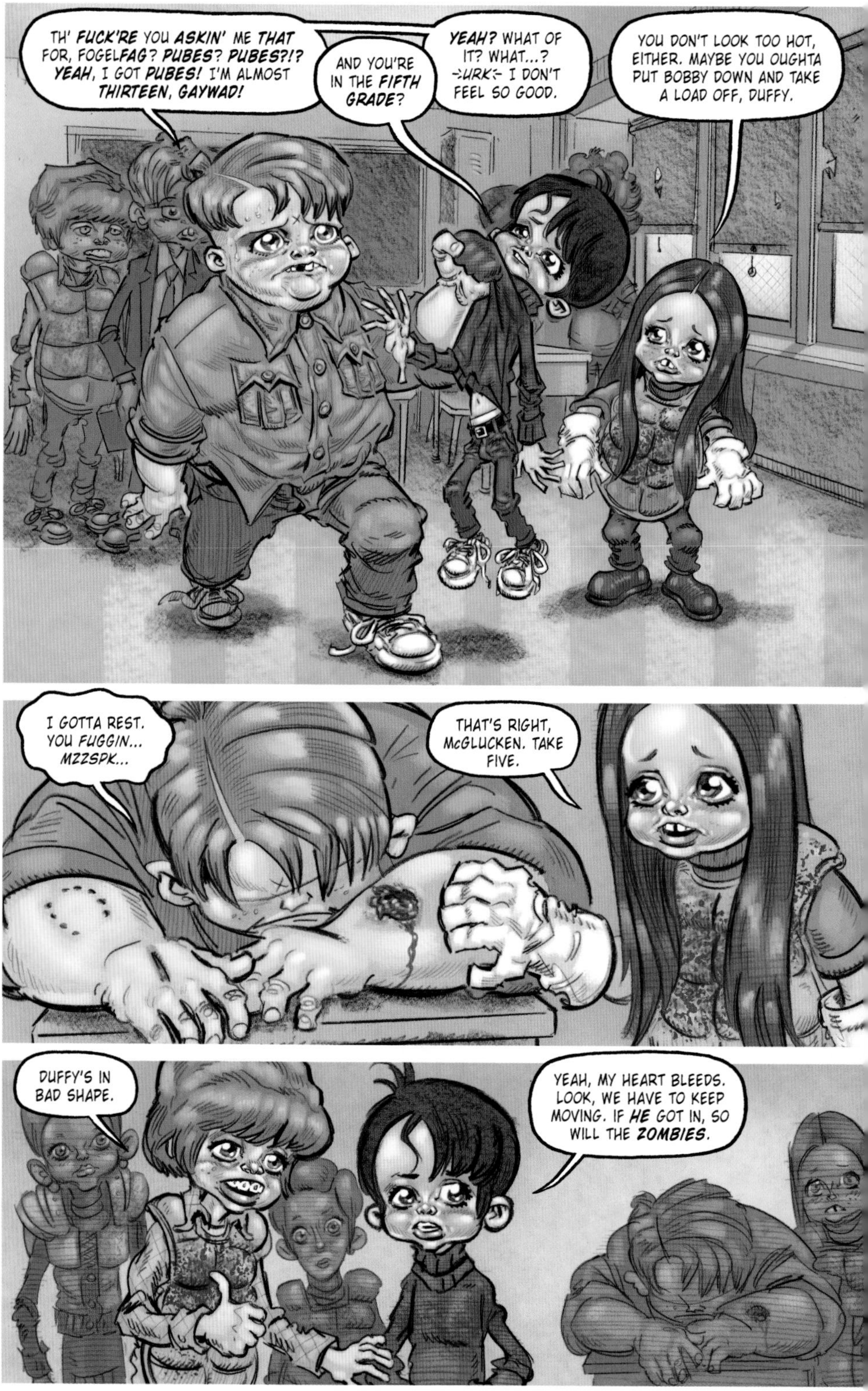
TH' FUCK'RE YOU ASKIN' ME THAT FOR, FOGELFAG? PUBES? PUBES?!? YEAH, I GOT PUBES! I'M ALMOST THIRTEEN, GAYWAD!
AND YOU'RE IN THE FIFTH GRADE?
YEAH? WHAT OF IT? WHAT...? -URK- I DON'T FEEL SO GOOD.
YOU DON'T LOOK TOO HOT, EITHER. MAYBE YOU OUGHTA PUT BOBBY DOWN AND TAKE A LOAD OFF, DUFFY.
I GOTTA REST. YOU FUGGIN... MZZSPK...
THAT'S RIGHT, McGLUCKEN. TAKE FIVE.
DUFFY'S IN BAD SHAPE.
YEAH, MY HEART BLEEDS. LOOK, WE HAVE TO KEEP MOVING. IF HE GOT IN, SO WILL THE ZOMBIES.

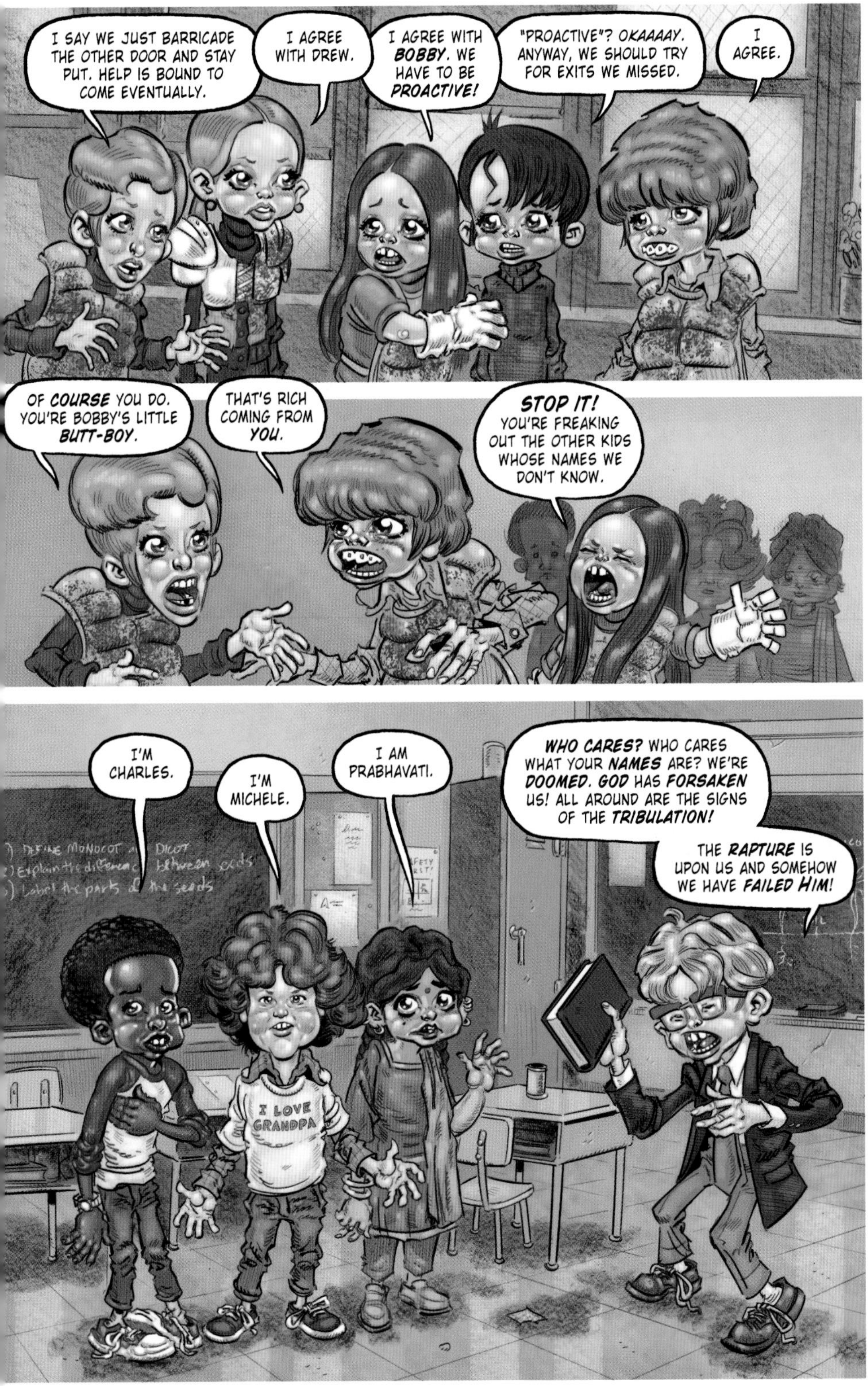
I SAY WE JUST BARRICADE THE OTHER DOOR AND STAY PUT. HELP IS BOUND TO COME EVENTUALLY.
I AGREE WITH DREW.
I AGREE WITH BOBBY. WE HAVE TO BE PROACTIVE!
"PROACTIVE"? OKAAAAY. ANYWAY, WE SHOULD TRY FOR EXITS WE MISSED.
I AGREE.
OF COURSE YOU DO. YOU'RE BOBBY'S LITTLE BUTT-BOY.
THAT'S RICH COMING FROM YOU.
STOP IT! YOU'RE FREAKING OUT THE OTHER KIDS WHOSE NAMES WE DON'T KNOW.
I'M CHARLES.
I'M MICHELE.
I AM PRABHAVATI.
WHO CARES? WHO CARES WHAT YOUR NAMES ARE? WE'RE DOOMED. GOD HAS FORSAKEN US! ALL AROUND ARE THE SIGNS OF THE TRIBULATION!
THE RAPTURE IS UPON US AND SOMEHOW WE HAVE FAILED HIM!
I LOVE GRANDPA

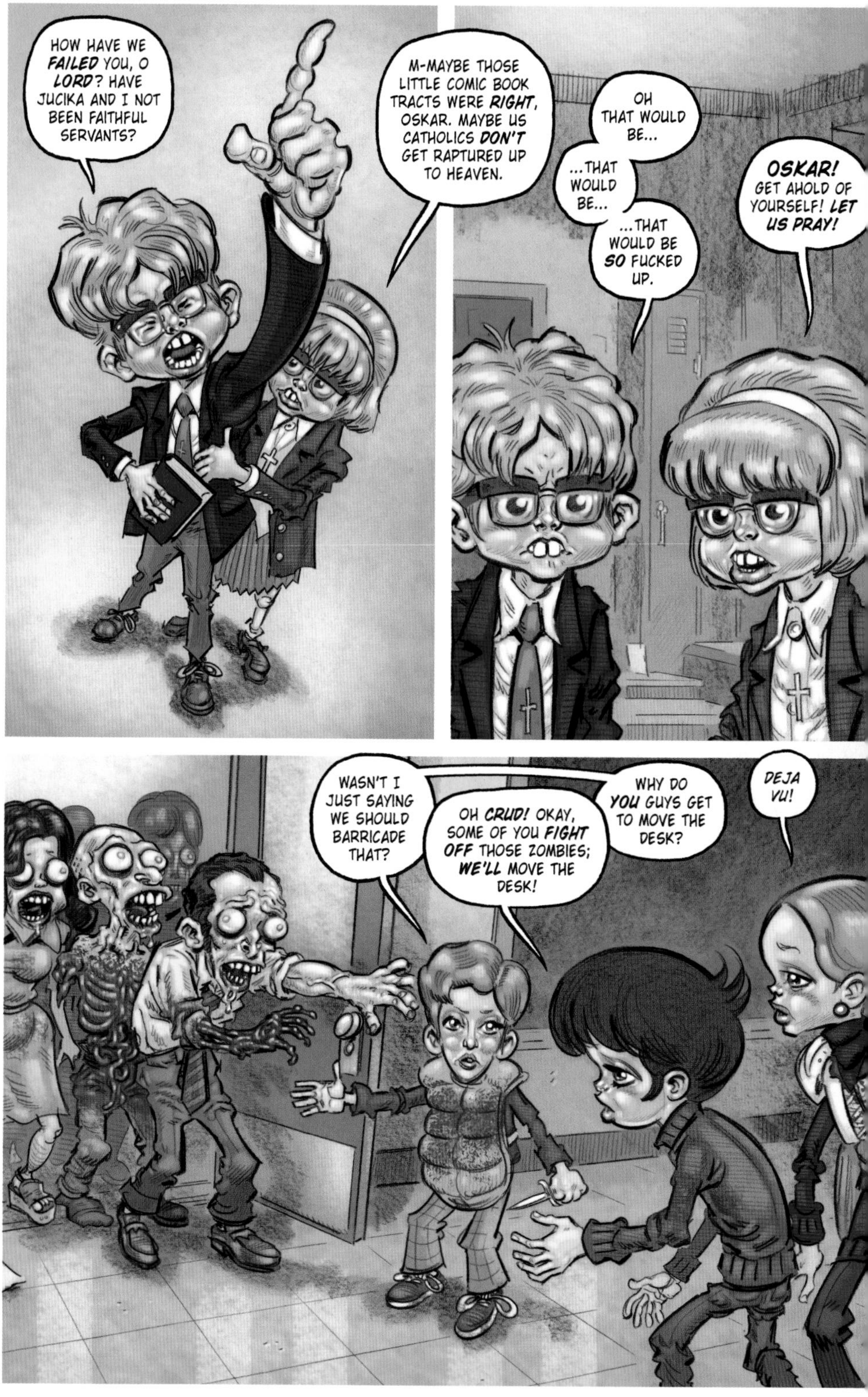
HOW HAVE WE FAILED YOU, O LORD? HAVE JUCIKA AND I NOT BEEN FAITHFUL SERVANTS?
M-MAYBE THOSE LITTLE COMIC BOOK TRACTS WERE RIGHT, OSKAR. MAYBE US CATHOLICS DON'T GET RAPTURED UP TO HEAVEN.
OH THAT WOULD BE...
...THAT WOULD BE...
...THAT WOULD BE SO FUCKED UP.
OSKAR! GET AHOLD OF YOURSELF! LET US PRAY!
WASN'T I JUST SAYING WE SHOULD BARRICADE THAT?
OH CRUD! OKAY, SOME OF YOU FIGHT OFF THOSE ZOMBIES; WE'LL MOVE THE DESK!
WHY DO YOU GUYS GET TO MOVE THE DESK?
DEJA VU!

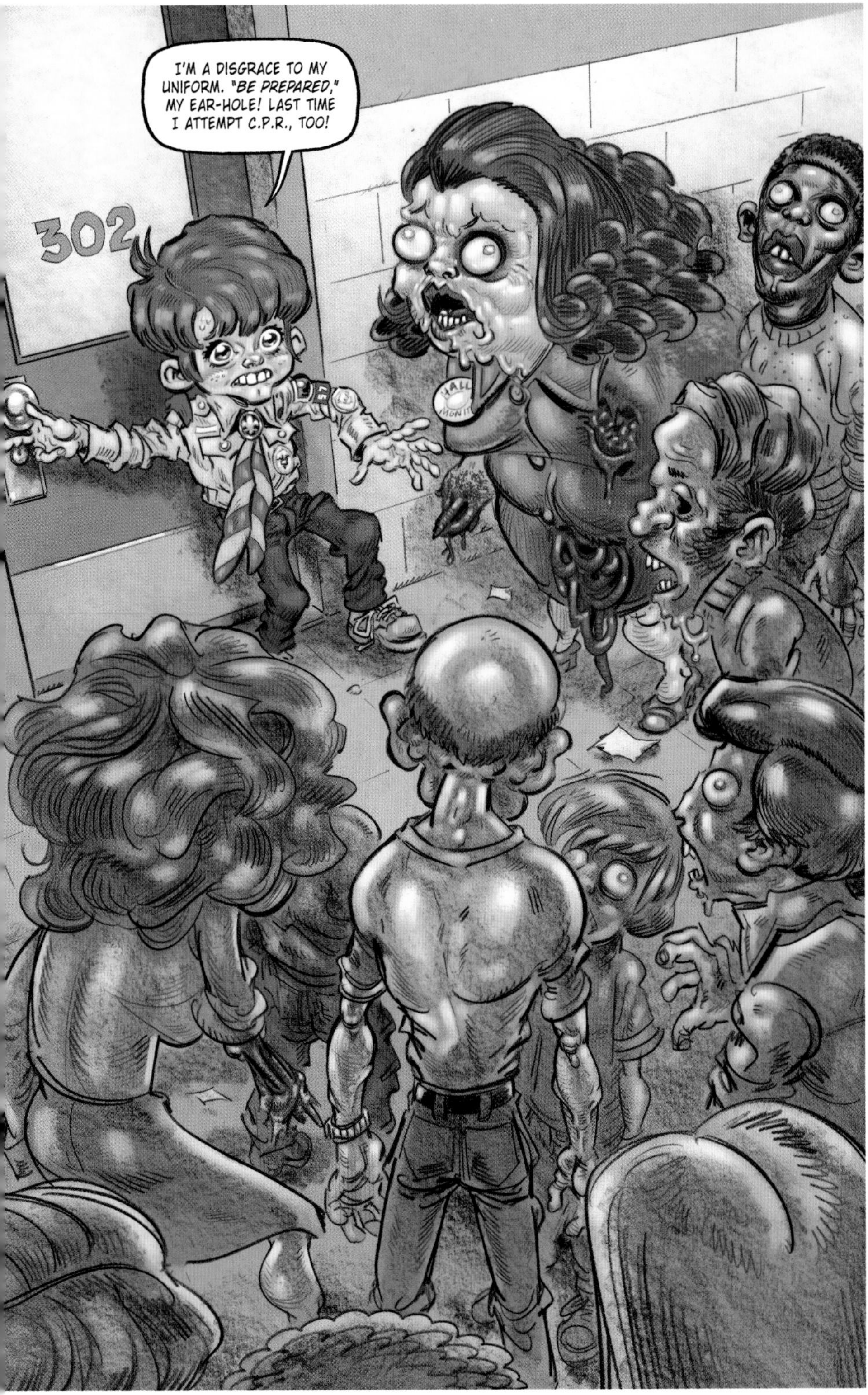
I'M A DISGRACE TO MY UNIFORM. "BE PREPARED," MY EAR-HOLE! LAST TIME I ATTEMPT C.P.R., TOO!
302

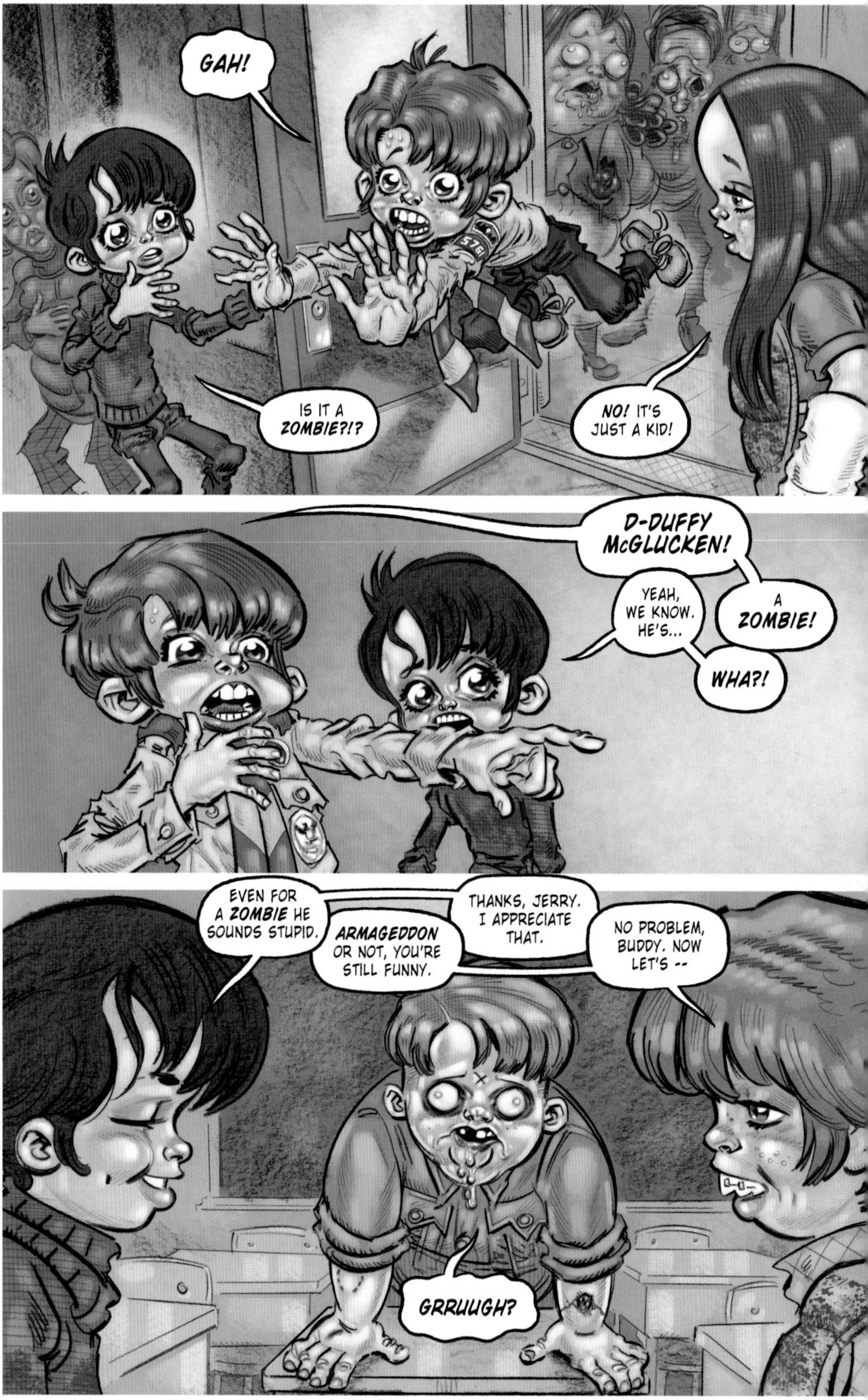
GAH!
IS IT A ZOMBIE?!?
NO! IT'S JUST A KID!
D-DUFFY McGLUCKEN!
YEAH, WE KNOW. HE'S...
A ZOMBIE!
WHA?!
EVEN FOR A ZOMBIE HE SOUNDS STUPID.
ARMAGEDDON OR NOT, YOU'RE STILL FUNNY.
THANKS, JERRY. I APPRECIATE THAT.
NO PROBLEM, BUDDY. NOW LET'S --
GRRUUGH?

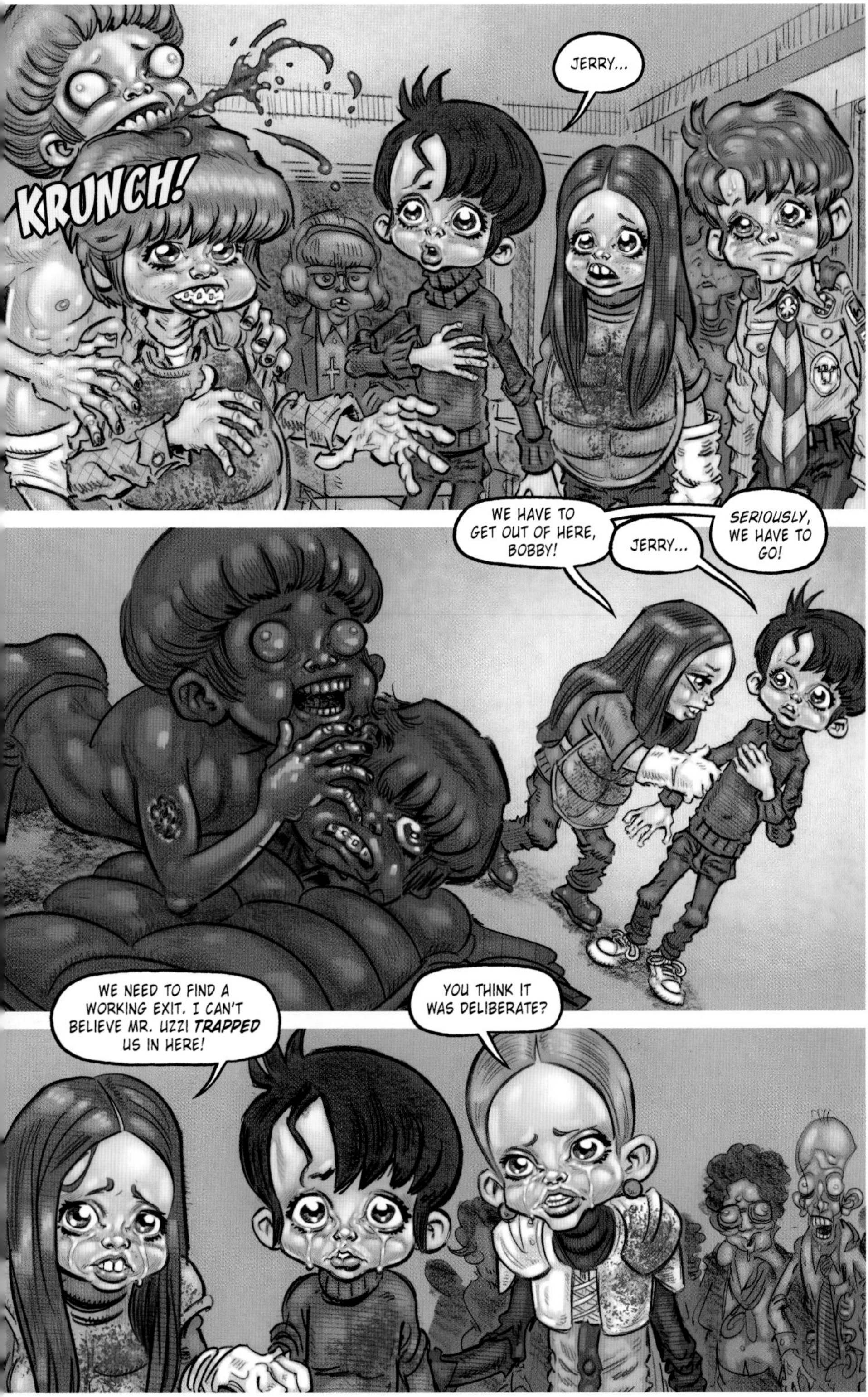
KRUNCH!
JERRY...
WE HAVE TO GET OUT OF HERE, BOBBY!
JERRY...
SERIOUSLY, WE HAVE TO GO!
WE NEED TO FIND A WORKING EXIT. I CAN'T BELIEVE MR. UZZI TRAPPED US IN HERE!
YOU THINK IT WAS DELIBERATE?

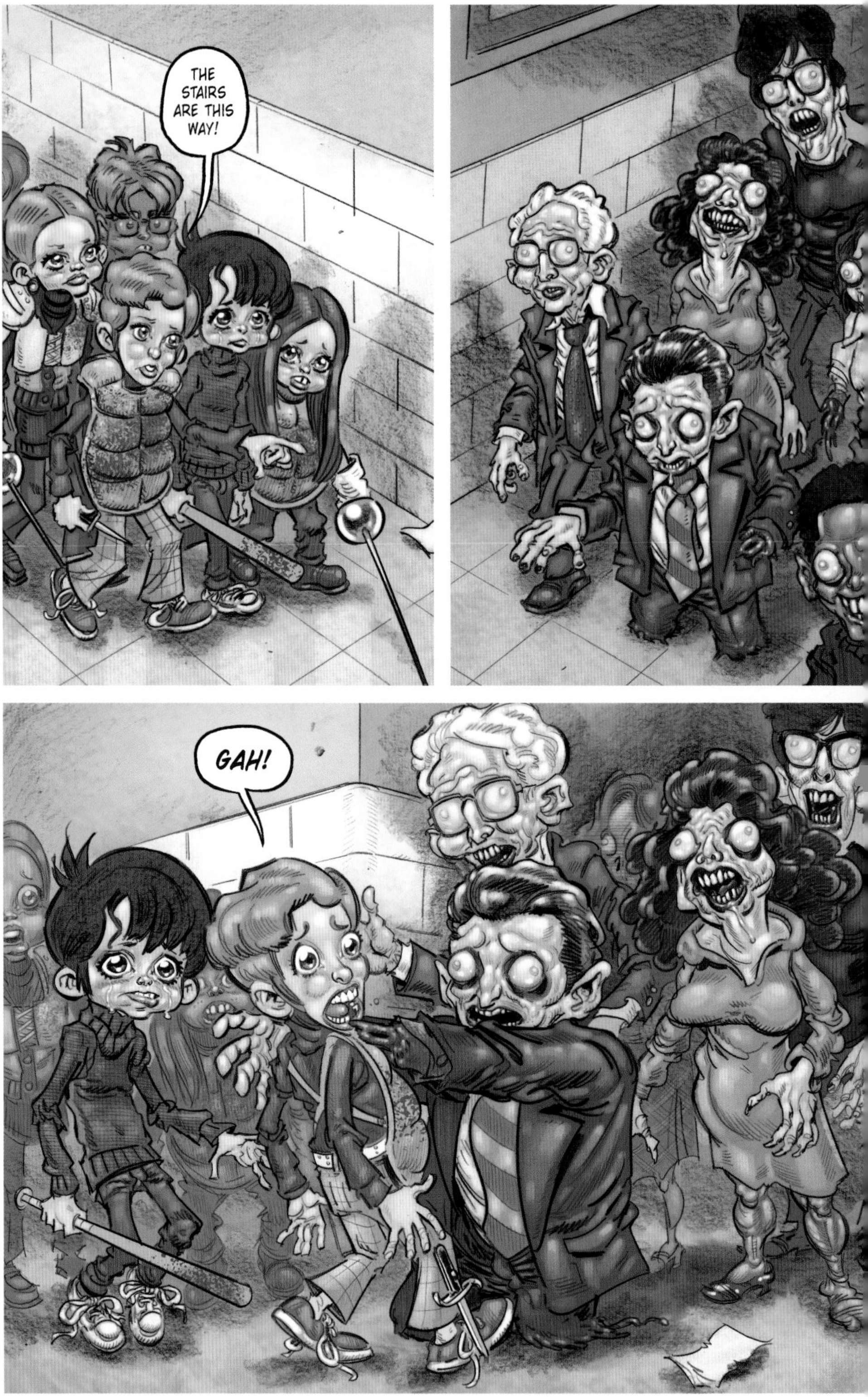
THE STAIRS ARE THIS WAY!
GAH!

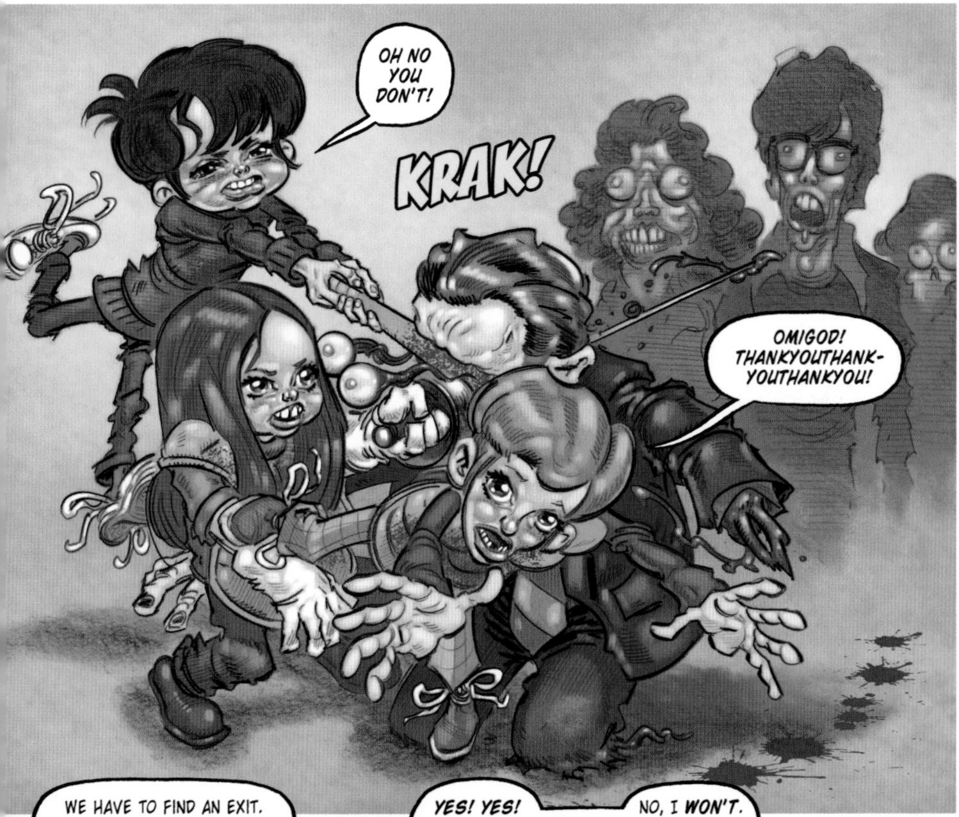
OH NO YOU DON'T!
KRAK!
OMIGOD! THANKYOUTHANK-YOUTHANKYOU!

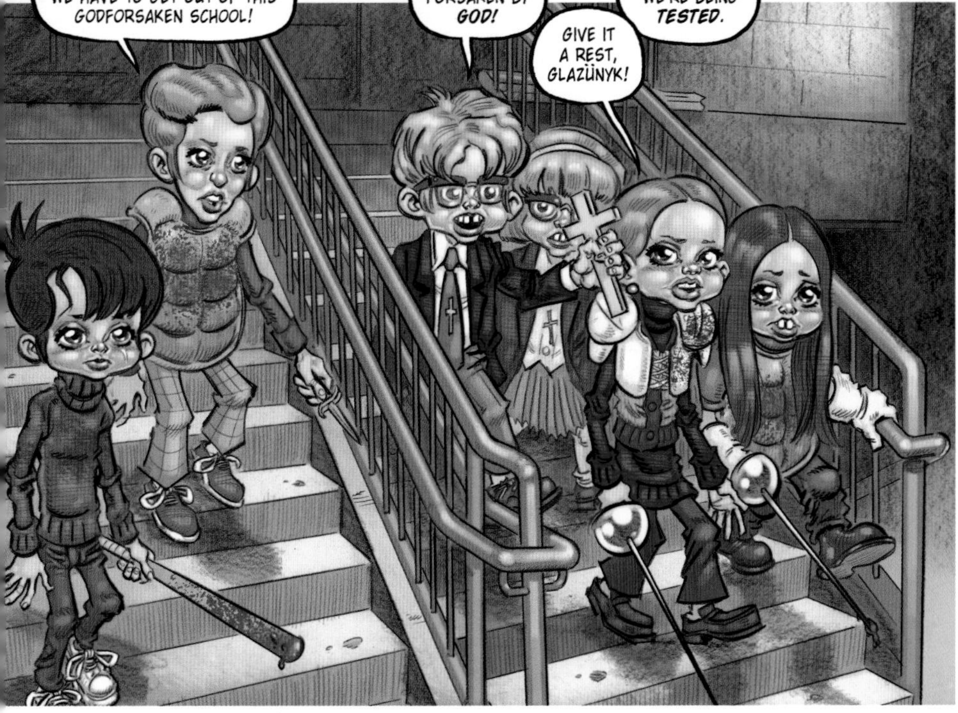
WE HAVE TO FIND AN EXIT. WE HAVE TO GET OUT OF THIS GODFORSAKEN SCHOOL!
YES! YES! FORSAKEN BY GOD!
NO, I WON'T. WE'RE BEING TESTED.
GIVE IT A REST, GLAZÜNYK!

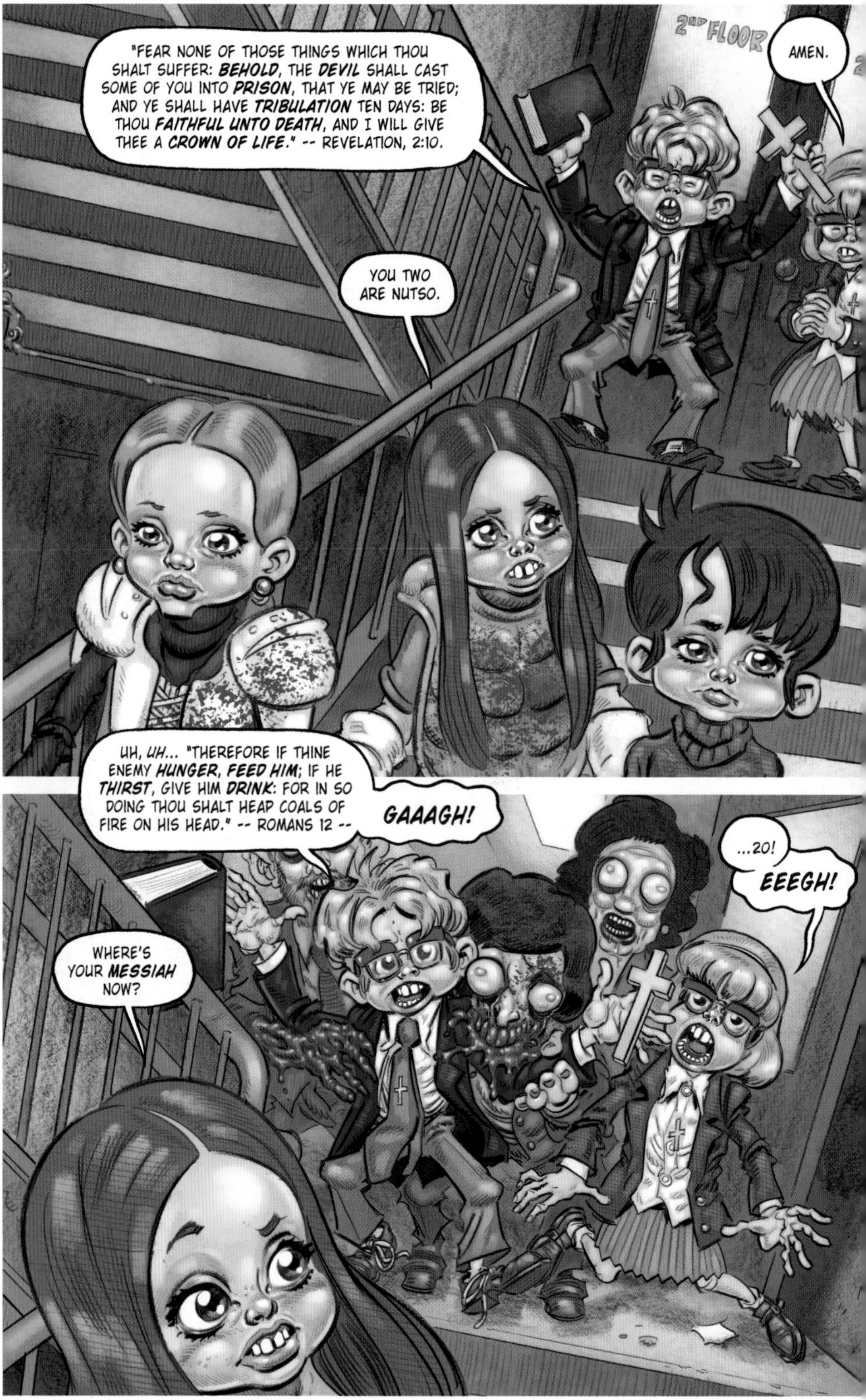
2ND FLOOR
"FEAR NONE OF THOSE THINGS WHICH THOU SHALT SUFFER: BEHOLD, THE DEVIL SHALL CAST SOME OF YOU INTO PRISON, THAT YE MAY BE TRIED; AND YE SHALL HAVE TRIBULATION TEN DAYS: BE THOU FAITHFUL UNTO DEATH, AND I WILL GIVE THEE A CROWN OF LIFE." -- REVELATION, 2:10.
AMEN.
YOU TWO ARE NUTSO.
UH, UH... "THEREFORE IF THINE ENEMY HUNGER, FEED HIM; IF HE THIRST, GIVE HIM DRINK: FOR IN SO DOING THOU SHALT HEAP COALS OF FIRE ON HIS HEAD." -- ROMANS 12 --
GAAAGH!
...20!
EEEGH!
WHERE'S YOUR MESSIAH NOW?

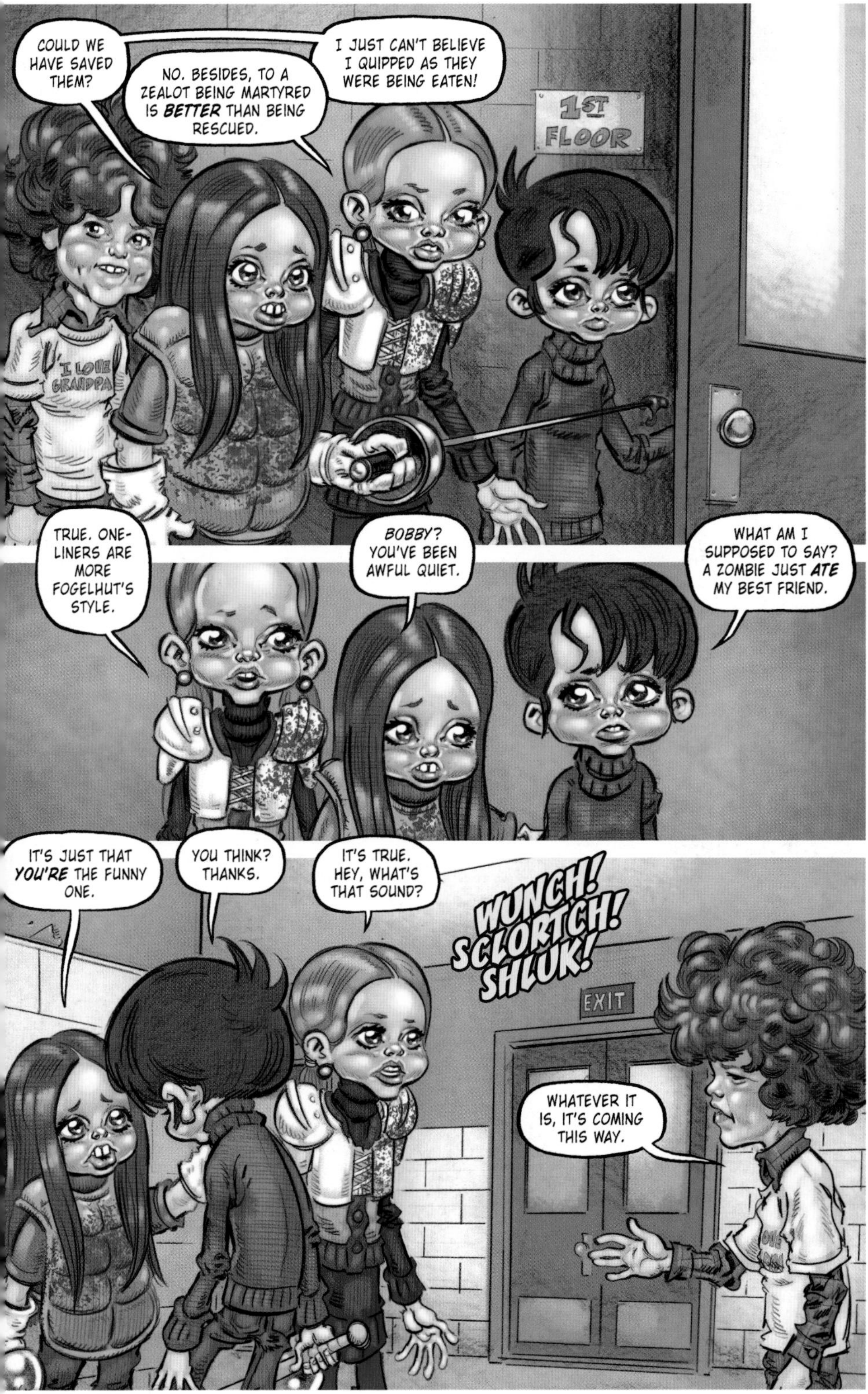
COULD WE HAVE SAVED THEM?
NO. BESIDES, TO A ZEALOT BEING MARTYRED IS BETTER THAN BEING RESCUED.
I JUST CAN'T BELIEVE I QUIPPED AS THEY WERE BEING EATEN!
1ST FLOOR
I LOVE GRANDPA
TRUE. ONE-LINERS ARE MORE FOGELHUT'S STYLE.
BOBBY? YOU'VE BEEN AWFUL QUIET.
WHAT AM I SUPPOSED TO SAY? A ZOMBIE JUST ATE MY BEST FRIEND.
IT'S JUST THAT YOU'RE THE FUNNY ONE.
YOU THINK? THANKS.
IT'S TRUE. HEY, WHAT'S THAT SOUND?
WUNCH! SCLORTCH! SHLUK!
EXIT
WHATEVER IT IS, IT'S COMING THIS WAY.

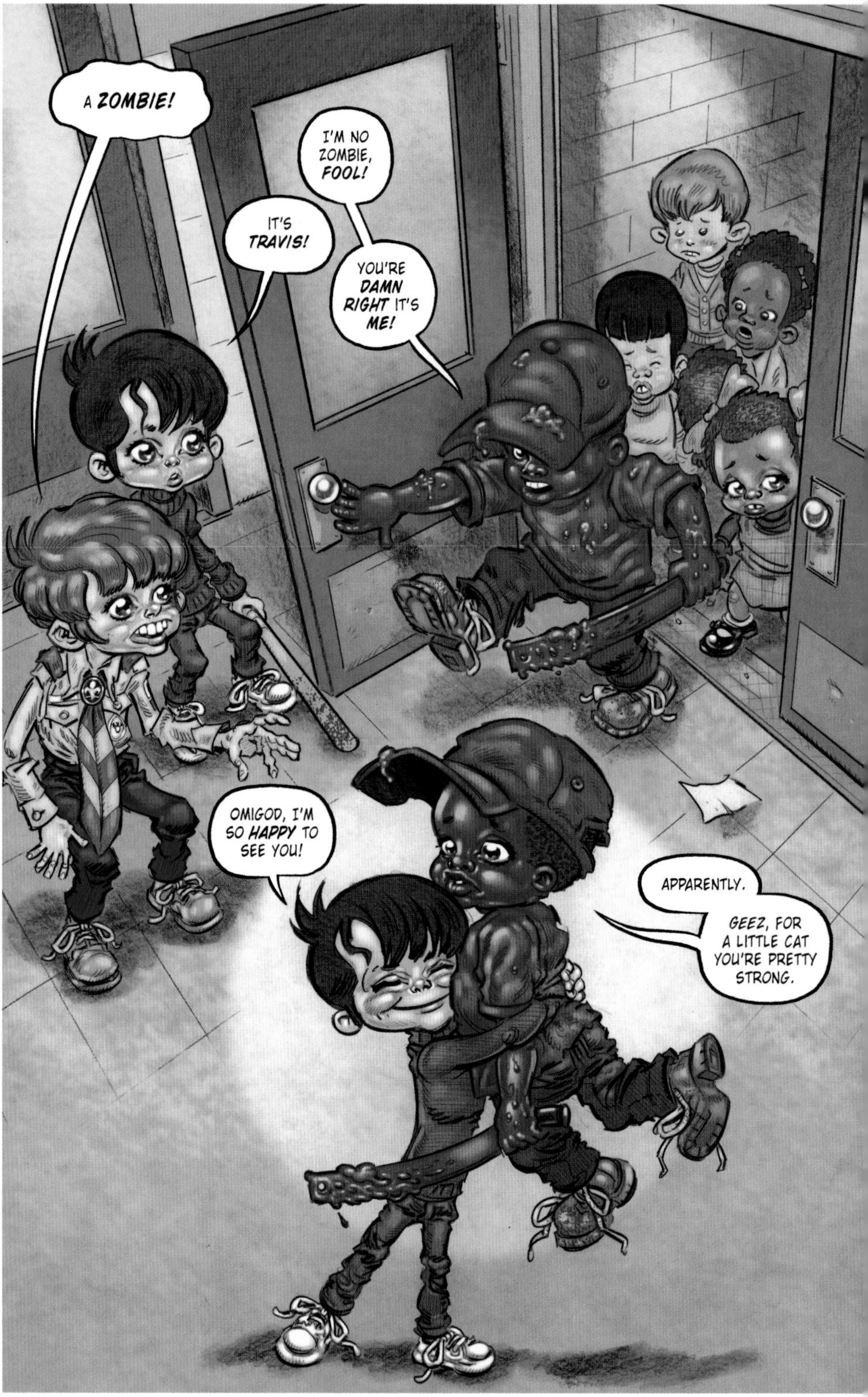
A ZOMBIE!
IT'S TRAVIS!
I'M NO ZOMBIE, FOOL!
YOU'RE DAMN RIGHT IT'S ME!
OMIGOD, I'M SO HAPPY TO SEE YOU!
APPARENTLY.
GEEZ, FOR A LITTLE CAT YOU'RE PRETTY STRONG.

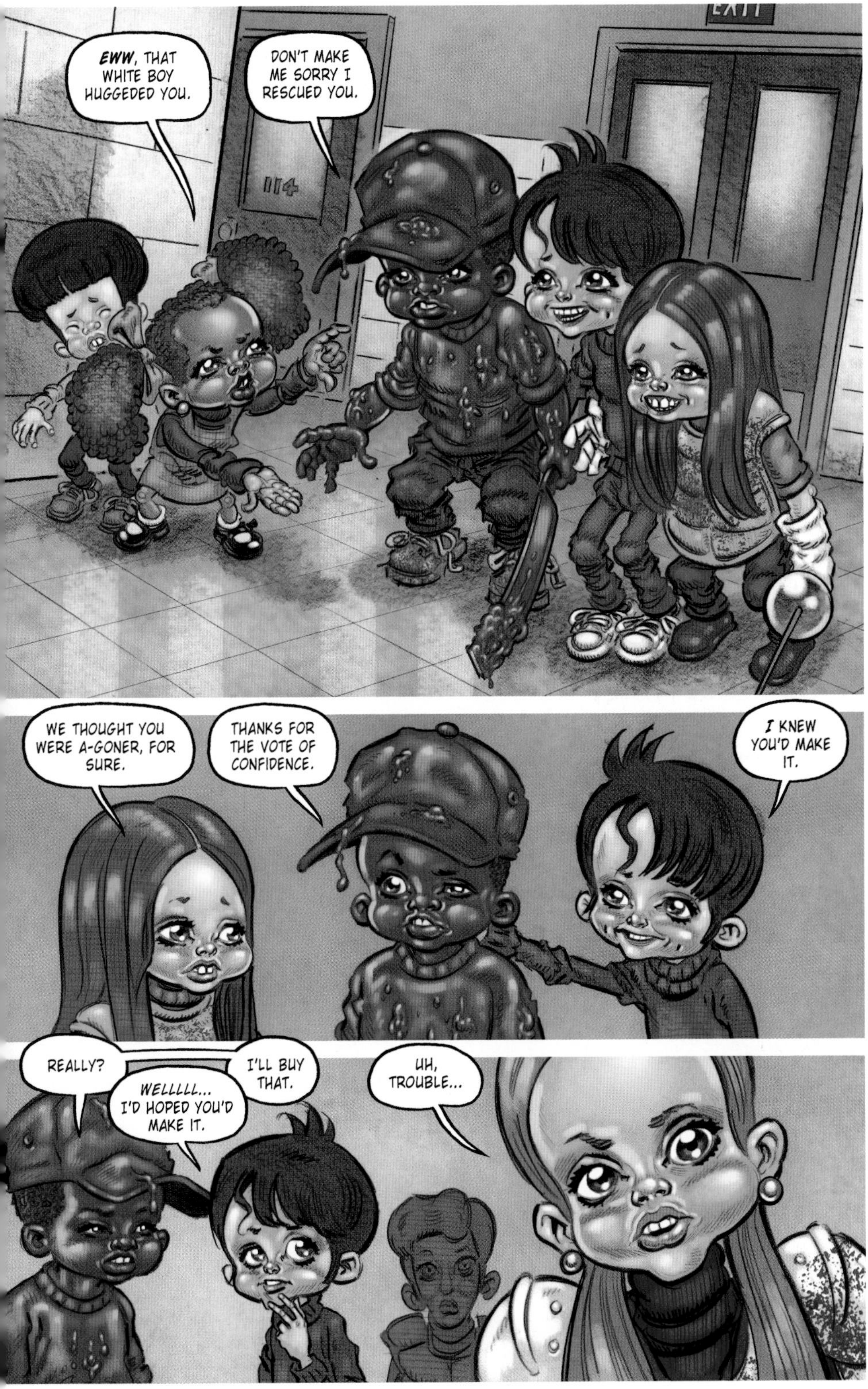
EWW, THAT WHITE BOY HUGGEDED YOU.
DON'T MAKE ME SORRY I RESCUED YOU.
WE THOUGHT YOU WERE A-GONER, FOR SURE.
THANKS FOR THE VOTE OF CONFIDENCE.
I KNEW YOU'D MAKE IT.
REALLY?
WELLLLL... I'D HOPED YOU'D MAKE IT.
I'LL BUY THAT.
UH, TROUBLE...

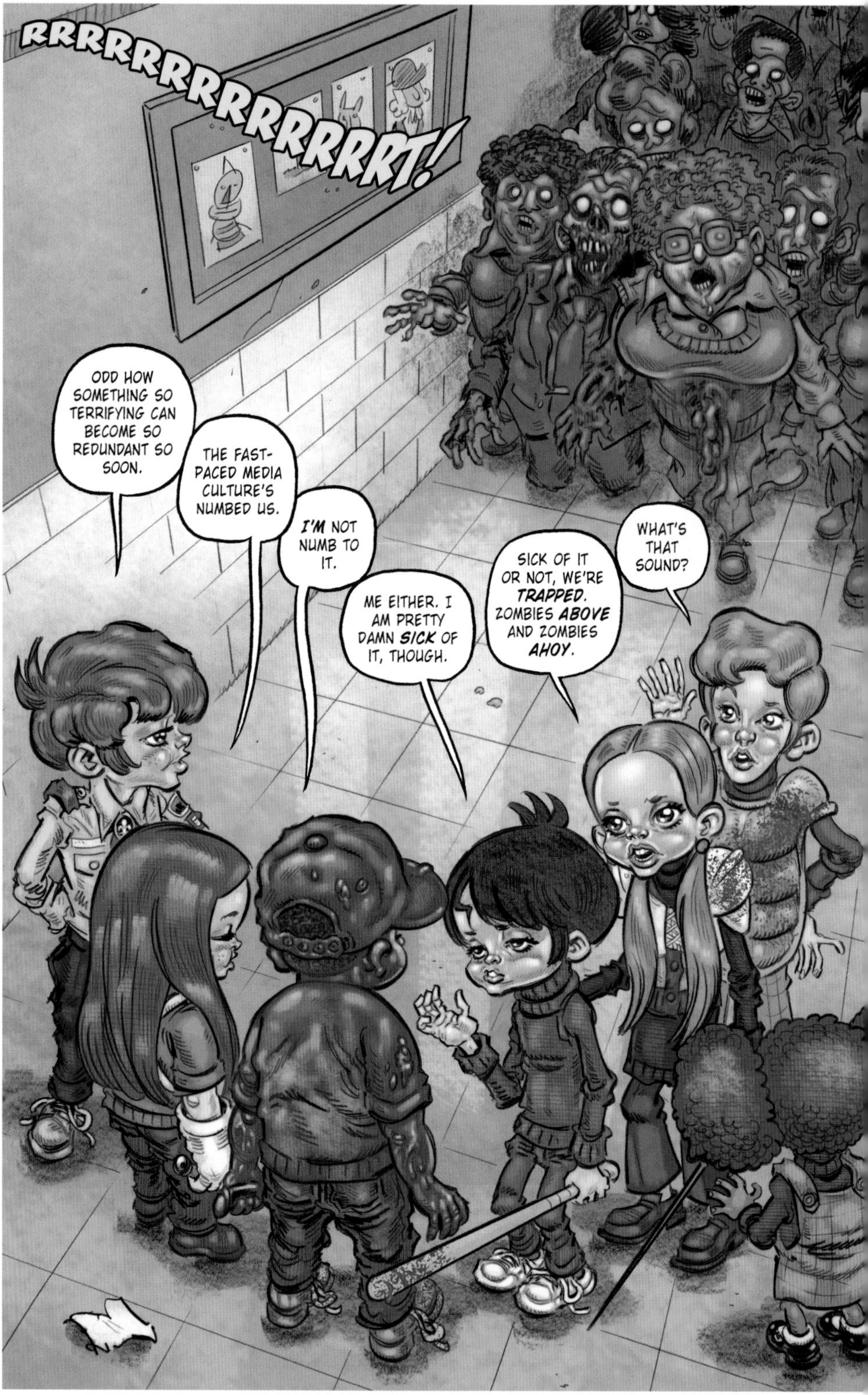
RRRRRRRRRRRRRRRRRRT!
ODD HOW SOMETHING SO TERRIFYING CAN BECOME SO REDUNDANT SO SOON.
THE FAST-PACED MEDIA CULTURE'S NUMBED US.
I'M NOT NUMB TO IT.
ME EITHER. I AM PRETTY DAMN SICK OF IT, THOUGH.
SICK OF IT OR NOT, WE'RE TRAPPED. ZOMBIES ABOVE AND ZOMBIES AHOY.
WHAT'S THAT SOUND?

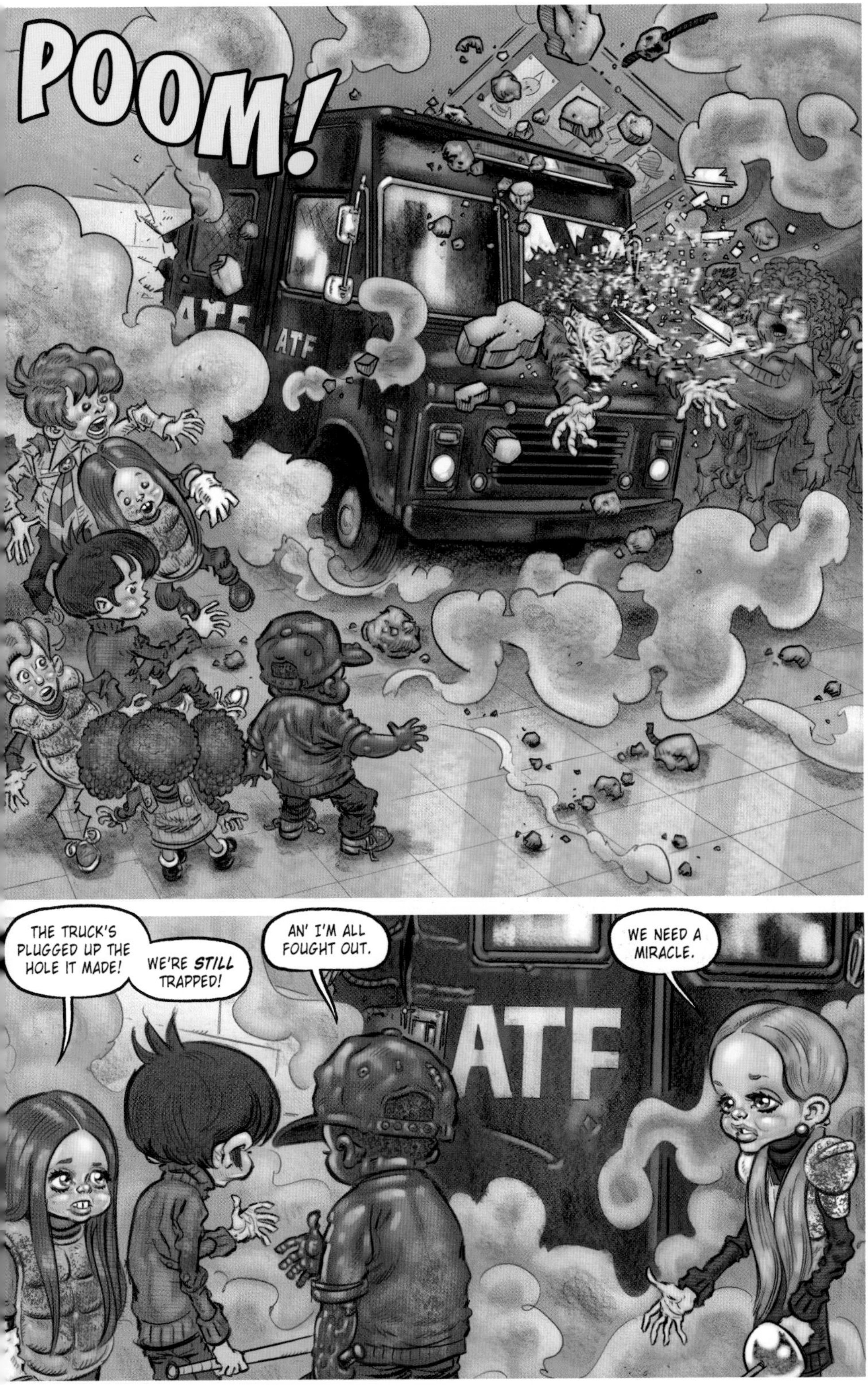
POOM!
ATF
ATF
THE TRUCK'S PLUGGED UP THE HOLE IT MADE!
WE'RE STILL TRAPPED!
AN' I'M ALL FOUGHT OUT.
WE NEED A MIRACLE.
ATF

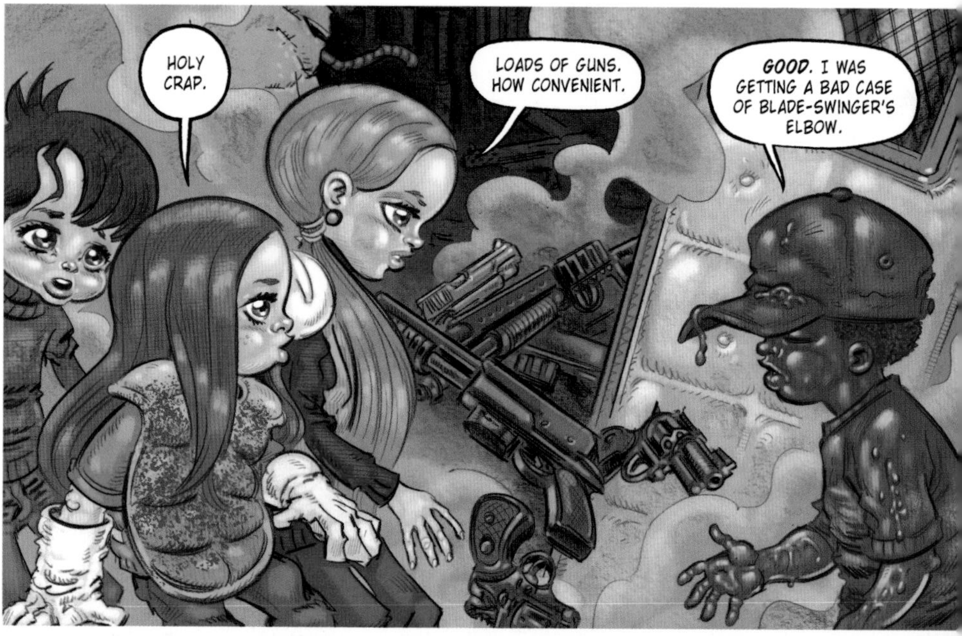
HOLY CRAP.
LOADS OF GUNS. HOW CONVENIENT.
GOOD. I WAS GETTING A BAD CASE OF BLADE-SWINGER'S ELBOW.

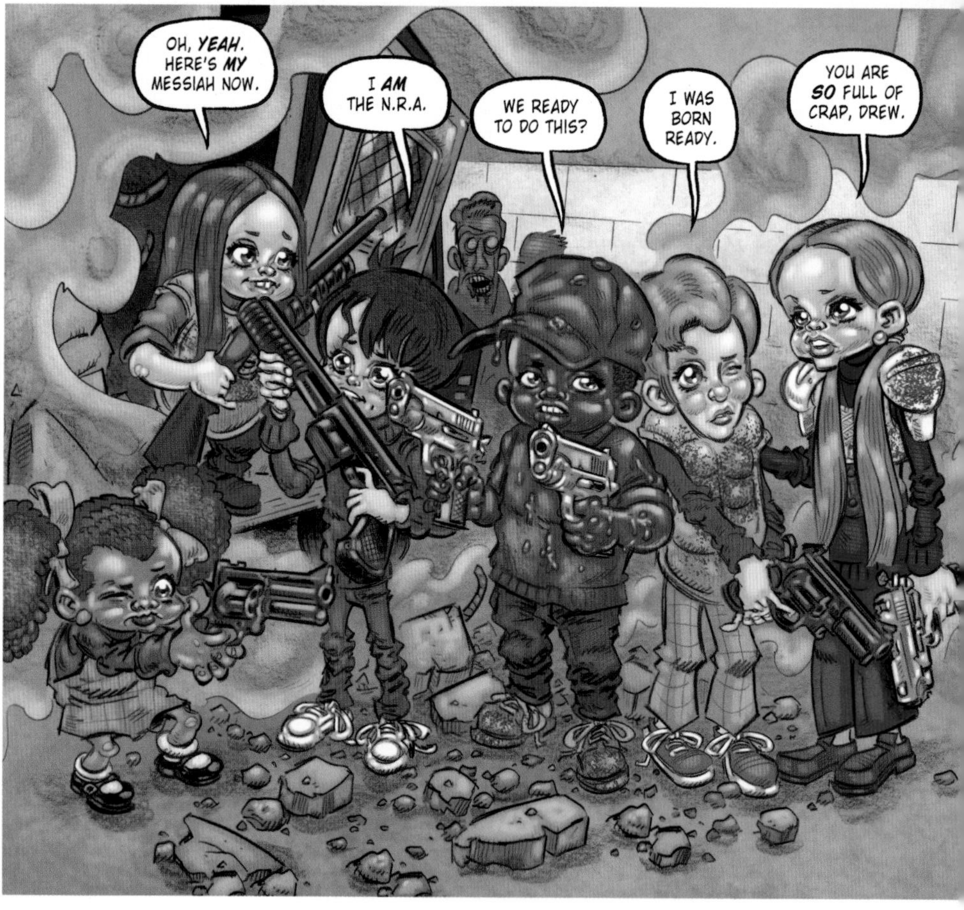
OH, YEAH. HERE'S MY MESSIAH NOW.
I AM THE N.R.A.
WE READY TO DO THIS?
I WAS BORN READY.
YOU ARE SO FULL OF CRAP, DREW.

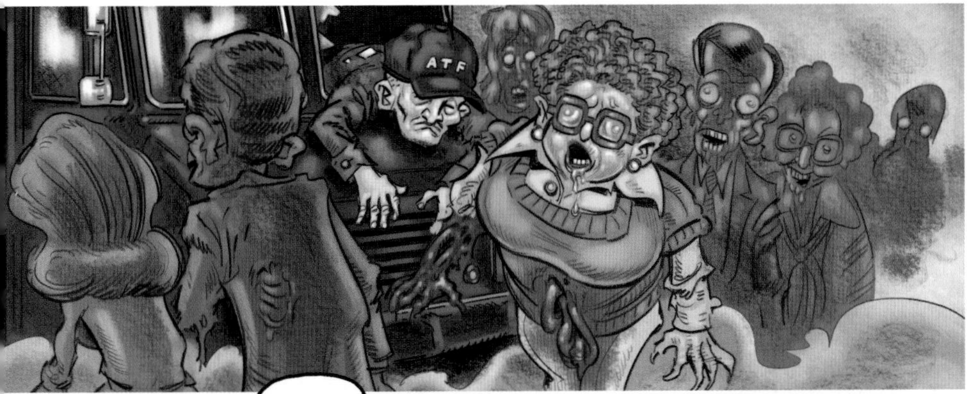

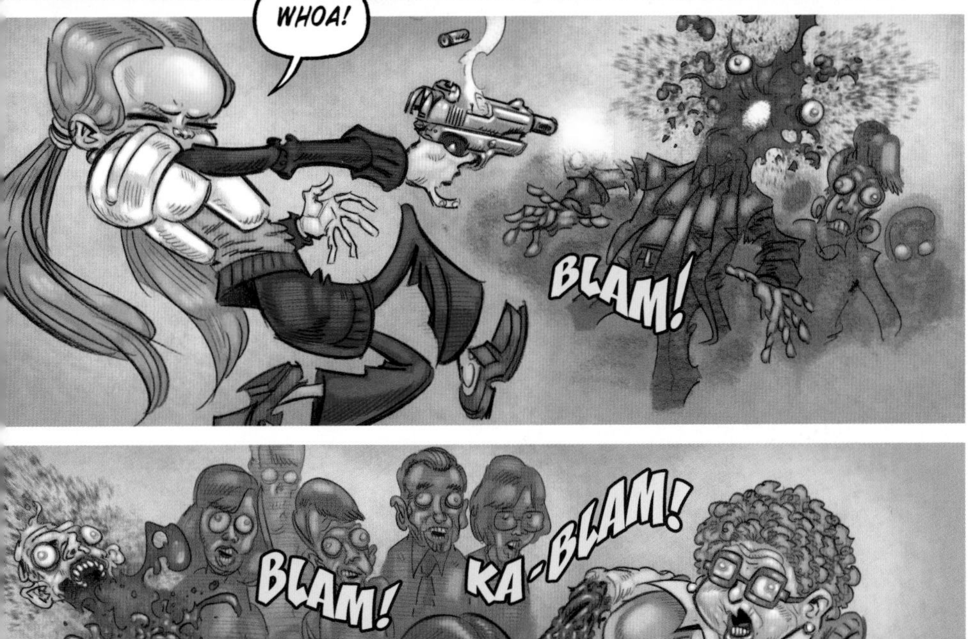
WHOA!
BLAM!

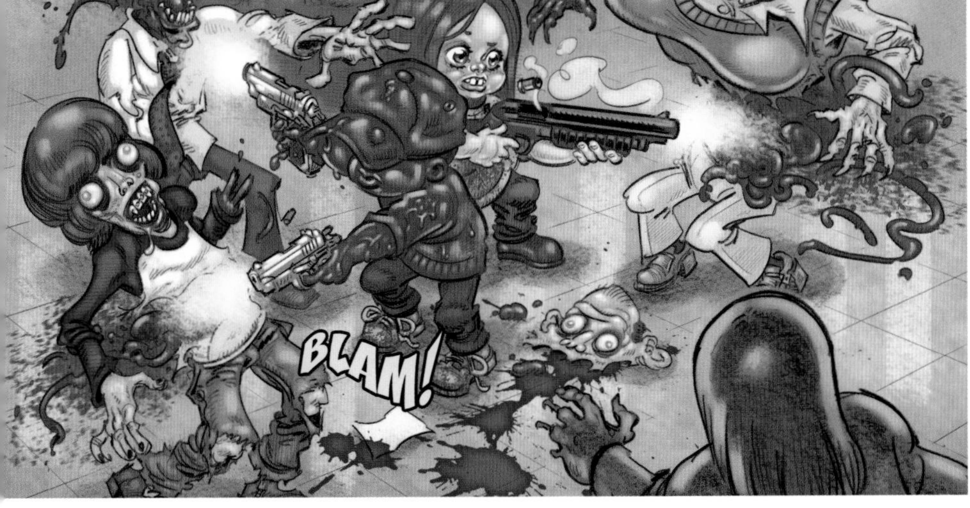
BLAM!
KA-BLAM!
BLAM!

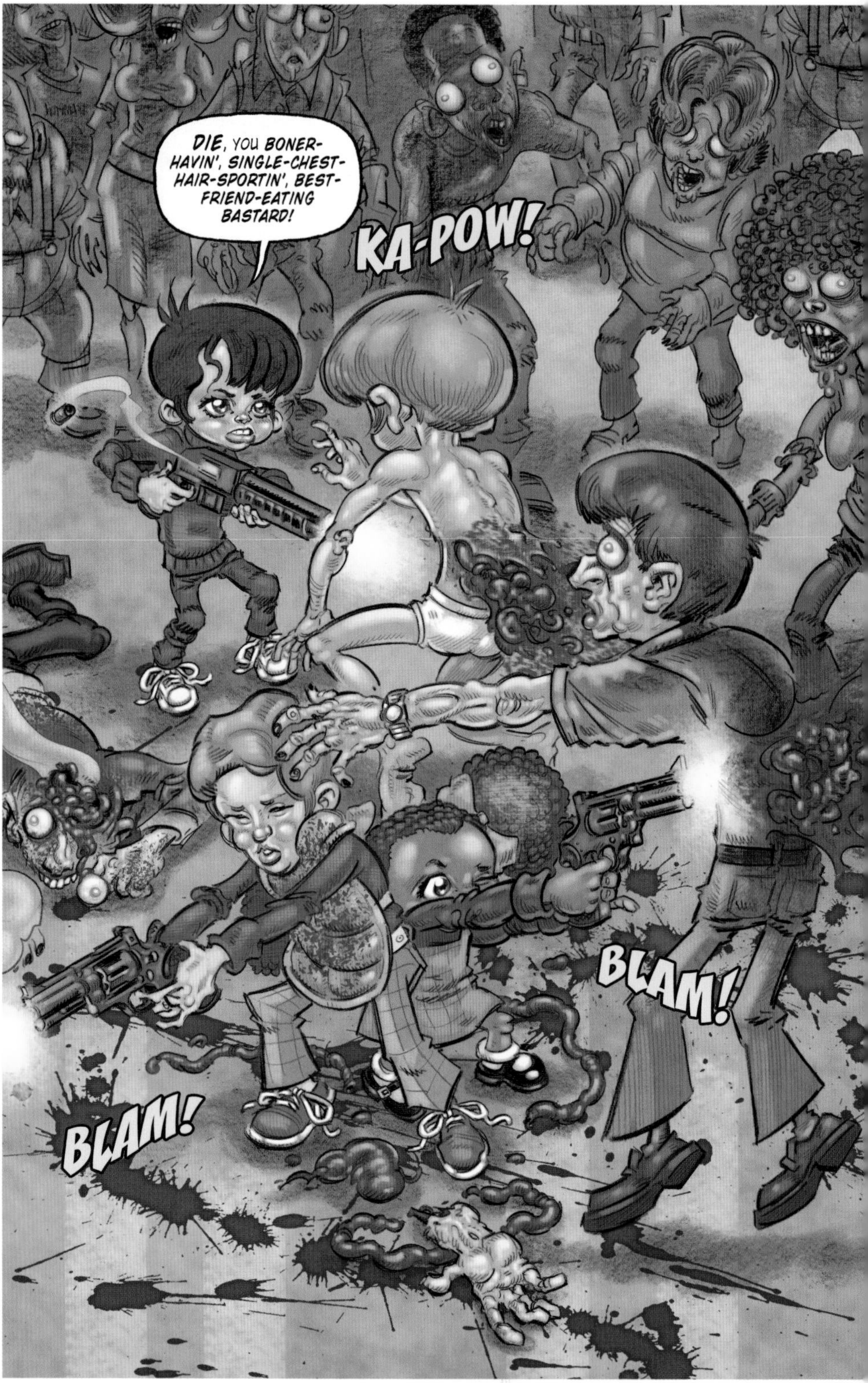
DIE, YOU BONER-HAVIN', SINGLE-CHEST-HAIR-SPORTIN', BEST-FRIEND-EATING BASTARD!
KA-POW!
BLAM!
BLAM!

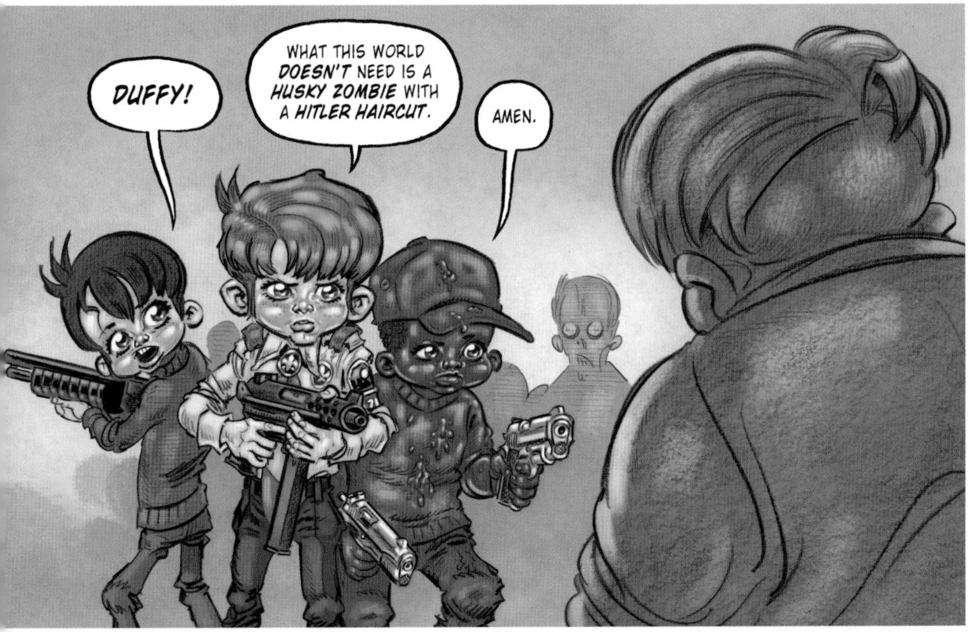
DUFFY!
WHAT THIS WORLD DOESN'T NEED IS A HUSKY ZOMBIE WITH A HITLER HAIRCUT.
AMEN.

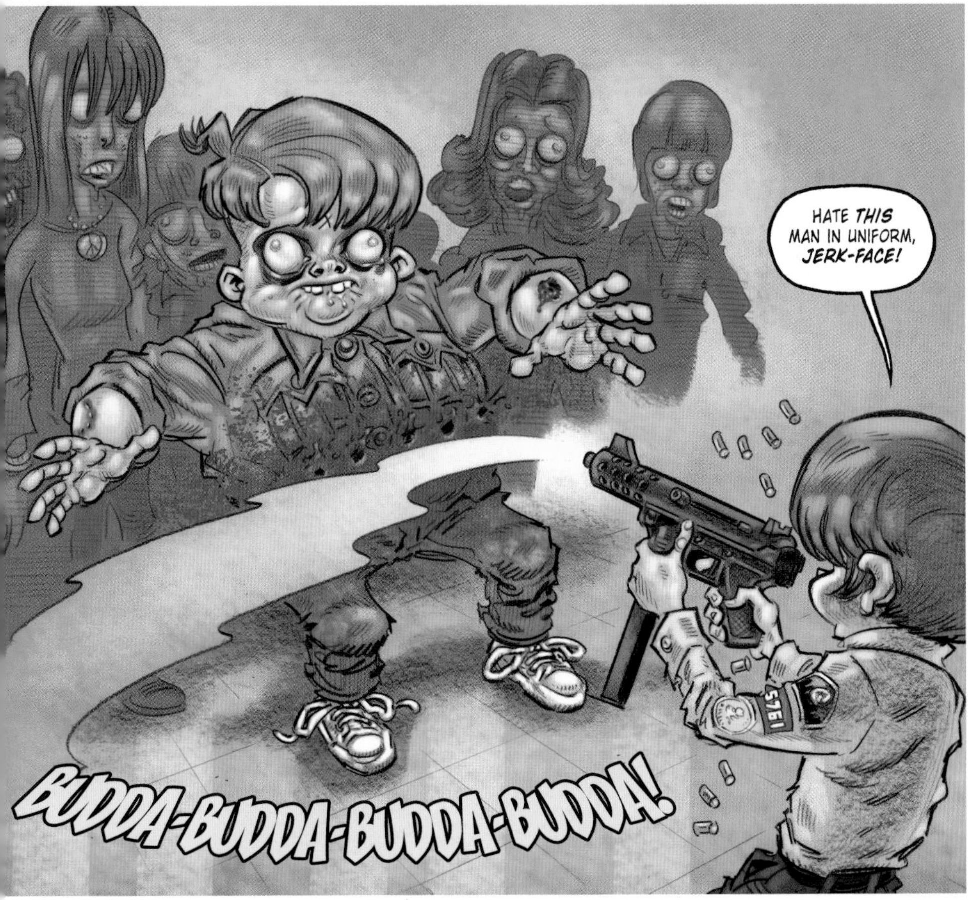
HATE THIS MAN IN UNIFORM, JERK-FACE!
BUDDA-BUDDA-BUDDA-BUDDA!

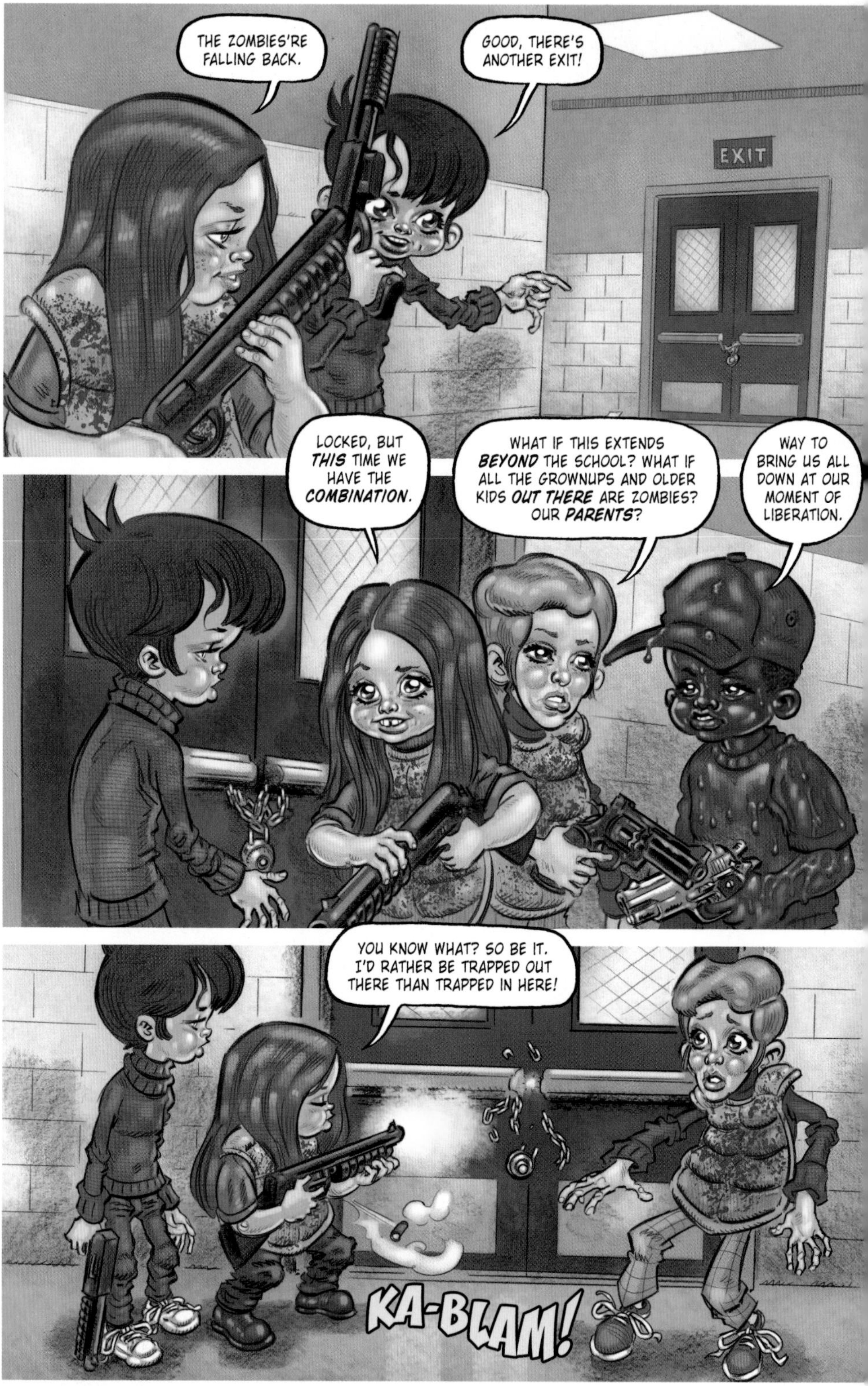
THE ZOMBIES'RE FALLING BACK.
GOOD, THERE'S ANOTHER EXIT!
EXIT
LOCKED, BUT **THIS** TIME WE HAVE THE **COMBINATION**.
WHAT IF THIS EXTENDS **BEYOND** THE SCHOOL? WHAT IF ALL THE GROWNUPS AND OLDER KIDS **OUT THERE** ARE ZOMBIES? OUR **PARENTS**?
WAY TO BRING US ALL DOWN AT OUR MOMENT OF LIBERATION.
YOU KNOW WHAT? SO BE IT. I'D RATHER BE TRAPPED OUT THERE THAN TRAPPED IN HERE!
KA-BLAM!

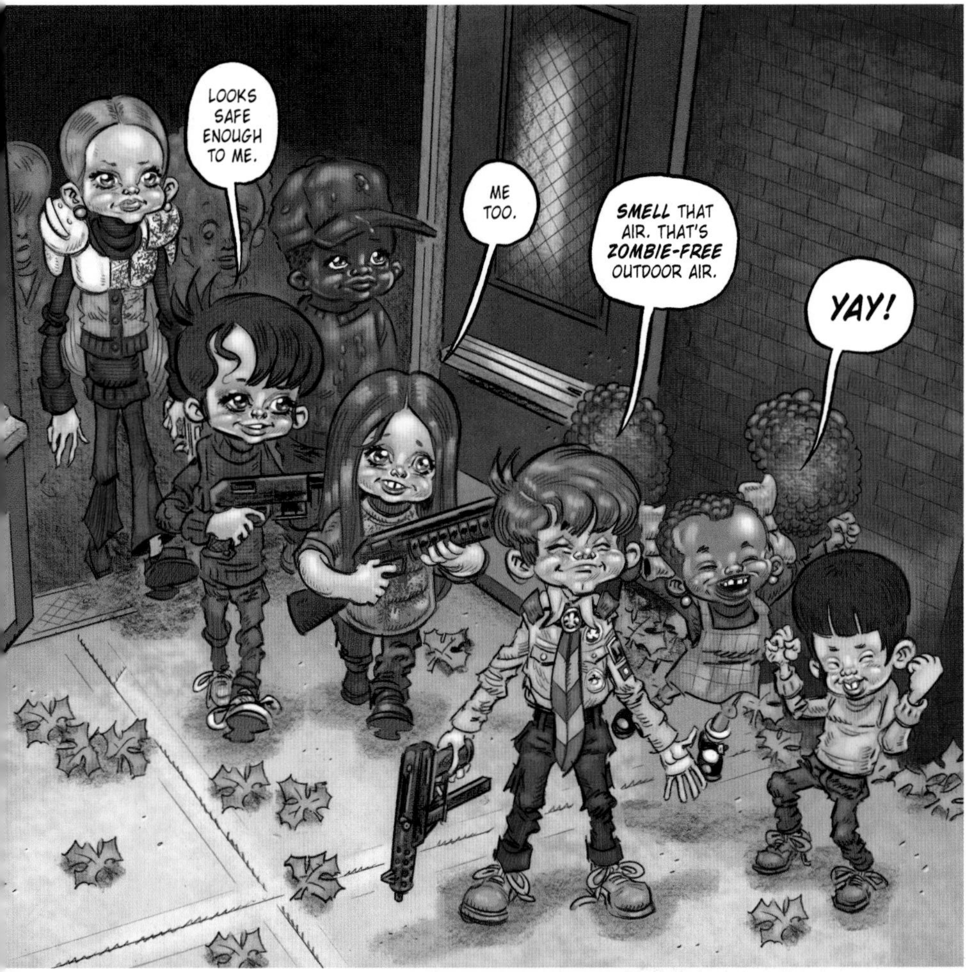
LOOKS SAFE ENOUGH TO ME.
ME TOO.
SMELL THAT AIR. THAT'S ZOMBIE-FREE OUTDOOR AIR.
YAY!

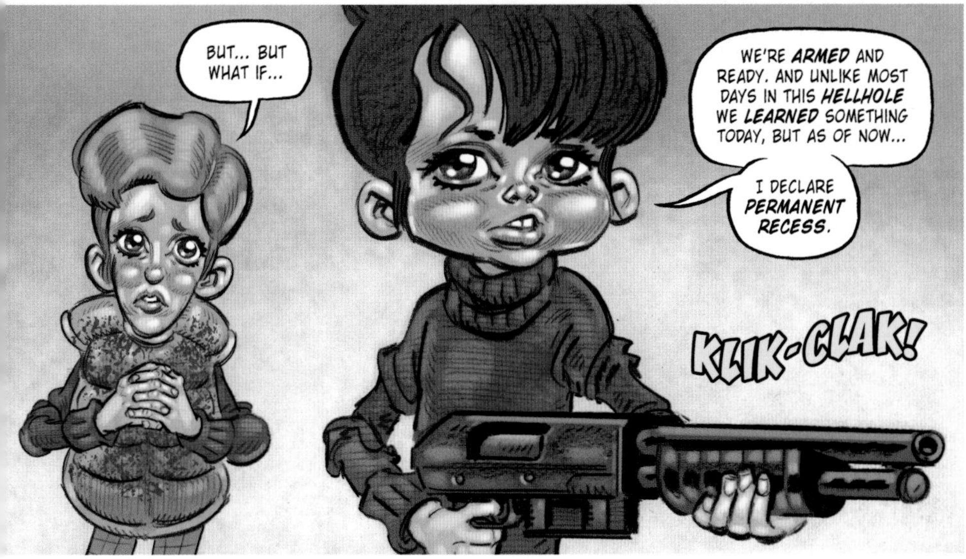
BUT... BUT WHAT IF...
WE'RE ARMED AND READY. AND UNLIKE MOST DAYS IN THIS HELLHOLE WE LEARNED SOMETHING TODAY, BUT AS OF NOW...
I DECLARE PERMANENT RECESS.
KLIK-CLAK!

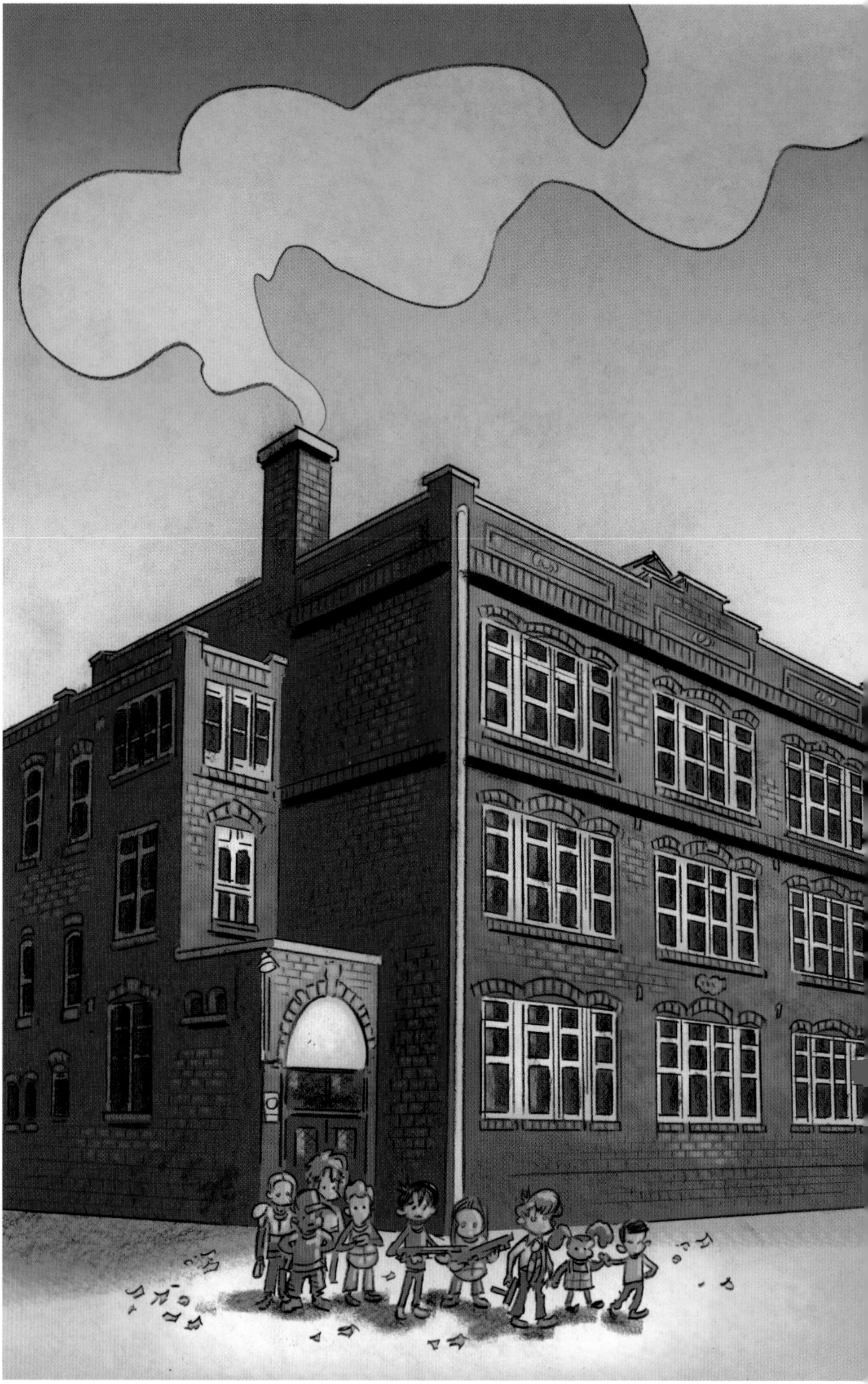

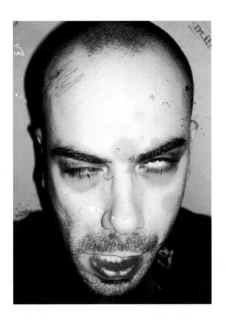

Bob Fingerman was fated to live, dream, and propagate zombies from a very early age. Edited-for-television viewings of *Night of the Living Dead* and *Children Shouldn't Play with Dead Things* recalibrated his psyche and cemented his fascination with all things undead. He is a veteran of the comics field, creator of such graphic novels as *White Like She* and *Beg the Question*. He authored the title story of *Zombie World: Winter's Dregs and Other Stories.* M Press will release his first prose novel, *BOTTOMFEEDER,* in November 2006.

He is married and lives in New York City.

ALSO FROM DARK HORSE BOOKS

you deserved it
Bob Fingerman

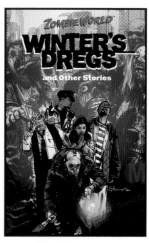

YOU DESERVED IT
Is Bob Fingerman a cynical misanthrope or a disappointed humanitarian? Dare we suggest maybe both? In *You Deserved It*, the sensitive creator of the acclaimed graphic novel *Beg the Question* accesses his darker side, serving up this caustic collection of comical cautionary chronicles.
ISBN: 1-59307-390-9 / $9.95

ZOMBIEWORLD
WINTER'S DREGS
and Other Stories

ZOMBIEWORLD: WINTER'S DREGS AND OTHER STORIES
Bob Fingerman and Tommy Lee Edwards take us into the subway tunnels of New York, where the rats aren't the only things that bite, in the critically acclaimed "Winter's Dregs," plus three other terrifying tales from Kelley Jones, Gordon Rennie & Gary Erskine, and Pat Mills & J. Deadstock.
ISBN: 1-59307-384-4 / $24.95

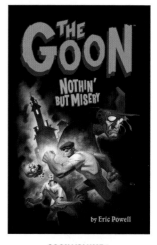

ZOMBIEWORLD
CHAMPION OF THE WORMS
Mike Mignola
Pat McEown

ZOMBIEWORLD: CHAMPION OF THE WORMS
Every year, publishers and movie studios churn out piles of new zombie yarns, but none have rivaled the originality of this tale about a reanimated priest from an ancient cult and the zombie outbreak he creates in order to sacrifice mankind to his dark gods.
ISBN: 1-59307-407-7 / $8.95

THE GOON
NOTHIN' BUT MISERY
by Eric Powell

GOON VOLUME 1: NOTHIN' BUT MISERY
The Goon is a laugh-out-loud, action-packed romp through the streets of a town infested with zombies. An insane priest is building himself an army of the undead, and there's only one man who can put them in their place: the man they call the Goon.
ISBN: 1-56971-998-5 / $15.95

AVAILABLE AT YOUR LOCAL COMICS SHOP OR BOOKSTORE
To find a comics shop in your area, call 1-888-266-4226
For more information or to order direct visit darkhorse.com or call 1-800-862-0052
Mon.-Fri. 9 A.M. to 5 P.M. Pacific Time
***Prices and availability subject to change without notice**